Global Governance Diplomacy

Global Governance Diplomacy

The Critical Role of Diplomacy in Addressing Global Problems

Jean-Robert Leguey-Feilleux

ROWMAN & LITTLEFIELD
Lanham • Boulder • New York • London

Published by Rowman & Littlefield
A wholly owned subsidiary of The Rowman & Littlefield Publishing Group, Inc.
4501 Forbes Boulevard, Suite 200, Lanham, Maryland 20706
www.rowman.com

Unit A, Whitacre Mews, 26-34 Stannary Street, London SE11 4AB

British Library Cataloguing in Publication Information Available

Library of Congress Cataloging-in-Publication Data

Names: Leguey-Feilleux, Jean-Robert, 1928- author.
Title: Global governance diplomacy : the critical role of diplomacy in addressing
    global problems/Jean-Robert Leguey-Feilleux.
Description: Lanham : Rowman & Littlefield Publishers, Inc., [2017] | Includes
    bibliographical references and index.
Identifiers: LCCN 2016051265 (print) | LCCN 2017000566 (ebook) |
    ISBN 9781442276574 (cloth : alk. paper) | ISBN 9781442276581 (pbk. : alk. paper) |
    ISBN 9781442276598 (electronic)
Subjects: LCSH: International relief. | Diplomacy.
Classification: LCC HV544.5 .L44 2017 (print) | LCC HV544.5 (ebook) |
    DDC 361.2/6—dc23
LC record available at https://lccn.loc.gov/2016051265

∞™ The paper used in this publication meets the minimum requirements of American National Standard for Information Sciences—Permanence of Paper for Printed Library Materials, ANSI/NISO Z39.48-1992.

Printed in the United States of America

To the memory of my mother, and to my wife Virginia
with gratitude for her patience as I worked on this book
To my children
Michèle
Monique and Joe
Suzanne
Christy
And to my grand children
Courtney
and Caroline

Contents

List of Acronyms

AMCEN	African Ministerial Conference on the Environment
ASEAN	Association of Southeast Asian Nations
APEC	Asia-Pacific Economic Association
AU	African Union. Formerly Organization of African Unity (OAU)
CAP	Consolidated Appeals Process
CEB	UN System Chief Executives Board
CERF	Central Emergency Response Fund
CGIAR	Consultative Group on International Agricultural Research
CMG	Conflict Management Group
COE	Council of Europe
CSCE	Conference on Security and Cooperation in Europe
CSD	Commission for Sustainable Development
CSIS	Center for Strategic and International Studies
CTC	Counter-Terrorism Committee
CTED	Counter-Terrorism Executive Directorate
CTITF	Counter-Terrorism Implementation Task Force
DEA	Drug Enforcement Administration
DPKO	Department of Peacekeeping Operations
ECOSOC	Economic and Social Council
EFA	Education for All
FAO	Food and Agriculture organization
FATF	Financial Action Task Force
G7	Group of Seven
G8	Group of Eight
G77	Group of Seventy-Seven
GAFSP	Global Agriculture and Food Security Program

GATT	General Agreement on Tariffs and Trade
GDACS	Global Disaster Alert and Coordination System
GEF	Global Environment Facility
GNI	Gross National Income
GNP	Gross National Product
IAEA	International Atomic Energy Agency
IASC	Inter-Agency Standing Committee
ICAO	International Civil Aviation Organization
ICBL	International Campaign to Ban Landmines
ICOC	International Code of Conduct against Ballistic Missile Proliferation
ICC	International Criminal Court
ICRC	International Committee of the Red Cross
I CSID	International Center for the Settlement of Investment Disputes
IFAD	International Fund for Agriculture and Development
ILO	International Labour Organization
IMF	International Monetary Fund
INCB	International Narcotics Control Board
INSARAG	International Search and Rescue Advisory Group
INSTRAW	International Research and Training Institute for the Advancement of Women
IOM	International Organization for Migration
IPCC	Intergovernmental Panel on Climate Change
ISDR	International Strategy for Disaster Reduction
ITO	International Trade Organization
MDGs	Millennium Development Goals
MIGA	Multilateral Investment Guarantee Agency
MNC	Multinational Corporation
MONUSCO	UN Organization Stabilization Mission in the Republic of the Congo
MTCR	Missile Technology Control Regime
NATO	North Atlantic Treaty Organization
OAS	Organization of American States
OCHA	Office for the Coordination of Humanitarian Affairs
OECD	Organization for Economic Cooperation and Development
ONUC	UN Operation in the Congo
OPEC	Organization of Petroleum Exporting Countries
OSAGI	Office of the Special Adviser on Gender Issues and Advancement of Women
OSCE	Organization for Security and Cooperation in Europe
PCA	Permanent Court of Arbitration
PCB	Program Coordinating Board

PECC	Pacific Economic Cooperation Council
REDD	Reducing Emissions from Deforestation and Forest Degradation in Developing Countries
SAARC	South Asian Association for Regional Cooperation
SEATO	Southeast Asia Treaty Organization
SECT	Southeast European Cooperative Initiative
SIU	Sensitive Investigative Unit
UNAIDS	Joint UN Program on HIV/AIDS
UNCED	UN Conference on the Environment and Development
UNCJIN	UN Crime and Justice Information Network
UNCITRAL	UN Commission on International Trade Law
UNCTAD	UN Conference on Trade and Development
UNDAC	UN Disaster Assessment and Coordination Service
UNDCP	International Drug Control Program
UNDG	UN Development Group
UNDP	UN Development Program
UNDSA	UN Department of Economic and Social Affairs
UNEP	UN Environment Program
UNEPTA	UN Experimental Program of Technical Assistance
UNESCO	UN Educational, Scientific and Cultural Organization
UNFDAC	Fund for Drug Abuse Control
UNFPA	UN Population Fund
UNHCR	UN High Commissioner for Refugees
UNICEF	UN Children's Fund
UNICRI	UN Interregional Crime and Justice Research Institute
UNIDO	UN Industrial Development Organization
UNIFEM	UN Development Fund for Women
UNITAR	UN Institute for Training and Research
UNODC	UN Office on Drug and Crime
UNOSOM	UN Operation in Somalia
UNPROFOR	UN Protection Force
UNRRA	UN Relief and Rehabilitation Administration
UNRWA	UN Relief and Works Agency for Palestine Refugees in the Near East
UNTAC	UN Transitional Authority in Cambodia
UNU	UN University
WFP	World Food Program
WHO	World Health Organization
WIPO	World Intellectual Property Organization
WMO	World Meteorological Organization
WTO	World Trade Organization

Chapter 1

Diplomacy and Global Governance

The world is confronted with an increasing number of international problems that cannot be solved single-handedly by states—for example, environmental degradation or the spread of disease.[1] Countries are thus impelled to seek collective ways of addressing them and diplomacy is a critical element in this endeavor. Moreover, most of these international problems cannot be solved once and for all. They require continuing attention, that is, continuing international cooperation in dealing with them. Many situations require some form of international *management* to keep them from deteriorating and getting out of hand. Many modes of diplomatic interaction are used for this purpose. And a large variety of international organizations are available to help. Making these organizations accomplish their objectives also requires a great deal of diplomacy, some of which is very different from what international society was accustomed to. New forms of diplomacy have been devised to meet changing needs, and this evolution of the diplomatic process needs to be examined. Global society is still primarily made up of nation states, each with its own culture, form of government, national priorities, and a fierce desire to act independently. It is going to take very skillful diplomacy to make some governments come around and cooperate even when is it obviously in their interest to do so. But this is not a new phenomenon: many governments fail to see the obvious.

Global governance does not imply the creation of some supranational government. The independent Commission on Global Governance defined global governance as "the sum of the many ways individuals and institutions, public and private, manage their common affairs. It is a continuing process through which conflicting or diverse interests may be accommodated and cooperative action may be taken. It includes formal . . . as well as informal arrangements that people and institutions have agreed to or perceive to be in their interest."[2]

It may be better understood as *international problem management.* Its scope need not be global. Labels can become misleading if taken too literally. In the rare cases when international bodies are given binding decision-making authority, for example, the UN Security Council (in some situations), the international distribution of power and the way in which the state system operates often make implementation problematic. In the end, when it comes to addressing international problems, some form of multilateral cooperation is usually needed given our growing interdependence.[3]

A complicating feature is the large number of independent states (some 200 of them[4]), many with divergent agendas, working at cross purposes, and some of them woefully governed. Global governance diplomacy can be very challenging. Furthermore, independent states are no longer the only actors in global society. In the nineteenth century, states began to create international organizations, for example, the European Danube Commission. These organizations are normally given international functions to perform and, in carrying out their responsibilities, they engage in international relations and practice diplomacy as international actors. After the Second World War, international organizations proliferated: special purpose institutions such as the World Bank, multipurpose organizations like the United Nations (UN), and regional entities such as the European Union (EU), although some are only marginally involved in world politics, for example, the International Bureau of Weights and Measures. In many of these organizations, member states engage in diplomacy, particularly in the decision-making process (e.g., lining up support for the next policy decision). The organizations themselves use diplomacy in dealing with states and with other organizations in carrying out their mandates, as seen in the work of UN officials, for example, the UN secretary-general. These organizations are of course very diverse but a number of them play a critical role in the diplomacy of global problem management.

Civil society must also be taken into account. Many of its components, such as nongovernmental organizations (NGOs), play an increasing role in global affairs.[5] Their political power is not comparable to what nation states or international organizations can do, but they are becoming more significant in global politics, maintaining transnational networks, insisting on being heard in diplomatic gatherings, mobilizing public opinion, and affecting the course of international events. They are a force that governments and international organizations must increasingly reckon with. Many NGOs are officially accredited with a large number of international organizations. They even participate in the decision-making process of a number of institutions, such as the World Bank and the Joint United Nations Program on HIV/AIDS (UNAIDS). Some are even officially involved in diplomatic negotiations as was the case in the 1996–1997 Land Mine Treaty diplomatic process (see chapter 4).

In addition, some non-sovereign territories are now occasionally invited to participate in international conferences. And some revolutionary movements are heard in international gatherings. Even when distrusted or seen as illegitimate, some of their representatives actually participate in the diplomatic process, as was the case with the Palestine Liberation Organization. International practices have become highly diversified. What was once unthinkable is now part of mainstream diplomacy. This is the new reality. But is it really diplomacy?

THE MEANING OF DIPLOMACY

Diplomacy is a term that has a number of connotations.[6] The "diplomacy" of a certain country is often understood as its foreign policy or its way of handling foreign relations.[7] This is particularly the case in the field of diplomatic history. In this book, the term *diplomacy* is used to identify a *method of interaction* between states or other international actors such as international organizations. It has to do, among other things, with maintaining contact, communicating, or negotiating. Over the years—diplomacy has a *long* history—some of its procedures have become enshrined in repeated government practice. A good deal of diplomacy is rooted in long-established tradition. But diplomacy is not frozen in the past. The world keeps changing and international actors turn to new methods of interaction as their needs evolve. Thus, diplomacy must be understood as a phenomenon with changing boundaries.

Diplomacy also implies *a mode of behavior*, a certain professional style. It facilitates transactions across political boundaries and bridges many differences—political, ideological, cultural, and economic. The practice of diplomacy thus requires caution, tact, and circumspection, particularly when the issues at hand are of some delicacy. Political entities are often sensitive, especially when approached to discuss issues they do not want to address. They are concerned about the defense of their interests (often narrowly defined), anxious to protect national honor, and international image. Finesse is required to handle complex international situations in which misunderstanding may easily occur, particularly when very different cultures are involved. A good understanding of psychology,[8] patience, and discretion are of profound value and so is integrity if trust is to be preserved. Other interpersonal skills, especially the ability to communicate, are essential. By analogy, behavior involving these attributes may be called *diplomatic* when encountered in other walks of life ("The matter was handled so diplomatically!"). These qualities are critical to permit dialogue in difficult relationships. The following must be added to the preceding qualities: adaptability—given the vast diversity of settings in which diplomacy is practiced—self-control, the ability to size up a situation (or one's counterpart), and imagination—to create alternatives in conflicting situations. Some of these traits are probably inherited, or acquired through the socialization process. Training undoubtedly can help. Ultimately, experience is of utmost importance, that is, practice is repeated until one acts almost instinctively. It may not be far-fetched to speak of the art of diplomacy. But diplomacy is part of the political process. It is another way of practicing politics. Diplomats must be politically aware, perceptive, resourceful, and realistic.

In the seventeenth century, Cardinal Richelieu[9] transformed much of what was done in the conduct of diplomacy, systematizing and reforming it so that it could be an effective tool to increase French influence. This eventually involved the training of a corps of professionals. Other countries saw merit in this systematic approach and proceeded to reorganize their diplomatic apparatus. A French diplomat François de Callières undoubtedly helped this development by writing, in 1716, a small manual on the subject, *On the Manner of Negotiating with Princes*,[10] which was widely used internationally. This form of diplomacy came to be a model for great powers from the seventeenth to the nineteenth century. The diplomats of the major states received the same type of training and even used French as the language of diplomacy. A fairly cohesive diplomatic culture could thus be detected in Europe. But as the world changed, new participants in world affairs moved away from the French model and greater diversity entered the practice of diplomacy.

The expanding subject matter of international relations is also having an impact on the diplomatic process. A large variety of issues that used to be exclusively domestic, such as health care, education, and human rights, need to be addressed internationally, and nations need to turn to *specialized personnel and experts* to negotiate issues in these areas. For example, the global effort to control the spread of disease requires the participation of health care specialists or medical personnel in the diplomatic process. Experts become critical components of international negotiations. Diplomacy without diplomats? These experts need to learn on the job. It is true that diplomatic delegations to negotiate technical issues will include, along with specialized experts, professional foreign service officers who will provide the political and diplomatic guidance that may be needed in the transactions concerned.

The changing diplomatic agenda has led to even more radical transformations in the conduct of foreign relations. Specialized government ministries (executive departments in the United States) are now increasingly involved in foreign relations (separately from foreign ministries, although consultation is a normal occurrence). For example, the US Department of Labor includes a Bureau of International Labor Affairs in charge of an Office of International Relations. This office has the lead role within the US government on policy and program issues pertaining to international labour affairs. For example, every year, US Labor Department officers represent the United States at the International Labour Conference of the International Labour Organization in Geneva. And it is to be noted that in contemporary global problem management, more specialized officials from around the world participate in the diplomatic process.

Another facet of the foreign relations of specialized executive departments is that agents from these departments (e.g., the Agriculture Department) are posted in some of their country's embassies.[11] In important embassies, some 60 percent of the professional staff is not connected with the foreign ministry. See chapter 2 for structure of the US Embassy in Paris.

Moreover, many specialized executive departments work directly with some of their counterparts in foreign capitals, for example, Justice Department officials from different countries harmonizing their counterterrorism strategies, or criminal law enforcement, often without leaving their desks in their national capitals, and without using the services of their foreign offices. This is often called "transgovernmental relations" (see chapter 2 section "An Example of Transgovernmental Work"). More and more specialized domestic departments are involved in this kind of international work, another consequence of interdependence and the blurring of the line between domestic and international functions. Despite the distance separating them and their cultural/political differences, these non–foreign service officials are likely to become colleagues with their foreign counterparts, developing diplomatic skills on the job without ever meeting face to face.

Adding to the diversity of the diplomatic process, *international organizations* and *NGOs* interact and negotiate with nation states and indeed practice diplomacy in a variety of international situations, for example, representatives of the International Committee of the Red Cross get involved in some international conflict resolution efforts. Thus, a surprising variety of diplomatic activity is taking place in the expanding field of global governance but the people involved in the process are not necessarily members of any foreign service. The greater need for international problem solving and the more complex nature of international society are likely not only to expand diplomatic interaction but to produce more innovations in the field. It must be pointed out that many of the people involved in this expanded diplomatic process are not officially recognized as diplomats (or even *perceived* as practicing diplomacy) and are not entitled to diplomatic privileges and immunities under international law.[12] Governments, however, frequently arrange, on an ad hoc basis, for the diplomatic protection of agents on special missions. Some international organization personnel are given diplomatic immunities in a number of conventions. Such is the case of UN diplomatic agents.

THE PROBLEM OF IDEOLOGY

One modern complication in the practice of diplomacy is found in ideology although the problem varies with the values held and the extent to which decision makers are intent on the promotion of these norms. Shared ideology may facilitate international cooperation. Ideological conflict, on the other hand, can lead to polarization as was seen during the Cold War. The normal task of diplomats is to facilitate communication and permit dialogue across political, cultural, and other differences. This implies an ability to work with people of different persuasions and to find possibilities for cooperation, which, in turn, implies some pragmatism. Ideological polarization produces the opposite. It emphasizes differences and tends to make diplomatic work more difficult. Ideology has pernicious tendencies. In the name of dedication to a value system, it may encourage intolerance and create barriers. It may foster tunnel vision—an inability to perceive what is not encompassed by the ideology. In more extreme cases, international issues are seen exclusively through the distorting lens of the ideology. Moreover, ideological zeal tends to infuse an emotional dimension complicating dialogue. A confrontational style makes it more difficult to explore what can be done collectively.

Polarization can also derail negotiations by bringing up irrelevant issues, thus poisoning the proceedings (e.g., using a conference on global warming to reopen the status of Jerusalem), literally hijacking the meeting. Some international actors will use any international gathering to remind the world of their plight. Rationality no longer enters the picture. Single issue fixations are of course extremely detrimental to any form of diplomatic dialogue, no matter how legitimate the issues. The age of mass communication has unfortunately made crusading stances more tempting to rally the faithful. Looking for accommodation can then be seen as a betrayal of one's cause—hardly promising for diplomacy.

NEGOTIATION

Negotiation is of immense importance in global governance. Addressing world problems requires making very disparate actors, particularly nation states, work together and find common strategies despite all that separates them.[13] Some of these actors will undoubtedly be more important in given situations, but many of them will usually be involved. Thus the number of participants will often be a challenge, and many of them will come to the task with their own, different, negotiating styles.[14] These will inevitably vary according to their culture, personal traits, and often, political systems. To complicate the process of negotiation, it must be acknowledged that many of the issues at hand are intricate, for example, environmental degradation, the management of the global economy, or the reduction of poverty. And a critical issue is, often, finding strategies that the actors involved can afford and are willing to finance. Moreover, the *number* of issues that need attention is staggering. Some of these may be interrelated and addressed together, but the global aggregate remains humbling. The second part of this book will examine what international actors are doing in specific problem areas and the role of diplomacy in this endeavor.

Various *kinds of negotiation* can be observed, many of them multilateral, but international actors also network bilaterally, seeking support for their proposals in larger forums. A more formal type of negotiation seeks to create binding obligations in the form of a treaty. A variety of names are used to identify this kind of legal instrument, sometimes interchangeably, for example, convention, international agreement, protocol, covenant, and charter. Often, a draft document will be prepared in advance to help the negotiating process. The wording of the treaty will be of special importance for legal application and interpretation. A special committee will often be used to present the result of the negotiations in the proper legal terminology. A treaty will normally require final ratification by the governments involved. Some treaties will be binding upon signature if specified in the text or indicated in the negotiators' credentials. A substantial number of states fail to ratify instruments they have signed, often as a result of domestic politics. Negotiations attempting to coordinate policy may not produce a binding instrument but the parties may be expected to act in accordance with what they have agreed to. Nonlegally binding agreements may be found useful as parties may want to abide by their commitments as they appreciate the importance of cooperation and wish to avoid working at cross purposes. A good example is found in the annual meetings of the Group of 7 (G7) (see chapter 2).

Summit negotiations are of several types. Some involve genuine negotiations at the summit level. The chief executives do the negotiating. Often, however, diplomatic representatives will engage in negotiations ahead of time, in preparation for the summit interaction. Chief executives seldom relish the thought of failing in their negotiations and therefore try to determine in advance how much can be agreed upon. Some important parts of an agreement may still have to be negotiated by the leaders themselves in the course of their meeting. Another reason for advance negotiations is that summits must remain relatively short, although some critically important summits, such as the 1978 Camp David meeting to broker peace between Egypt and Israel, have taken close to two weeks of intense negotiations. These are rare. And then, there are symbolic summits, such as the 1992 Earth Summit, in which the bulk of the diplomatic work is done by the conference delegates before the arrival of the heads of state or government. The presence of the chief executives, in this case, is used to emphasize the significance of the event. Summit meetings are now more frequent and chief executives do a great deal of traveling. President Bill Clinton undertook 133 foreign visits during his eight years in office and Presiding George W. Bush 140[15] (and this does not include the visits of foreign chief executives received in the White House). A good many of these, however, are goodwill visits—diplomatically useful—but not negotiation missions.

High government officials or cabinet ministers, particularly foreign ministers, may join their chief executives and engage in negotiations of their own during some summit meetings (depending upon the issues at hand). Often, summit meetings open the way for post-summit diplomacy. Some summits provide for follow-up action. For example, the diplomats who are to prepare for the next G7 summit usually hold a meeting shortly after the annual gathering to review what was accomplished and what needs to be carried out. Later summits may continue the dialogue on certain agenda items. Summit meetings that are an integral part of the decision-making process of international organizations (e.g., the EU) are even more likely to generate follow-up diplomacy. Independently of summit meetings, foreign ministers and executive department heads are now more involved in meetings of their own, consulting and negotiating—another form of high-level diplomacy and an expanding method of global problem management. It is often thought, particularly in UN circles, that involving high-level decision makers in negotiations may generate faster action since many have greater latitude to make decisions than rank and file diplomats (hence negotiations are frequently mandated to be held "at the highest level"). It needs to be noted that this approach does not always work as heads of departments having other pressing business to handle at home, may just decide to send a representative to participate in the negotiations.

A different kind of negotiation is found in third-party involvement, particularly in conflict resolution.[16] This is often presented as *mediation*, but it is done in a vast variety of ways, involving at times as little as facilitating the discussion and as much as formulating an entire settlement program. The goal is always to have the parties reach an agreement (by contrast to arbitration or judicial settlement in which the decision of the third party is binding). Mediation requires great diplomatic skill and imagination to provide alternatives for what separates the disputants. One reason for the difficulty is often the depth of distrust and enmity between the conflicting states. Between 1925 and 1945, in ten disputes that took place in Latin America, thirty-five countries tried to mediate; after 1945, in just thirteen disputes, there were sixty-three mediation attempts.[17] But the procedure remains widely used. If little animosity is involved in the dispute, the states concerned may take the initiative to seek the help of a mediator to settle their difference. Frequently, third parties take the initiative of offering their help, particularly when it appears that the parties in conflict are not making any progress. Some disputes are so envenomed that even getting the conflicting states to talk to a mediator may be difficult.[18]

Mediation is extremely flexible and is a great asset as state conflicts are so diverse. It may be offered by a government, or a head of state. A professional diplomat will normally acts as mediator in the leader's name, although several US presidents actually participated in Middle East mediation (assisted by their secretaries of state and other specialists). Much depends on how much trust the mediator can inspire, or the incentives that can be offered (at Camp David the United States offered security guarantees and several billion dollars in economic assistance to both Egypt and Israel to accept a peace agreement). International organizations, for example the UN, can be particularly helpful when no state is offering to mediate or when it fails to win the cooperation of the disputants. Private-sector actors and NGOs have also been effective mediators, often because they are seen as more impartial or devoid of ulterior motives.[19]

It may be pointed out that an offer of good offices is a diplomatic variant in providing third-party assistance in international conflicts. Technically, the procedure of good offices involves an offer of facilities that will help the disputants in their own negotiations. For example, a neutral state such as Switzerland may make an estate or a castle available where the conflicting states can negotiate their differences. The party offering good offices normally does not participate in the negotiations. In practice, the provider of good offices may become a facilitator and even mediate as the need arises and negotiations evolve. Both mediation and good offices have an official, formal dimension. But success is often dependent on a great deal of informal interaction, initiatives taken, and suggestions made as the talks progress.

In international affairs there is a great deal of totally informal negotiations. And these may need to be categorized separately. Often presented as *consultations*, particularly at the UN, or even as "conversations," they enable international actors to determine to what extent they may be able to work together. These actors may even modify their initial outlook depending upon the course of the conversations. Often, in such "conversations," the parties are subtly negotiating. And this is demonstrated, for example, at the UN when a committee has failed to agree on what it was negotiating. The committee chair, at this point, is likely to declare a short recess for the membership to engage in "consultations"—and the whole group engages in conversations, moving about the room, going from one party to the next, and working out its differences. There is a good deal of this sort of informal interaction in diplomatic gatherings, in the margin of the formal diplomatic process. Personal relationships between the delegates are often an important element in such consultations.

THE IMPACT OF TECHNOLOGY

Technology is transforming the world. Nations are more interconnected than ever before and this is fueling an expansion of global governance diplomacy. Spectacular advances in technology, particularly in the fields of communication, are making global society more interdependent; for example, one can witness the remarkable chain reaction of popular uprisings in the Middle East against authoritarian rulers triggered by mass demonstrations in Tunisia in late 2010. *Interdependence* is a consequence of the evolution of human society.[20] Technology cannot be wished away nor modern communication renounced. Society has derived enormous benefits from technological development fostering more research, more invention, and more interdependence. Other factors have contributed to its accelerated growth—among them, no doubt, the interaction itself and the awareness of interdependence. These factors of course lead to increased traffic across international boundaries and activities on a global scale.

Interdependence is at the root of *globalization* and globalization generates more interdependence. Russett, Starr, and Kinsella have identified globalization as "a process whereby economic, political, and cultural transactions are less and less constrained by national boundaries and the sovereign authority of national government."[21] The changes taking place are spectacular. Already in 1975, Alex Inkeles could write: "Recent decades reveal a general tendency for many forms of human interconnectedness across national boundaries to be doubling every ten years."[22] The International Monetary Fund reports that "since 1995, global capital flows have tripled to $6.4 trillion, reaching about 14.5 percent of world GDP,"[23] and roughly $1.5 trillion worth of global currencies are traded each day, up from less than $200 billion in 1986.[24]

Another aspect of the phenomenon is the proliferation of problems that no one nation can solve through simple self-reliance. The maintenance of economic stability needs to be addressed internationally. A crisis anywhere can threaten the most prosperous countries. Drug traffic, organized crime, the migration of people in search of a decent existence, and so many other problems cannot be contained without concerted efforts on the part of a large number of states, and not just the rich and powerful, although, doubtless, they have more to contribute. This points to the globalization of international problem solving and calls for diplomatic efforts on an unprecedented scale.

It is important to note, however, that extensive as interdependence and globalization may be, this dual phenomenon is unevenly manifested around the world. For example, in the realm of communication, the average number of television sets per 1,000 people is 735 in high-income groups worldwide, 326 in the medium income category, and only 91 among low-income people. The difference is even more pronounced with regard to personal computers (and roughly the same for Internet users): 467, 45, and 8, respectively.[25] This does not invalidate global trends. But global society retains elements of profound disparity and these are going to keep states from working together as interdependence would seem to warrant. No nation state is self-sufficient; but some states are more sheltered from global influences than others. Geography, the uneven distribution of natural resources, and particular traits of national culture are factors that create differences in the interdependence of societies. Nations experience different needs, a situation which complicates the task of achieving international cooperation. The world remains badly divided into nation states, all too reluctant to work together. Cultural, economic, and political differences emphasize separateness. Self-centeredness continues to hamper the process of managing common problems.

Another aspect of interdependence and globalization is the *expansion of the diplomatic agenda*. A multiplicity of issues that used to be confined to the domestic order must now be addressed internationally. In 1975, Secretary of State Henry Kissinger observed, "Dealing with the traditional agenda is no longer enough. A new and unprecedented kind of issue has emerged. The problems of energy, resources, environment, population, the uses of space and the seas now rank with questions of military security, ideology and territorial rivalry which have traditionally made up the diplomatic agenda."[26] And the range of issues dealt with internationally keeps growing.

Since a good deal of diplomacy has to do with communication, the *"communication revolution"* has of course left its mark. Written communications remain important in international affairs, but more diplomatic work is now done by telephone from one capital to the next. The hotline between Washington and Moscow made history when the superpowers realized during the Cuban Missile Crisis that in a nuclear confrontation rapid communication could be critical.[27] A number of enemy countries eventually established their own hotlines. Telephone communication is now frequent among a number of chief executives—and not limited to emergency situations. It is now widely used in diplomatic negotiations.

For example, in the process of implementing the Oslo peace agreements, Dennis Ross, the US Middle East negotiator, was on the phone three or four times a day for two weeks in September 1995, talking to the chief Israeli negotiator, and then to his Palestinian counterpart, explaining to each of them the terms that the other side was insisting upon to win the support of its domestic constituency—mediation by telephone. And then came a crisis: On September 24, Yasir Arafat stormed out of the negotiations in Taba, Egypt, screaming that Israel was trying to shove down his throat totally unfair territorial terms. At 3:00 a.m., Ross received a call at his home, near

Washington, DC, from Israel's chief negotiator, asking for help in calming Arafat. From 3:15 to 6:00 a.m., Ross spoke with Arafat, the Israeli foreign minister, the chief Palestinian negotiator, and Israel's chief negotiator, trying to convince them that they were just a few steps away from an agreement and that they should not throw away a year of hard work. The two sides agreed to make concessions. At 7:00 a.m., Arafat and the Israeli foreign minister called the US secretary of state and announced that agreement had been reached. Then came President Bill Clinton's turn to get on the phone. He called the Israeli prime minister and Arafat to congratulate them and invite them to the signature ceremony in Washington; and he called King Hussein of Jordan, King Hassan II of Morocco, and President Hosni Mubarak of Egypt to invite them to attend the ceremony. A small piece of history was thus written between telephone conversations.[28]

Teleconferencing is now making its own contribution to diplomatic negotiations. Gordon Smith reported in 1999 that the military in many countries had been holding virtual meetings using secure video links "for some time."[29] In 2007, when Hamas defeated Fatah in Gaza, creating an unexpected crisis, the quartet of peace brokers (the United States, the EU, Russia, and the UN) held an emergency teleconference on June 15 to review the grim realities of the new situation.[30] Now, the Internet is transforming relations between field missions (including embassies) and their foreign ministries back home. In the mid-1980s, the US Department of State was reporting that message traffic with the field had been increasing by 100,000 communications a year since 1980 and had reached 1.8 million in 1986.[31] By the turn of the century, it was electronically processing over 140,000 official records and 90,000 data messages each day, supporting more than 250 diplomatic posts around the world. Over 20 million electronic messages were posted annually by State Department personnel.[32] The Center for Strategic and International Studies in Washington, DC, predicted that the Internet would become "the central nervous system of international relations."[33]

As early as 1979, digital technology gave US negotiators a remarkable advantage in the course of the World Administrative Radio Conference held in Geneva by the International Telecommunication Union, a Specialized Agency of the UN that deals with radio channel allocations. Among the 150 national delegations, the US mission alone had the advantage of knowing the status of each of the thousands of proposals generated each day pertaining to the conference agenda. As each of them was negotiated, changes were recorded on a desktop computer at the US delegation office, thus permitting a fast and effective way of sorting out and accessing a vast array of data. Having a timely and accurate record of any progress made in the negotiations gave the US delegates a critical advantage in developing their negotiation strategy.[34]

eDiplomacy

In 2003, the US Department of State launched the Office of eDiplomacy in the Bureau of Information Resource Management. Its Diplomatic Innovation Division was designed to work with US government's foreign affairs agencies, other nations' diplomatic institutions, and entities involved in international relations.[35] One of the most prominent programs of the Office of eDiplomacy is Diplopedia Wiki launched in 2006. It is a Wikipedia-style unclassified online encyclopedia of diplomacy and foreign relations running on the Department of State's internal Intranet. It provides practical job knowledge to US foreign affairs personnel and State Department units, both domestic and abroad, with State Intranet access. It is also available to the US intelligence community and national security organizations on a read-only basis. It is not open to the public.

State Department personnel who can access Diplopedia are invited and encouraged to contribute knowledge in the form of articles, discussion, or editing of material submitted by others. It is fast becoming a reference tool on all topics of interest to the US foreign affairs community.[36] It is particularly important for officers who are regularly rotated to new posts. They can thus obtain basic information on their new location, city, or country—information which would normally take time to acquire after arrival, by other means of inquiry and phone calls. In just four years, it has grown to more than 40,000 articles written and edited by the foreign affairs community. In Diplopedia, users must be registered and editing is not anonymous.[37] The State Department believes that Diplopedia offers a way to thwart the embarrassing publication of diplomatic cables on the WikiLeaks website. These cables have now been replaced by Diplopedia's highly secure system by which ambassadors and their staffs can compare notes, pass tips, offer candid observations on world leaders, or exchange any other information.[38]

Other projects of the Office of eDiplomacy include the following: The Sounding Board is a project started by Secretary Hilary Clinton that enables domestic and overseas employees to submit ideas for Department innovation and reform. Senior Department officials review both the initial proposal and management response to determine if additional action or implementation is feasible and necessary. Virtual Student Foreign Service is a program to permit new forms of diplomatic engagement for university students in the United States. American students working virtually (eInterns) are given online assignments with US embassies. Virtual Presence Posts help the State Department to broaden its outreach abroad in key foreign cities of regions having no access to US embassies or consulates. Most Virtual Presence Posts have a website and American diplomats in the region may use public outreach programs, media events, or online webchats to create a "virtual" presence for local populations.[39]

Communication technology offers remarkable possibilities for global governance diplomacy if skillfully used, particularly in networking with NGOs and other members of civil society. It must be noted, however, that many government bureaucracies are slow in adjusting to the new modes of communication. Many countries cannot afford to invest in these expensive systems. Diplomacy, too, remains attached to well-established traditions long after they have outlived their usefulness. Often, a cultural change is needed before diplomacy can make effective use of the new technology. Change is taking place, obviously, but unevenly around the world.

Geographic Information Systems

Satellite imagery and geographic information systems are used to facilitate international negotiations as well as coordination of joint fieldwork between governments, international organizations, and NGOs. The technology involves computer systems capable of storing, processing, and displaying data according to their geographical location using various types of imagery acquired by orbiting satellites.[40] Complex diplomatic work involved in the deployment and control of multinational peacekeeping forces can be enormously facilitated by this type of technology. The success of many of these operations is heavily dependent upon negotiations to win the consent of distrustful contending factions in situations fraught with uncertainty. Geographical details are usually of great importance in convincing one's opponents of the demands and limitations of given situations on the ground, or in deciding who will be allowed to enter specific areas and the resultant implications for the maintenance of cease-fires or the disengagement of military units. This technology can also be useful in negotiating other types of international monitoring and supervision—matters of critical significance in this age of ethnic conflict.

Cybersecurity

Expanding the use of information and communication technology in global diplomacy raises the issue of communication security. In a 2003 study of computer security, more than half of the twenty-four US federal agencies surveyed received a grade of D or F.[41] The Department of Homeland Security's division in charge of monitoring cybersecurity, received the lowest overall score. Also earning an F was the Justice Department the agency charged with investigating and prosecuting cases of hacking and other forms of cybercrime.[42] In global diplomacy, maintaining confidentiality is of course of particular importance, aside from the matter of protection from disruption and incapacitation of electronic systems. Cybersecurity will thus remain a continuing quest; but as soon as a new defensive measure is in place, hackers, assorted code-breakers, and perhaps foreign agents, will be busy finding new ways of attaining their objectives. The addition of cyber communication to the global diplomatic process makes the effort evermore tempting.

Cyberterrorism is widely discussed among information technology professionals. Attacks by hackers give an idea of the damage that can be done by means of computer break-ins, swarming (i.e., bombarding targets with thousands of messages at once), and computer viruses and worms, among other techniques. Greater security efforts are thus urgently needed; and it must be remembered that during the North Atlantic Treaty Organization (NATO) operations to evict Serbian forces from Kosovo, businesses, public entities, and academic institutions in NATO countries received virus-laden e-mails from a range of Eastern European nations.[43]

Humanitarian Applications of Geographic Information Technology

Satellite imagery and geographic information technology have been put to good use in humanitarian operations (e.g., earthquake relief) involving agencies of multiple governments, international organizations, and civil society personnel, particularly NGOs, that have widely different information needs. Satellite images are processed and analyzed according to the specific requirements of the institutions concerned, and are distributed to personnel in the field and to decision makers in regional offices and headquarters. Geographically organized information can include details on the availability of food and medical resources, population distribution in affected areas, weather conditions, and so much more.[44] Some relief operations take place in underdeveloped, unfamiliar, or poorly mapped areas, for example, in places where refugees stream across mountainous regions in Eastern Afghanistan, or where victims of earthquakes were trapped in isolated villages in Pakistan. The many agencies trying to provide relief have an acute need for accurate geographical information about the disaster areas or places where people may be safely relocated.

The UN is extensively involved in disaster relief and it endeavors to achieve global coordination of relief efforts. For that purpose, its Office for the Coordination of Humanitarian Affairs (OCHA) in Geneva has created the Virtual On-Site Operations Coordination Center (Virtual OSOCC), whose main object, through the ReliefWeb site, is to facilitate decision making for a widespread response to disasters around the world, by means of near real-time information exchange, among all international actors involved in such operations, including a variety of international organizations, governments, and NGOs.[45] All agencies and field staffs have access to the information pertaining to specific operations and can provide comments on existing situations and discuss issues of concern with other participants. Disaster information can be exchanged continuously and simultaneously from anywhere in the world.

ReliefWeb was launched in October 1996. It maintains three offices (New York, Geneva, and Kobe, Japan) to update the website around the clock and has seen a steady growth of traffic from its inception. In 2002, ReliefWeb received 1.5 million hits (visits to the website) per week; in 2004, it received 1 million hits per day. Shortly after the December 2004 tsunami disaster in southern Asia, it received an average of 3 million hits per day. In addition, in 2009, ReliefWeb serviced 152,000 subscribers, providing resources specifically targeted to relief professionals and received almost 10 million visits to the website (a 12 percent increase over 2008).[46]

Early Warning and Crisis Management

Rapid communication technology offers the possibility of better early warning for crisis management and preventive diplomacy before problems are out of control. For example, the Helsinki Summit of the Conference on Security and Cooperation in Europe (July 1992) agreed to improve its capability for early warning, conflict prevention, and crisis management.[47] The US Agency for International Development/Famine Early Warning System provides information about food security situations throughout the world and issues alerts to decision makers, helping in preparedness and response.[48] The EU has probably made the most concerted effort to create a comprehensive crisis management capability but acknowledges that further advances in relevant technologies are needed (e.g., early warnings, real-time news, and geo-spatial information) to ensure effectiveness.[49]

Organizations such as the US Institute of Peace and the Crisis Management Initiative have done research to improve interoperability, that is, the ability of emergency responders (governments, international organizations, and NGOs) to communicate and work seamlessly. The OCHA with its Virtual OSOCC and ReliefWeb has achieved a good measure of interoperability. The US government, in 2004, launched the RapidCom program to achieve better emergency response interoperability. Awareness of its importance is spreading.[50] However, states often hesitate to respond to early warning when the danger seems uncertain or still somewhat remote. International organizations and NGOs show fewer inhibitions, but effective prevention is more problematic without the support of influential states. Early warning needs to achieve greater credibility. Information and communication technology can make a difference by providing more specificity to the warning and greater reliability in its sources of information.

Network Power

The significant development of information and communication technology is also magnifying the role of civil society in global affairs. Mass access to technology, even in the developing world, has led to greater political awareness at the grassroots level and has contributed to the growth of activism in global civil society. NGOs have been a major factor in this phenomenon. They mobilize opinion, exercise leadership, and thanks to digital technology, network around the world. NGOs are becoming more aggressive and resorting to their own diplomatic outreach to achieve their objectives, especially in international organizations. All interconnected groups can instantly receive the latest information and instructions on what needs to be done. Massive responses to international events, conferences, meetings of international organizations, and governmental action, can be coordinated. The most impressive example of network power in action is provided by the International Campaign to Ban Landmines (ICBL), a network of more than 1200 organizations around the world. Under the leadership of Jody Williams, it influenced governments and their diplomacy. NGO representatives even participated in the negotiations that produced the 1997 landmine treaty. See details in chapter 4.

Networking is also taking place between international organizations and NGOs. Even governments and their diplomats are now routinely doing the same. During the summer of 2010, Africa's mobile phone enthusiasts were racing to develop better mobile phones in the "Apps <4> Africa" contest sponsored by the US State Department and three local technology communities (the Nairobi-based iHub, Kampala-based Appfrica Labs, and the Social Development Network, which works throughout East Africa). In today's interconnected world, individuals and organizations can play a defining role in international affairs and the State Department is capitalizing on this new landscape.[51] Information and communication technology are transforming the international political process—and this transformation has only just begun.

Espionage

Unfortunately, technology is also adding a wrinkle to the conduct of diplomacy. Espionage, of course, is as old as world affairs, but technology is now making it easier to obtain illegal access to confidential diplomatic exchanges, and such efforts are not limited to states engaged in international conflict. British spying on UN secretary-general Kofi Annan was revealed in late February 2004 in an interview with Clare Short, an outspoken former member of Tony Blair's cabinet who resigned in the summer of 2003 and called on Blair to do the same. She said that Britain had regularly spied on the secretary-general and that transcripts of his conversations had circulated freely in the British Cabinet. Interestingly, in a BBC interview, one day after the Clare Short revelations, former UN secretary-general Boutros Boutros-Ghali acknowledged: "From the first day I entered my office, they told me, 'Beware, your office is bugged, your residence is bugged.' It is the tradition that member states that have the technical capacity to bug will do it without hesitation." Richard Butler, former weapons inspector in Iraq, interviewed in the same BBC program, declared: "There is abundant evidence that we were being constantly monitored." He added that when he had something sensitive to discuss, "I had to go to the basement café in the UN where there was heaps of noise or I'd go and take a walk in Central Park."[52]

In 2003, Katharine Gun, a linguist working for one of Britain's intelligence agencies, reported that "she had seen an American request for British help in bugging the diplomats of six Security Council members whose votes were being courted" for the resolution that the United States sought to authorize the war against Iraq.[53] Shortly thereafter, the EU uncovered a bugging operation directed at five of its members, France, Germany, Britain, Austria, and Spain. Listening devices were found in the offices of their delegations in the EU headquarters building in Brussels. This occurred when EU leaders, particularly from France and Germany, were sharply critical of the Bush administration's decision to use force against Iraq.[54] While espionage has always been a factor in the conduct of foreign relations, advanced technology is making the matter more dangerous, thus complicating the work of the diplomatic profession—and the problem will become worse as technology becomes more sophisticated.

STRUCTURE OF THE BOOK

The objective of this inquiry is to study how diplomacy serves global governance, how the diverse international actors use it, and what it accomplishes. The multilateral dimension of much of this work adds to its intricate nature and so does the complexity of many of the problems it seeks to address. This book focuses on diplomatic practice and the methods used by the international actors involved.

J. David Singer observed that "in any area of scholarly inquiry, there are always several ways in which the phenomena under study may be sorted out and arranged for purposes of systematic analysis,"[55] emphasizing that an accurate description of the phenomena under consideration is necessary, presenting as complete and undistorted a picture of reality as possible. The task is facilitated by selecting appropriate levels of inquiry. Singer chose two for his analysis of international relations: the international system and the national state. Other research projects will need different levels of analysis.

Kenneth Waltz, seeking to examine the major causes of war, divided his investigation into three categories: people, the structure of the separate states, and the global system. He called his three components "images of international relations," (his units of analysis), and organized his book around them.[56] It is to be noted that each level of analysis not only identifies the boundaries of what is examined, but it also offers a different perspective, a distinctive vision, of the phenomenon under investigation. For example, global issues are likely to look different when seen from a national and from a transnational vantage point.

James Rosenau, examining foreign policy, used five analytical categories: (1) individual, (2) role, (3) governmental, (4) societal, and (5) a systemic set of variables. He called his categories "philosophies of analysis."[57] Others have selected levels of analysis to meet the specific needs of their inquiry, for example, by adding a regional level.[58] Bruce Russett, Harvey Starr, and David Kinsella made very successful use of six levels in their analysis of world politics: (1) individual decision makers, (2) decision makers' roles, (3) structure of decision makers' government, (4) characteristics of the decision makers' society, (5) relations between the decision makers' nation state and other international actors, and (6) the world system.[59]

This kind of analytical method is useful in the study of diplomacy as an instrument of global governance. The subject matter of this study is of course more specialized. Also, diplomacy does not necessarily change in its application with every configuration of the global system. Four levels of analysis are used in the present study.

The first level of analysis is the state level and includes the role of the nation state in global governance. The state remains the most critical global actor even when it cannot solve global problems by itself. The state often chooses to act independently to protect its national interest. Even when participating in collective endeavors, the national perspective remains a significant element in the diplomacy of global governance.

The second level of analysis looks at intergovernmental institutions and its critical importance in global governance diplomacy. International organizations are both a forum for multilateral diplomacy and a major set of international actors still growing in significance for global governance diplomacy. Some of these organizations are multipurpose, others are specialized. In addition, a multiplicity of regional or limited membership institutions play a role in global governance.

The third level of analysis is the transnational level including the increasing role of civil society institutions and NGOs. This is where new kinds of international actors are found, unevenly contributing to global governance diplomacy beyond the control of public authorities and increasingly determined to play a role in international affairs.

The fourth level is the functional level where the term *functional* is used in a broad sense. Here, the role of diplomacy is examined in the five areas of global governance studied in part II of this book: (1) peace and security, (2) economic affairs, (3) social issues, (4) human rights, and (5) environmental protection. Each of these presents different challenges for global governance diplomacy. They require the development of different diplomatic strategies. Some of the issues are more amenable to global governance while others, such as the eradication of global poverty, remain fairly intractable.

NOTES

1. See Thomas G. Weiss, ed. *Thinking About Global Governance: Why People and Ideas Matter* (New York: Routledge, 2011).

2. Commission on Global Governance, *Our Global Neighbourhood: Report of the Commission on Global Governance* (New York: Oxford University Press, 1995), p. 2.

3. See Craig Murphy, "The Emergence of Global Governance," in Thomas G. Weiss and Rorden Wilkinson, eds. *International Organization and Global Governance* (New York: Routledge, 2014).

4. See Bruce Russett, Harvey Starr, and David Kinsella, *World Politics: The Menu for Choice* (8th ed. Belmont, CA: Thomson / Wadsworth, 2006), pp. 73 ff. and Appendix B, pp. 535 ff. Also in 10th edition, 2012.

5. See Michael Edwards and John Gaventa, eds. *Global Citizen Action* (Boulder, CO: Lynne Rienner, 2001).

6. Pauline Kerr and Geoffrey Wiseman, eds. *Diplomacy in a Globalizing World: Theories and Practices* (New York: Oxford University Press, 2012). Corneliu Bjola and Markus Kornprobst, *Understanding International Diplomacy: Theory, Practice, and Ethics* (New York: Routledge, 2013).

7. For example, Robert L. Hutchings, *American Diplomacy and the End of the Cold War: An Insider's Account of U.S. Policy in Europe, 1989–1992* (Washington, DC: Woodrow Wilson Center; Baltimore, MD: Johns Hopkins University Press, 1997).

8. See Harvey J. Langholtz and Chris E. Stout, *The Psychology of Diplomacy* (Westport, CT: Greenwood Publishing, 2004).

9. Chief minister, 1624–1642, of France's Louis XIII.

10. Still in print today. François de Callières, *On the Manner of Negotiating with Princes: On the Uses of Diplomacy; the Choice of Ministers and Envoys; and the Personal Qualities Necessary for Success in Missions Abroad* (translated from the French by A. F. Whyte [1716] Notre Dame, Indiana: Notre Dame University Press, 1963. Reprinted by University Press of America, by arrangement with the University of Notre Dame Press).

11. The US Agriculture Department maintains a Foreign Agricultural Service to deal with US foreign agricultural relations. www.usembassy.gov and www.usda-france.fr (Accessed August 27, 2010).

12. Lord Gore-Booth, ed. *Satow's Guide to Diplomatic Practice* (5th ed. New York: Longman, 1979), pp. 120–160.

13. Frances Mautner-Markhof, "International Negotiations: Mechanisms for the Management of Complex Systems," in *Processes of International Negotiations* (Boulder, CO: Westview, 1989), pp. 65–78. Also, Brigid Starkey, Mark A. Boyer, and Jonathan Wilkenfeld, *International Negotiation in a Complex World* (4th ed. New York: Rowman & Littlefield, 2015).

14. See United States Institute of Peace series on national negotiating styles. See for example Emily Metzgar, *French Negotiating Style* (April 2001).

15. http://history.state.gov/departmenthistory/travels (Accessed June 1, 2011).

16. Thomas Princen, *Intermediaries in International Conflicts* (Princeton, NJ: Princeton University Press, 1992).

17. Princen, *Intermediaries*, p. 5.

18. See for example Christopher S. McMullen, *Resolution of the Yemen Crisis: A Case Study in Mediation* (Washington, DC: Institute for the Study of Diplomacy, School of Foreign Service, Georgetown University, 1980).

19. I. William Zartman and Saadia Touval, "International Mediation in the Post-Cold War Era" in *Managing Global Chaos: Sources of, and Responses to, International Conflict*, edited by Chester A, Crocker, and Fen Osler Hampson, with Pamela Aall (Washington, DC: US Institute of Peace, 1996), pp. 445–461; see also chapter 4.

20. See Robert O. Keohane and Joseph S. Nye, *Power and Interdependence* (2nd ed. Glenview, IL: Scott, Foresman, 1989), Part I. "Understanding Interdependence," pp. 1–60.

21. Russett, Starr, and Kinsella (2006), 432.

22. Alex Inkeles, "The Emerging Social Structure of the World," *World Politics* Vol. 27 (July 1975), p. 479.

23. www.imf.org/external/pubs/ft/survey/so/home (Accessed November 10, 2010).

24. Russett, Starr, and Kinsella (2006), p. 434.

25. World Bank, *World Development Indicators 2004* (Washington, DC: World Bank, 2004).

26. Henry A. Kissinger, "A New National Partnership," *Department of State Bulletin* (February 17, 1975), p. 199.

27. See Robert F. Kennedy, *Thirteen Days: A Memoir of the Cuban Missile Crisis* (New York: Norton, 1969).

28. Stephen Greenhouse, "Mideast Shuttle's New Twist: U.S. Aide Mediated by Phone," *New York Times* (September 25, 1995), pp. A1, A4.

29. Gordon S. Smith, *Reinventing Diplomacy: A Virtual Necessity* (Washington, DC: US Institute of Peace, 1999), p. 8.

30. *New York Times* (June 16, 2007), p. A7.

31. Eric Schmitt, "Of Diplomacy and Software," *New York Times* (April 18, 1986), p. 12.

32. Wilson Dizard, Jr. *Digital Diplomacy: US Foreign Policy in the Information Age* (Westport, CT: Praeger, 2001), p. 100.

33. Center for Strategic and International Studies, Advisory Panel on Diplomacy in the Information Age, Washington, DC. *Reinventing Diplomacy in the Information Age* (Washington, DC: Center for Strategic and International Studies, 1998), pp. x–xi.

34. Dizard, p. 107.

35. US Department of State, Office of eDiplomacy, "About eDiplomacy," www.state.gov/m/irm//ediplomacy (Accessed June 6, 2011).

36. www.state.gov/m/inn/ediplomcy/115847 (Accessed June 2, 2011).

37. "Diplopedia—Wikipedia-style Diplomacy—A Success at US Department of State," www.sciencedaily.com/2010/05/100520112345 (Accessed June 2, 2011).

38. http://fcw.com/articles/2010/12/07/state-department-diplopedia (Accessed June 6, 2011).

39. For other programs of the Office of eDiplomacy, see www.state.gov/m/irm/ediplomacy/c23840 (Accessed June 2, 2011).

40. Einar Bjorgo, *Space Aid: Current and Potential Uses of Satellite Imagery in Humanitarian Organizations.* Virtual Diplomacy Report No. 12 (Washington, DC: US Institute of Peace, 2002).

41. Conducted by the US House of Representatives, Government Reform Sub-Committee on Technology.

42. Gabriel Weimann, *Cyberterrorism: How Real Is the Threat?* Special Report No. 119 (Washington, DC: US Institute of Peace, 2004), p. 8.

43. Weimann, *Cyberterrorism,* p. 5.

44. Bjorgo, *Space Aid,* pp. 1ff.

45. www.reliefweb.int/virtualosocc (Accessed September 17, 2010).

46. www.reliefweb.int/stats/rw_annual_stats_2009 (Accessed September 17, 2010).

47. www.ena.lu/helsinki_summit_document_extract_concerning_early_warning_conflict_prevention_crisis_management (Accessed September 20, 2010).

48. www.fews.net (Accessed September 20, 2010).

49. http://globesec.jrc.ec.europa.eu/institutional-actions (Accessed September 20, 2010).

50. See *Interoperability Today: A Quarterly Newsletter* www.safecomprogram.gov/SAFECOM/interoperability/default (Accessed September 21, 2010).

51. Sam duPont "Digital Diplomacy," *Foreign Policy* (August 3, 2010). www.foreignpolicy.com/articles/2010/08/03/digital_diplomacy (Accessed September 16, 2010).

52. Warren Hoge, "On Bugging News, Annan Had Low-Key Reaction to Old Practice," *New York Times* (February 28, 2004), p. A6.

53. "Tony Blair's Iraq Hangover," *New York Times* (February 28, 2004), p. A26.

54. *New York Times* (March 20, 2003), p. A7.

55. J. David Singer, "The Level-of-Analysis Problem in International Relations," in *International Politics and Foreign Policy: A Reader in Research and Theory*, edited by James N. Rosenau (rev. ed. New York: Free Press, 1969), p. 20.

56. Kenneth N. Waltz, *Man, the State, and War: A Theoretical Analysis* (New York: Columbia University Press, 1959), p. 12.

57. James N. Rosenau, *The Scientific Study of Foreign Policy: Essays on the Analysis of World Politics* (rev. ed: New York: Nichols, 1980), pp. 128–129.

58. Timothy J. Lomperis, *Flawed Realism: Hans Morgenthau and Kenneth Walts on Vietnam—the Case for a Regional Level of Analysis* (Unpublished. St. Louis: Saint Louis University, 2005).

59. Russett, Starr, and Kinsella (9th ed. 2010), Chapter 1.

Part I

INTERNATIONAL ACTORS AND THEIR DIPLOMACY

Chapter 2

The Role of State Diplomacy in Global Governance

States remain the most significant players in international politics and in the diplomatic process. This is not intended to deny that other international actors play important roles—as will be seen later—but states wield power and authority. They can mobilize national resources—seldom inconsequential even for small states—and they make independent decisions, for better or worse. Of course, states now face more constraints as global interdependence increases, and the world becomes incredibly more complex. Often states feel stymied facing a multiplicity of problems and seldom with enough resources to satisfy all their needs.

States are still overwhelmingly focused on their own national interests. It may be pointed out that serving the global common good is in the national interest, but states do not necessarily see it that way. Furthermore, they frequently disagree as to what the common good is at a given time. They may have their own special vision of it; or, then again, they may not care. International cooperation is not always easy and unilateral action remains an important mode of global governance as many see it: states respond individually to international situations according to their sense of what will serve their purpose.

Great powers are probably more inclined to act unilaterally (even when they do not have to), seeing it as "taking the lead" in approaching questions of concern to them, perhaps inviting others to follow them or join them. They are often resented for not consulting other actors *before* embarking upon their own courses of action. It must be noted, however, that this kind of unilateral initiative may be the only mode of global governance available when apathy prevails, or when a deadlock prevents collective action. And it is true that there are situations in which collaborative approaches are not critical. Unilateral humanitarian assistance to a neglected region, for example, Somalia, may be beneficial even when a collective approach might accomplish more. As for quick assistance, unilateral action may in fact be preferred, while efforts are made to achieve international cooperation. Thus, global governance is by no means limited to collective decisions even though collective decisions are becoming more important. Many modes of diplomatic interaction are available.

TRADITIONAL DIPLOMATIC MEANS

Diplomacy is still importantly carried out by means of resident diplomatic representation: a government is often represented in a foreign capital by a resident diplomatic mission, usually an embassy. This takes care of the bilateral diplomatic relations of the governments concerned. When faced with issues of global governance, pairs of governments may use their resident missions to explore the kind of cooperation they may be prepared to engage in to address the matter. When several nations are affected by a particular situation, they may still explore the possibility for joint action by means of a series of bilateral contacts, discussing, for example, what the participants might contribute to a collective effort. Nations do a good deal of consulting and networking by means of their resident missions, and some of them have multilateral objectives.

States may also prefer to send special envoys traveling to several capitals to discuss future joint efforts. Special envoys can focus on a single issue, travel to different capitals, and engage in elaborate negotiations over lengthy periods of time, as US envoys to the Middle East do periodically, seeking accommodation in this deeply divided region. Special envoys are well suited to mediation work. States may also engage in bilateral consultation to coordinate their diplomatic efforts in multilateral forums or to settle differences arising in the course of multilateral negotiations taking place elsewhere. For example, if the British representative at the UN in New York is unwilling to support the US position on an issue before the Security Council, the US ambassador in London may be directed by the US secretary of state to discuss the matter with the British foreign minister in London. This is parallel diplomacy or auxiliary diplomacy. Given the increase in the volume of multilateral diplomacy in contemporary international affairs, national embassies in foreign capitals have a larger amount of work relating to issues negotiated in some multilateral forums. It must be acknowledged, however, that a large number of states today maintain a very limited number of resident missions in foreign capitals.

Bilateral Permanent Representation in Foreign Capitals

23 states maintain *no* embassy in any foreign capital
72 states maintain 1 to 5 embassies in foreign capitals

30	maintain	6 to 10
14	maintain	11 to 15
18	maintain	16 to 25
22	maintain	26 to 50
8	maintain	51 to 75
2	maintain	76 to 100

4   maintain more than 100. They are, in ascending order, Japan, the United States, France, and Canada. Canada has more than 175.[1]

Thus, 95 states (just about half of the states of the world) maintain no more than five embassies in foreign capitals. 125 maintain no more than 10. For many of the developing countries, this is a matter of economy and also the result of limited relations with most other countries. These nonrepresented states routinely use their memberships in international organizations, particularly the UN, to maintain diplomatic contact with the countries in which they have no permanent missions.

STATES USING INTERNATIONAL ORGANIZATIONS FOR GLOBAL GOVERNANCE

International organizations are a diplomatic tool created by states to meet their needs and particularly to address international problems. Their multilateral character is highly practical. Some organizations are specialized (e.g., health), while others are multipurpose. Starting in the nineteenth century, these institutions have proliferated. There are now 244 global and regional intergovernmental bodies. But if we add special purpose organizations, such as UNAIDS, and subsidiary bodies, the total reaches more than 1,800.[2] This can be taken as an indication of how states perceive the need for global governance.

Useful as many of these institutions are, however, they cannot always meet the needs of global society. Member states' cooperation is not always available when needed, as can be witnessed in the problems of piracy in Somalia, and the use of child soldiers in Africa. Many aspects of our international society remain beyond reliable forms of governance. The role of states in the effectiveness of international organizations (i.e., in ensuring the fulfillment of their missions) is insufficiently appreciated—to the point of condemning the League of Nations for failing to prevent the Second World War when its *member states* irresponsibly refused to use it to ensure collective security. Its structure was imperfect, to be sure, but the main flaw was in the inept policies of the very states that created it. No organization will achieve the objectives of its founders if the member states fail to carry out their obligations. This is the instrumental dimension of international organizations—and member-state diplomacy is critical in this respect. States remain in the driver's seat. Their diplomacy, the way they interact within the organization, is critical in the role international organizations will play in international affairs. This is the first condition for institutional effectiveness in global governance.

The second condition is to give the organization the means it needs to do its job, especially financial, and these must be provided by the member states. Reluctance to pay is a perennial problem. Insistence that the funds be properly administered is of course vital. But the nickels and dimes approach often used by member states is not the way to achieve effectiveness in global governance. Many states—even some of the richest—can be blamed for this myopic approach.

The third condition of effectiveness is the willingness of the member states to *implement* the decisions made collectively in the organization, or, in other words, to honor their commitments. Unfortunately, many states support collective decisions but fail to do their part in carrying them out. This gap between profession of intent and execution has been an enormous cause of cynicism concerning institutional arrangements for global governance. Technical issues of limited political or ideological import ("functional" matters in which cooperation is a question of obvious practicality) are easier to carry out, for example, simplifying postal service in the Universal Postal Union. This is particularly true of programs that can be directly administered by international agencies without much assistance from national governments, for example, vaccination programs carried out by the World Health Organization and the United Nations Children's Fund. In the case of controversial political issues, much skillful diplomacy may be needed to achieve cooperation.

Member states must also work together and negotiate the details of all it takes to keep their organizations functioning: selection of officers, effective administration, approval of the budget, and so much more, all of which requires constant diplomatic work and bridging state differences. The specifics of international organization diplomacy are discussed in the next chapter. International organizations have enabled less-developed states to be heard and to participate in global governance. Even the weakest, least-developed states can use their membership to place issues on the international agenda—issues that the dominant states might prefer to ignore. Major powers, of course, play a key role. Many use their prominence to sway other members. But lesser states now readily network and form coalitions that increase their international influence. And it must be noted that major powers, too, use the setting of international organizations to network and promote their own global agendas.

INTERNATIONAL CONFERENCES

International conferences are another diplomatic tool used by nation states to address international problems. As far back as the dawn of history, leaders have met to address common problems or bring wars to an end. What is new is the vast increase in the use of this medium. Technology and the extraordinary increase of interdependence are important factors in this development. Travel is easier, faster, and more problems need to be approached collectively. Conferences and international meetings can be more practical than resorting to international organizations. Conferences can be given a more specialized focus; participants can be invited according to their involvement in a given issue, or their readiness and ability to work together. The use of conferences has thus dramatically increased.

Total Number of International Conferences, Worldwide, 1840–1939[3]

1840–1849	5
1850–1859	22
1860–1869	75
1870–1879	149
1880–1889	284
1890–1899	469
1900–1909	1,082
1910–1919 (First World War)	974
1920–1929	2,913
1930–1939	3,655[4]

So many international conferences are held worldwide, year by year, that electronic search engines cannot produce reliable current statistics. In the early 1960s, the United States sent close to 2,800 delegates annually to attend international conferences, and this number has now escalated.[5] One important limitation of conference diplomacy is the relatively short time available for interaction. Most large conferences meet for less than two weeks. Beyond that, a conference may reconvene after a lapse of several months. But even a short conference may have an enduring impact—for example, when negotiating a treaty that will affect international relations for an indefinite period of time. A conference may also have a more lasting effect by creating an international organization. It may also lead participating states to agree on policy that will produce its effects for some time in the future. But the conference time for diplomatic interaction will remain essentially limited.

An alternative has been found in the practice of reconvening regularly, for example, agreeing to meet once a year—as happens in a number of summit meetings, such as the G7. This is discussed in further detail in the next section. Reconvening regularly can be seen as a kind of institutionalization of the conference. Some conferences may even be given a permanent Secretariat to prepare for the regular sessions. Some international conventions make provision for a periodic Conference of the Parties (often annually) in the course of which convention parties review how the agreement is working, discuss changes, or negotiate additional protocols.

Very large conferences may be scheduled three to four years in advance to permit extensive preparation, including preconference diplomacy. This may take the form of a preparatory committee open to all states invited to participate in the conference. Some preparatory committees meet three or four times and often start diplomatic negotiations of the very issues to be addressed at the conference. Many states start consulting other states (on their own) in preparation for the conference through preconference networking, coordination of efforts, and creation of coalitions that will support common positions during the conference. Some conferences lay the groundwork for follow-up diplomacy. Thus, although conference time may be limited, a great deal of diplomacy may take place, focused on issues of global governance.

SUMMIT AND MINISTERIAL DIPLOMACY

States are now more frequently contributing to global governance by means of summit and ministerial-level diplomacy. In fact, because of interdependence and globalization tendencies, high-level decision makers are more extensively involved in international relations. What is happening abroad frequently affects national affairs and the distinction between international and domestic becomes blurred—another development changing the character of diplomacy. What does high-level diplomacy contribute to global governance? Chief executives are more authoritative, they have more latitude to make international commitments. Their decisions carry more weight, although they have their own domestic constraints (e.g., parliament), and other dimensions of domestic politics. Heads of state or government interact in different ways. Many of them network. They visit one another in their respective capitals, seeking support, exploring how they can approach common problems, and, perhaps, work together in multilateral negotiations. Chancellor Helmut Kohl of Germany noted that he had met with President François Mitterand of France in excess of eighty times.[6] Depending upon personal affinity, language, and cultural compatibility, they may remain in close contact beyond their mutual visits—for example, Zbigniew Brzezinski, who was President Jimmy Carter's national security adviser, recalled: "I was many times in the Oval Office when the president would reach for the telephone and phone the Prime Minister of the United Kingdom or the Chancellor of Germany. The chances were that we probably wouldn't even bother to tell our ambassador that such a conversation took place because it was so frequent."[7]

Opportunities for multilateral summit interaction are now extensive. The UN convenes global summit conferences focused on particular global governance issues (see part II of this book). Some conferences are only partially at the summit level in the sense that chief executives join the conference only during the last few days of the program, perhaps to sign documents negotiated earlier by national diplomatic delegations. The presence of heads of state or government serves to advertise the significance of the conference although these chief executives may actually participate only in parts of the proceedings. The UN favors calling meetings "at the highest level," for example, for special sessions of the General Assembly.[8] Regional organizations too, hold summit meetings. A number of these organizations have institutionalized such summits in their own governance structures, for example, the European Union. Another form of summit diplomacy has gained international prominence: regular meetings of the chief executives of the main economic powers—a form of diplomatic networking. These summit meetings were initiated in 1975 and continued annually to discuss current international issues and came to be known as the G7.[9] In 1997, Russia was officially added to the group (renamed G8), and then expelled in the wake of Russia's seizure of Crimea. These meetings are generally not intended to reach binding decisions. They seek informal cooperation and policy coordination to keep the member nations from working at cross purposes.

These annual summits have little administrative structure of their own and no permanent Secretariat or bureaucracy. The presidency of the group rotates annually. The country holding the presidency is responsible for planning and hosting the summit. The agenda varies as the international situation evolves. Personal representatives of the chief executives usually meet ahead of the summit in preparation for the conversations. More than thirty-five of these annual meetings have been held. The president of the European Commission (the EU executive) has been attending all meetings since he was first invited in 1977, and so has the chief executive of the country that holds the rotating presidency of the EU.

Meetings of G7 finance ministers and central bank governors were initiated by the G7 summit of 1986, adding another level of diplomatic dialogue and informal networking for more effective financial management. They now meet four times a year.[10] In 1998, the G7 finance ministers and central bank governors invited the ministers of a number of emerging economies to participate in their conversations, which led, in the wake of the Asian financial crisis, to the creation of a new group to engage in annual consultations. This new group received the name of G20, although it met at the ministerial level.

In 2005, the G8, at Britain's initiative, invited the leading emerging economies (Brazil, China, India, Mexico, and South Africa) to join the summit talks in order to create a more representative group (G8 + EU + 5). In 2007,

Germany and France attempted to institutionalize this expansion, but the G8 did not support this proposal.[11] In 2008, the new economic crisis led to a special meeting of the G20 at the summit level on "Financial Markets and the World Economy." This launched a new set of summit meetings. The G20 summit met twice in 2009 and twice in 2010, but only once a year starting in 2011. In 2010, France suggested the creation of a permanent Secretariat for the G20.[12] The composition of these meetings will probably change again as some argue that the group is still not representative enough. In fact the rotating president typically invites states that are not members of the G20 as well as executives of international organizations. Spain has been regularly invited. However, diplomatic dialogue tends to be more effective when the number of participants remains limited.

In the meantime, ministerial meetings continue to be a major instrument of global governance diplomacy. In 2009 the G20 finance ministers and central bank governors were scheduled to meet twice, their deputies were to meet thrice, and they planned three "Official Workshops" on special topics (e.g., "Sustainable Financing for Development"). They also used "working groups" as needed. In 2009, the G8 summit, hosted by Italy, also convened a meeting of finance ministers and central bank governors. Italy in fact showed enthusiasm for ministerial meetings and convened seven more (labor, agriculture, environment, energy, justice and home affairs, development, and foreign affairs). Each meeting included a number of representatives of non-G8 members and an assortment of international organizations.[13]

More partnerships are likely to develop as new international problems arise. For example, the 2007 G8 summit received a proposal from the EU for a worldwide initiative on energy efficiency. In 2008, a meeting of the energy ministers of the G8 countries, the EU, China, India, and South Korea, established the International Partnership for Energy Efficiency Cooperation (IPEEC), a fifteen-member organization including the EU.[14] The energy ministers of the Asia-Pacific Economic Cooperation hold their own periodic meetings and in 2010 supported IPEEC's purpose.[15] The IPEEC Secretariat is hosted by the Secretariat of the International Energy Agency in Paris, created in 1974 by the Organization for Economic Cooperation and Development (OECD)—additional evidence of international cooperation and networking.

Convening summits and ministerial-level meetings require much more diplomacy than publicly reported. The personal representatives of the heads of state and government, and of the ministers involved, play a key role in the elaborate preparations for the annual consultations and follow-ups to these meetings. These representatives are known as "sherpas" and are invited to take part in several working meetings in the host country where they prepare the agenda and subsequently process its results. Implementation of what has been agreed upon may also require more diplomatic activity. In 2008, the G8 summit (in Japan) had as its follow-up an international conference on Global Action for Health System Strengthening (November 3–4, 2008), which published its policy recommendations in January 2009.[16]

TREATY MAKING AS AN INSTRUMENT OF GLOBAL GOVERNANCE

Treaty making is widely used by states to engage in global governance (and other aspects of their foreign relations). A very large number of international agreements (by far the most numerous) have a narrow, highly specialized, or short-term function, for example, a commercial transaction. They are written in contractual terms of exchange of rights and obligations and are not usually considered tools of global governance. But many treaties enable states to establish complex relationships; some have regulatory functions; many are multilateral. In fact, this tool of international administration long antedated the development of international organizations and remains extremely important for global governance. Over 507 major multilateral treaties were deposited with the UN secretary-general as of 2006.[17] Some agreements create international legal norms (law-making treaties).

The diplomatic process leading to the formulation of international agreements is extremely diverse ranging from negotiations by resident diplomatic representatives in foreign capitals to plenipotentiaries sent to multilateral conferences, as well as simple exchanges of notes (without meetings). It may also involve summit meetings, meetings of foreign ministers or heads of other executive departments. The negotiations may be initiated by individual states or by decisions of international organizations—all of which contributes to the diplomacy of global governance and shows the role of states in the process.

ROLE OF DIVERSE DOMESTIC AGENCIES IN GLOBAL GOVERNANCE DIPLOMACY

Because of the expansion of the diplomatic agenda, states are increasingly using a multiplicity of executive agencies other than their foreign ministries in dealing with other states with regard to specialized issues of international governance. These agencies recruit and train personnel for this purpose. For example, the US Department of Labor has a Bureau of International Labor Affairs headed by a deputy undersecretary of labor. It has projects in more than seventy-five countries and has three divisions:[18] (1) the Office of International Relations, which represents the US government at the ILO in Geneva and in the labor components of other international organizations;

(2) the Office of Trade and Labor Affairs composed of three divisions dealing respectively with trade policy and negotiations, trade agreement administration, and economic and labor research. This office has, in particular, a program to address HIV/AIDS in the workplace in more than thirty countries; (3) the Office of Child Labor, Forced Labor, and Human Trafficking. It funds technical assistance projects in Africa, the United States, Asia, and Europe, especially to eliminate the worst forms of child labor as defined by the ILO (ILO Convention No.182), including the recruitment of child soldiers with projects in Afghanistan, Liberia, Sierra Leone, and Uganda.

Of the 2,800 or so US delegates involved annually in international conference work, only about 40 percent of these represent the Department of State.[19] It also demonstrates the extraordinary expansion of the diplomatic agenda and the complexity of global governance—complexity that will increase as global affairs become more elaborate. The involvement of departments other than foreign ministries in global governance is demonstrated also in the changing composition of the personnel of embassies in foreign capitals: a large number of specialized departments (e.g., justice or agriculture) station officers in the national embassy. See for example the structure of the US Embassy in Paris:

The American Embassy in Paris

Department of State personnel:

Ambassador
Deputy Chief of Mission (DCM)

Major Embassy Sections:

Political Affairs (a minister-counselor)
Economic Affairs (a minister-counselor)
Public Affairs (a minister-counselor)
Press Office and Cultural Affairs Office
Consular Affairs (a minister-counselor)
Administrative Affairs (a minister-counselor)
Agricultural Affairs (a minister-counselor)
Commercial Affairs (a minister-counselor)
Scientific, Technological, and Environmental Affairs (a counselor)
Africa Regional Services (a branch of the State Department's Bureau of African Affairs)
Regional Security Office (a branch of the State Department's Bureau of Diplomatic Security: Responsible for providing security services to all US missions, personnel, and facilities in France)

Personnel representing other departments:

Defense Attaché (Department of Defense)
Tax Attaché (Department of the Treasury)
Customs Attaché (US Customs and Border Protection, US Department of Homeland Security)
Space Attaché, European Representative, National Aeronautics and Space Administration (NASA)
Voice of America Finance Office for Europe and Africa
Foreign Agricultural Service (Department of Agriculture)
Commercial Service (Department of Commerce)
Internal Revenue Service (Department of the Treasury)
Office of Defense Cooperation (Department of Defense)
National Science Foundation, Europe office (Head of Office)

Other posts under the authority of the US Embassy:

Consulates General in Marseille and Strasbourg
Limited consular facilities called "American Presence Posts"

Two US Missions in Paris are separate and independent from the embassy:

US Mission to the Organization for Economic Cooperation and Development (OECD)
US Mission to the UN Educational, Scientific, and Cultural Organization (UNESCO).[20]

TRANSGOVERNMENTAL OPERATIONS

As a consequence of the expansion of the diplomatic agenda and the proliferation of national government agencies involved in international relations, new forms of interaction are taking place across international boundaries. Transgovernmental work entails direct cooperation between specialized government departments of different countries bypassing usual diplomatic channels. The communication revolution is simplifying this kind of activity; government officials of different countries work together—some of them interacting even without leaving their desks in their respective capitals—but they still need a common language and an ability to cooperate across cultural divides. Others work with their foreign colleagues abroad, in various types of visits, or in field projects. A degree of cordiality and an interest in cooperating between the political systems or governments concerned is necessary. Highly centralized or authoritarian systems are likely to impose restrictions on the freedom of their government ministries to engage in transgovernmental operations.

Geographical proximity often increases relations, thus neighboring countries normally engage in a great deal of joint activities that lend themselves to direct interaction between many segments of their governmental bureaucracies. But transgovernmental work is not limited to neighboring states.

These are additional channels of global governance. Do they amount to "diplomacy without diplomats?" These officials do not have foreign service preparation, but experience acquired on the job (or other international experience or aptitude gained elsewhere) permits this form of interaction to become effective and highly practical. The vast expansion of international relations leads to new forms of transgovernmental work.

An Example of Transgovernmental Work

The Drug Enforcement Administration (DEA) of the US Department of Justice maintains extensive relations with foreign law-enforcement authorities and other government agencies in countries dealing with international drug traffic and participates in a large number of multilateral enforcement programs. In Washington, the DEA has an Office of International Operations within the US Department of Justice, and maintains 79 offices in 58 countries. The main components of the DEA's international operations are its 29 Sensitive Investigative Units (SIUs) operating in 9 countries, and investigating major drug trafficking organizations and money-laundering operations in cooperation with the law-enforcement agencies of each host country. Illustrating this type of work, the SIU in Thailand carried out a multinational investigation involving the DEA and law-enforcement agencies in Thailand, China, and Hong Kong, culminating in April 2002 with the seizure of some 700 pounds of heroin and the arrest of 13 traffickers with ties to an international insurgent organization.

The DEA takes a variety of international initiatives, such as counternarcotics training, using mobile training teams that offer both in-country and regional training programs. It works very closely with counternarcotics agents in Peru, Bolivia, and Thailand.[21] It also organizes international operations. For example, in February 2002, the DEA brought together representatives from 25 countries in Ankara, Turkey, to develop a coordinated, post-Taliban counterdrug strategy to deprive international terrorist groups of the financial resources for their operations. This project also targeted weapons, ammunition, and currency. The participants agreed on joint efforts of law enforcement and customs authorities in Central Asia, the Caucasus, Europe, and Russia, in operations coordinated by the Southeast European Cooperative Initiative (SECI) Regional Center for Combating Transborder Crime in Bucharest, Romania, and the Bishkek Command Center in Bishkek, Kyrgyzstan.[22] SECI is noteworthy in that customs and police authorities of Albania, Bosnia/Herzegovina, Bulgaria, Croatia, Greece, Hungary, Macedonia, Moldova, Montenegro, Romania, Serbia, Slovenia, and Turkey work together in direct cooperation on collective projects.[23]

THE CHANGING NATURE OF THE NATION-STATE SYSTEM

In the eighteenth century and much of the nineteenth, lesser states hardly participated in global governance. European powers dominated international relations. But things have drastically changed. *Small states are now playing a significant part in global affairs.* Great powers have lost their monopoly—which is not meant to imply that they do not try to control international politics. Their power undeniably gives them many opportunities to dominate. Small states are anxious to play a role in global affairs although many of them are very small and underdeveloped. For example St. Kitts and Nevis, in the Caribbean, has a population of 41,000 and a national territory of 116 square miles; Nauru, in the Pacific, has a population of 10,000 and a territory of 8 square miles. Forty-six nation states show similar limitations.[24] The World Bank lists 65 states having a gross national income (GNI) per capita of $745 or less (which compares with 52 countries with a per capita GNI of $9,206 or more at the other end of the scale[25]).

International organizations have given weak states the means to be heard, to take initiatives, and to participate in decision making. The formation of voting blocs gives them power. When they manage to unite, they can produce 120–130 votes out of a UN membership of 193. This can make great powers pay attention to small state preferences. But forming coalitions or voting blocs is not as easy as it sounds. Small states have their differences and overcoming them requires a good deal of diplomacy—and those efforts do not always succeed. Coalitions are also made outside international organizations. Small states learned to unite in the decolonization process, in their search for development assistance and in their efforts to avoid being pawns in the Cold War. They formed potent associations; for example, at the 1955 Bandung Conference of Asian and African states, or at the 1961 Belgrade Conference where 25 countries, mostly former colonies, founded the Non-Aligned Movement, and at the 1964 UN Conference on Trade and Development, creating the Group of 77 (G77). Decolonization added to their ranks (numbering now more than 130[26])—and all of this changed the dynamics of global diplomacy. Great powers became interested in winning the cooperation of less-developed states—less so today than during the Cold War, but their support is often seen as valuable, for example, in tracking down al-Qaeda recruiters.

The sheer number of state actors—about 200 of them, depending upon how one counts[27]—makes the conduct of diplomacy and the formation of global policy more complex. More states want to be heard—and they have their own ideas as to what needs to be done. Global governance is thus a more elaborate endeavor and requires greater diplomatic skill. And all these newcomers are not always fond of the international system that excluded them for so long. Some of them go out of their way to show that they do not have to fall in line. Greater cultural diversity, too, affects the diplomatic process. Different negotiating styles need to be accommodated. The international diplomatic environment has changed. More significantly, however, different political orientations and conflicting national interests often make it difficult for states to work together. Diplomacy is thus even more critical to bridge all these differences and tackle global challenges.

NOTES

1. Consulates and other posts are excluded from this count. www.embassyworld. com/embassy/directory (Accessed June 10, 2011).

2. *Yearbook of International Organizations 2006/2007* (43rd ed. Munich: Saur, 2006) Vol. 1B, Appendix 3, Table 1a, p. 3024. Categorizing and counting international organizations is a complex endeavor. See the elaborate categorization in the same yearbook, Appendix 2, pp. 3021–3023. And it remains uncertain as to what is counted in what category.

3. Daniel S. Cheever and H. Field Haviland, Jr. *Organizing for Peace: International Organization in World Affairs* (Boston: Houghton Mifflin, 1954), p. 32.

4. Daniel S. Cheever and H. Field Haviland, Jr., *Organizing for Peace: International Organization in World Affairs* (Boston: Houghton Mifflin, 1954), p. 32.

5. Elmer Plischke, *US Department of State: A Reference History* (Westport, CT: Greenwood, 1999), p. 568.

6. G. R. Berridge, *Diplomacy: Theory and Practice* (3rd ed. London: Palgrave, 2005), pp. 182–183.

7. David H. Dunn, "What Is Summitry?" in *Diplomacy at the Highest Level: The Evolution of International Summitry*, edited by David H. Dunn (New York: St. Martin's, 1996), p. 7. See also, Zbigniew Brzezinski, *Power and Principle: Memoirs of the National Security Advisor, 1977–1981* (New York: Farrar, Straus, and Giroux, 1983).

8. In January 2002, the UN held its first-ever Security Council meeting at the level of heads of state or government. Boutros Boutros-Ghali, "Challenges of Preventive Diplomacy," in *Preventive Diplomacy: Stopping Wars Before They Start*, edited by Kevin M. Cahill (New York: Basic Books, 1996), p. 18.

9. They were Canada, France, Germany, Italy, Japan, the United Kingdom, and the United States.

10. Andrew Baker, "The Group of Seven," Global Monitor Series, *New Political Economy* Vol. 13, No. 1 (March 2008), p. 104.

11. G8 History. Official website. www.g8italia2009.it/G8/Home (Accessed June 15, 2011).

12. www.g20.org/G20 (Accessed June 15, 2011).

13. www.g8italia2009.it/G8/Home (Accessed July 23, 2009).

14. www.ipeec.org (Accessed August 25, 2013).

15. www.ipeed.org/history (Accessed June 16, 2011).

16. www.who.int/healthmetrics/news (Accessed July 24, 2009).

17. *Multilateral Treaties Deposited with the Secretary-General* (St/Leg/Ser/E). http://treaties.un.org/Pages/DB (Accessed February 10, 2009). Article 102 of the UN Charter specifies that "every international agreement entered into by any Member of the United Nations . . . [shall] be registered with the Secretariat and published by it."

18. www.dol.gov/ilab/programs (Accessed March 3, 2009).

19. Plischke, *U.S. Department of States*, p. 568.

20. Fifty-three US government agencies are attached to the three US missions in Paris. www.embassyworld.com and www.state.gov (Accessed March 4, 2009).

21. www.justice.gov/dea/programs/fci (Accessed September 27, 2010).

22. www.dea.gov/pubs/cngrtest. See also DEA major operations, 2000–2008 at www.usdoj.gov/dea/major/major (Accessed March 5, 2009).

23. www.secicenter.org/m106/About_SECI (Accessed September 27, 2010).

24. Russett, Starr, and Kinsella, Appendix B.

25. http://web.worldbank.org/WBSITE/EXTERNAL/DATASTATISTICS (Accessed March 6, 2009).

26. Russett, Starr, and Kinsella, 8th ed., p. 458.

27. For example, the Palestinian Authority is not a recognized state, but it is an active participant in some Middle East diplomacy. Even Hamas, ostracized as it is in many political circles, is an international actor.

Chapter 3

International Organizations as Instruments of Global Governance

International organizations involve a type of diplomacy that is of particular importance for global governance. It is distinct from the diplomacy practiced by embassies in foreign capitals. These maintain relations with the host state. Their work is bilateral in essence. Embassies do not maintain formal diplomatic relations with the other missions in the capital. By contrast, a state's diplomatic delegation to an international organization is intended to interact with the other national missions there and with the officers and Secretariat members of the organization. This is *multilateral* diplomacy. In this environment, diplomats represent a wide range of political systems, each with its own perception of the world and its own priorities. All of these representatives must contend with a greater variety of political outlooks, cultural differences, and diplomatic styles. Multilateral diplomacy is thus more complex than the traditional bilateral type.

Another kind of diplomacy needs to be acknowledged: the diplomacy of international organizations as international actors (distinct from the diplomacy of member-state delegates). International organizations are given functions to perform by the treaties that created them or by the membership itself through its decision-making process. In carrying out their mandates (using their own personnel), organizations become international actors. They participate in the diplomatic process with other international actors (e.g., nation states and other international organizations). This kind of diplomacy will be examined in a separate section, later in this chapter. It will also be seen in action in part II of this book.

DIPLOMACY OF NATIONAL REPRESENTATIVES
IN A MULTILATERAL SETTING

Many aspects of international organizations affect this diplomacy. *The structure of a given organization* is an important element and it varies a great deal. Large organizations are often complex.[1] Much of the diplomatic work is usually done in a diversity of bodies made up of national representatives. These bodies vary in size. One of the consequences of extensive committee work is that national delegations need additional personnel to represent their country in all these bodies. Another diplomatic consequence of the committee structure is that members of national delegations often specialize in the work of specific committees. This gives them greater substantive latitude and responsibility, but requires more delegation staff meetings to ensure that all representatives of a given nation present a coherent expression of their country's foreign policy.[2]

A modern practice in large organizations is the creation of *voting blocs* or diplomatic coalitions. It must be noted that in this way, multilateral diplomacy has enabled small states to play a role (often significant) in global politics. Some of these blocs remain informal. All kinds of factors will bring national delegations together, among them shared interests, regional affinity, and ideology. Other blocs become institutionalized as in the UN General Assembly. Keeping independent states aligned is a task in itself, requiring a good deal of continuing diplomacy (intra-bloc negotiations). Some voting blocs even create their own structures to help maintain bloc cohesion, with bloc officers, periodic meetings, and even bloc committees. Bloc members may engage in "negotiations" with their own governments, or at least try to convince them to adopt policies that will mesh with the needs of the voting bloc (government leaders back home may not be all that alive to the needs of voting blocs in some distant forums). Blocs may also negotiate with other blocs in the same organization through their officers or representatives. Some missions select some of their members to act as liaisons with given blocs, to keep track of the positions adopted by these blocs and perhaps also try to influence them. It may be noted that heads of international bodies (e.g., the UN secretary-general or the UN General Assembly president) may endeavor to remain in contact with voting blocs to guide the operations they are responsible for. Thus, they frequently add bloc leaders or representatives to their contact groups (i.e., advisory bodies created by institution leaders to remain in touch with important subgroups). Multilateral diplomacy can easily be compared to a three-ring circus (although it may not be diplomatic to say it aloud).

Another important feature of diplomacy in international organizations is that many nations, including the major powers, are *impelled to participate in the discussion of issues they would prefer to ignore*, such as environmental degradation or the plight of the destitute. They are drawn into diplomatic interaction when such matters are placed on the agenda, particularly when some form of international action is contemplated. This is one more factor causing an expansion of the diplomatic dialogue. *Severe time pressure* is a frequent characteristic of organization diplomacy. Periodic sessions of major organs and subsidiary bodies are normally given a specific amount of time to complete their work. The closer one gets to the end, the more hectic the process becomes.[3] Chairs press their group members to wind up their negotiations; toward the end they even schedule night meetings; controversial issues create deadlocks causing havoc in any work schedule. Stress becomes a part of one's daily life. There are deadlines for everything: to get material into the hands of the Secretariat for translation, duplication, and distribution before an upcoming meeting; to come up with resolutions to present before the parent institution; and, of course, to meet the ultimate deadline set by the end of the meeting or session. Both diplomats and members of the Secretariat are experiencing the same ugly pressure, even when there is no crisis. The impending adjournment becomes the crisis. Diplomacy, then, lacks the gentility that the public imagines from afar. Often enough, the imminent deadline pushes negotiators to reach agreements—or to make mistakes.

Because of the complexity of large proceedings, *elaborate rules of procedure* are needed.[4] And a skillful use of these rules can be an important element in the conduct of diplomacy (e.g., for matters of precedence, presentation of resolutions, closing the debate, or determining the order in which voting is to take place). Nothing comparable is to be found in bilateral diplomacy unless one includes rules of protocol and local diplomatic usage. Large national parliaments have long faced the challenge of complexity and, quite naturally, international organizations have borrowed from them a variety of techniques (floor action procedures, decision making, and more).

In turn, this has led to the notion of *parliamentary diplomacy*, which some have decried as a corruption of diplomacy. Undoubtedly, the process of open-floor debate amply covered by the media, adds a dimension to international interaction, which needs to be taken into account by diplomats; but a great deal of diplomacy—real diplomacy, away from the limelight—is conducted in the margin of the debates. It is needed in preparation for what will be debated, and as a consequence of what was said in the debate. Debating the issues is now part of the multilateral interaction, and it is done by diplomats, as an added dimension of their professional responsibilities. Those diplomats that have oratorical skills have an advantage, as Adlai Stevenson did at the UN; but diplomatic skill remains indispensable to attain one's objectives in this multilateral environment. It is true that taking a position publicly in the course of a debate adds rigidity to a situation. The give and take of negotiations cannot be done in public. Debating can also lead to hostile language, not conducive to accommodation. In a public debate, too, statements are often made for public consumption—again, not helpful in the diplomatic process. These are drawbacks that large-scale multilateral work needs to face. And multilateral gatherings attract the media. Diplomats must therefore be more cautious in their interaction. Confidentiality and the maintenance of trust remain important elements of diplomacy. Debating issues may be inevitable but it may complicate the interaction.

It must be noted also that the process seldom amounts to a true "debate," although that is what it is generally called. What happens is often more akin to a series of monologues. Presentations frequently entail a right of reply following established procedures that seldom permit instant responses (as in a debate). More likely, respondents must place their names on a speakers' list and wait until they are called (after many have addressed the issue as previously scheduled). By the time one's turn comes, it may be necessary to remind the assembly of the original point that was objected to. This hardly amounts to a spirited debate although it may still entail plenty of rhetoric and certainly permits the presentation of competing views. A closer approximation of a debate can take place in smaller meetings, especially when the person in charge (e.g., chair or president) calls for an informal exchange of views, which he or she will moderate, recognizing people who wish to speak; and this type of interaction need not be public. This is more likely to happen in committee meetings, some of them large, testing the skill of the chair, where requests to be heard are by show of hand.

Open presentations are, of course, not a substitute for diplomacy. They are a part of the multilateral process and affect the course of the proceedings. But extensive diplomacy occurs before and even during speech making, and it continues afterward. Diplomacy takes place in the corridors, over lunch, at receptions, and even in assembly halls as other representatives are making speeches. Some delegates move about while meetings are in session, gather at desks to confer with other representatives, or caucus in the back of the room (important speeches *will* have general attention). And diplomacy is also conducted on the phone and by exchange of messages. Thus, what has been called "parliamentary diplomacy" has not killed plain old diplomacy.

Another dimension of multilateral diplomacy is *diverse decision making*. In the nineteenth century as international organizations began to be created, the basic norm of international relations was that of the sovereign equality of nation states. They were of course very unequal but, as a rule, decisions had to be by unanimity and on the basis of one state, one vote. The practice was so established that it was also adopted for the League of Nations. Fortunately, the League Assembly was also given the power to formulate "wishes" by simple majority, and League members got into the habit of expressing their preferences by means of wishes instead of resolutions (which in any case were not binding).

As nations became accustomed to international organizations and their usefulness, they turned to more practical forms of majority for a variety of decisions. Article 18 of the UN Charter, after specifying that each member of the General Assembly shall have one vote, states that decisions "on important questions shall be made by a two-thirds majority of the members present and voting."[5] And it proceeds to indicate some of the questions to be included among "important questions," such as recommendations with respect to the maintenance of international peace and security, the admission of new members to the United Nations, and budgetary questions. Decisions on other questions are to be made by a majority of the members present and voting. Even in the Security Council, only the five permanent members have a veto power on matters that are other than procedural. In the words of the Charter, these decisions "shall be made by an affirmative vote of nine members including the concurring votes of the permanent members."[6] Decisions on procedural matters are to be made by an affirmative vote of nine members. These are called decisions by qualified majority. Some organizations, interestingly, have even abandoned the sacrosanct principle of one state one vote. The IMF, for example, was given a system of weighted voting based on the financial commitment of each member to the Fund. Thus, the United States casts 371,743 votes (16.74 percent of the total) and Palau 281 votes (0.013 percent).[7]

A substantial proportion of the diplomacy taking place in international organizations is focused on lining up the votes for upcoming decisions, trading political inducements, exchanging commitments, and creating coalitions or voting blocs. Rare are votes by secret ballot. In large organizations voting is now electronic, with members pressing a button on their desks. Some votes are recorded (a list of how each representative voted is issued); others are unrecorded (only the outcome of the vote is shown); and *some decisions are made by consensus*, thus eliminating the need to vote. Informal diplomacy is the main element in such decisions. Consensus is, essentially, accepting not to oppose a decision. Delegates do not have to indicate whether they support the decision or abstain. In the conversations that precede the decision, the delegates are consulted informally. If no one indicates an intent to oppose the decision (and the price for that may be the object of negotiations, e.g., a reformulation of the proposition), the chair of the meeting is informed. When the time has come to formulate a decision, the chair simply announces that it is his/her understanding that there is a consensus for the proposition on the table, and the chair usually asks "Is there any disagreement?" At this point, if anyone has a change of heart, or was left out of the conversations exploring the feasibility of a consensus, all that is needed is a statement to that effect— and a vote must then be taken. (Thus, refusing to accept consensus does not amount to vetoing the proposition since a vote will be taken). If no one speaks up, the chair simply acknowledges that a consensus has been reached and the matter is thus decided. No vote is taken; the matter is closed.

Decision by consensus simplifies international action, and this procedure has become popular. Indeed, if the assembled delegates are by and large unwilling to make an issue of the proposition on the table, a number of negative votes would not defeat it. It is thus understandable that when the dissenters see that they are not going to win they would not bother to ask for a vote. Some may of course still want to show their opposition, perhaps for ideological purposes. Otherwise, decisions by consensus avoid emphasizing differences, and there are diplomatic benefits for this kind of approach, hence, its increasing use.

As international organizations now address a multiplicity of specialized or highly technical issues, *experts and specialists in many fields participate in diplomatic interaction* along with foreign service officers. This development affects the style and substance of diplomatic proceedings. Some experts have no diplomatic experience. This can be a handicap even when members of their own foreign service are on hand to help. When these experts are used regularly enough on international assignments, they can learn on the job; but countries concerned about the effectiveness of their foreign relations need to do something more systematic about their training and fitness for international work.

Although state representatives in international organizations deal primarily with delegates of other states, they will *work with organization personnel*. This pertains primarily to clerical assistance (circulation of documents, their translation, production of transcripts, and thousands of other services), but a number of organization officials have diplomatic functions including facilitating proceedings and working for the smooth functioning of the organization (e.g., heads of agencies, particularly the organization's chief executive). Some Secretariat personnel are both administrators and diplomats. They help state representatives reach agreements and work together in carrying out international functions. They may serve as mediators and exercise leadership in getting states and their representatives to address international problems.

State representatives will also interact with *agents of other types of international actors*. Some organizations, such as the UN, accept various kinds of observers, even some from revolutionary movements. NGO representatives are now more frequently found in international organizations. Observers and nonstate agents do not vote, but they may be allowed to address some meetings (still rare for NGOs). They have access to all documentation, may occasionally circulate documents of their own, and, in any case, engage in diplomacy. They do not need permission to do that once they are allowed to attend organization proceedings and intermingle with the regular delegates (thus expanding the realm of diplomatic interaction).

It is to be noted that as a consequence of the growth of civil society and private-sector activism, NGO representatives are playing a greater role globally. The World Bank, for example, is now including some NGO representatives in the planning and decision making pertaining to a variety of economic and social development programs amounting to full diplomatic participation. Some states have even included NGO representatives in their delegations to international functions. The multilateral diplomatic process has thus been a significant factor in increasing the role of civil society in global governance. In addition, officials of *other* international organizations (i.e., organizations other than the one in which the diplomatic process is taking place) participate in a multiplicity of diplomatic activities along with state representatives. Many organizations cooperate in international programs and are invited to send representatives to international functions, often as full participants, speaking for their own organization. A variety of international actors can thus be involved in multilateral diplomatic work.

Nonagenda diplomacy must also be acknowledged. As the name indicates, some international actors, particularly member states, interact in a given organization on issues that are not on the organization's agenda. They use the organization forum to conduct business of their own having nothing to do with the organization for a variety of reasons (e.g., convenience, or lack of other venue when states do not maintain regular diplomatic relations).[8] On occasion, states will resort to this procedure to ensure low visibility in delicate transactions.

State representatives in an international organization may, on occasion, act in a *non-national role*, that is, in a role other than the normal one of representing their state. Organization sub-bodies elect their officers from the ranks of their state membership, for example, chairs of committees. These officers play an important role in ensuring that the work gets done. The elected officers are expected to serve impartially, despite the fact that they are national representatives. If the committee is to take up an issue involving the chair's own state, the chair is expected to turn the leadership over to someone else, perhaps a vice-chair, for this part of the agenda. This is a fairly routine matter.[9] Many diplomats in a multilateral environment contribute to the effective functioning of the organization even without being officially in charge of anything, becoming facilitators in complex diplomatic relationships, mediating differences, taking initiatives when the occasion arises, all of it on their own, that is, when their instructions do not prevent it. In large multilateral forums, there is room for constructive initiatives and facilitation. In the complex environment of multilateral diplomacy, interaction tends to be less structured and diplomats have greater latitude for independent action.

It must be noted that one of the special characteristics of multilateral diplomacy (particularly in large forums) is its *fluidity* (referring to the *rapidly changing character of diplomatic situations*). This phenomenon is rooted in the large amount of diplomatic interaction taking place not only in official gatherings, but also in the margin of meetings, in corridors, and beyond official premises. When agreement is unexpectedly reached between key players, the political balance may be altered and the other players need to adjust to the new circumstances. The next round of negotiations may thus be very different from the one that preceded it. Fluidity is normal in this kind of environment, although each agenda item may have its own dynamics. There is a greater element of unpredictability. As an example of diplomatic fluidity, I remember a negotiating session in a UN Committee, during a meeting of the General Assembly, that took a whole day to produce an understanding on just one point of a much larger agenda. At the end of the day, the delegates had overcome their differences—or at least had come to the conclusion that it was time to move on—and all went home. When the session resumed the next morning, the presiding officer opened the proceedings by reassuringly observing, "It seems we have reached agreement on this issue. Does anyone wish to add anything before we take a vote?" (Chairs do not want to give the impression that they are trying to rush things.) At this point, an elderly delegate, who had arrived late and was just reaching her desk, cleared her throat and asked—very tentatively, without any sign that she intended to challenge anyone or anything—"Does this paragraph, then, mean that . . . ."—whatever it was. Well . . . as it turned out, a number of delegates let it be known in no uncertain terms that it was *not* the intent *at all.* And they were off and running. The negotiations had to start all over again, which goes to show that it may sometimes be unwise to seek too many clarifications.[10]

Finally, a significant part of multilateral diplomacy is focused on the organization itself, that is, *the diplomacy of member states concerning the effectiveness of the institution*, for instance in the selection of officers. The functioning of the organization affects the diplomatic process, and leadership is often a critical issue. Thus a great deal of diplomacy is focused on effective administration, the budget, and the performance of a multiplicity of subsidiary organs. The Fifth Main Committee of the UN General Assembly (Administrative and Budgetary) addresses these issues on a regular basis.

DIPLOMACY OF INTERNATIONAL ORGANIZATIONS AS INTERNATIONAL ACTORS

International organizations play an increasingly important role in global governance as international actors. They run international programs, work with other international actors, practice diplomacy in addressing international issues and are internationally responsible for what they do. Organizations create subsidiary bodies to carry out some of their international activities, for example, the General Assembly created UNICEF to meet the needs of suffering children. The UN with all its related bodies is the most active and potent international actor. But states have created other international organizations to perform specific tasks requiring collective efforts.

Some international organizations now accept nonstates as full members,[11] for example, the Union for the Conservation of Nature. Its membership now includes 84 nation states, 121 government agencies, 108 international NGOs, and 874 national NGOs.[12] Some organizations, formally recognized as international actors in international documents and involved in international projects do not include any nation state in their membership. An example is the Consortium of International Agricultural Research Center Community (CGIAR), originally created as the Consultative Group on International Agricultural Research.[13] It is made up of 15 research centers around the world. Its constituent document specifies that it is an international entity endowed with international legal status. Its headquarters agreement with France (the host state), stipulates that it is entitled to diplomatic immunity. CGIAR is funded by 64 donors including governments, private foundations, and international organizations. It is sponsored by three UN Specialized Agencies (the Food and Agriculture Organization, the International Fund for Agricultural Development, and the World Bank) plus the United Nations Development Program (UNDP). The Consortium Fund is administered by the World Bank as a trustee.[14] CGIAR maintains relations with the states in which the research is carried out. It also organizes global conferences for agricultural research and development.

Some NGOs become international actors as a result of the part they play in international affairs. For example, the International Committee of the Red Cross (ICRC) is a Swiss NGO which owes its international status to its prominent role in the conduct of international warfare and its contribution to the development of international humanitarian law. Some of its international functions are spelled out in the four Geneva Conventions of 1949 and its three protocols of 1977 and 2005.

International Organization Partnerships

Many international organizations network informally with other international organizations as well as with nation states or civil society entities in implementing their projects. On occasion, however, international organizations create more formal partnerships in which cooperation may involve joint bodies such as coordinating committees. These partnerships can be very helpful for global governance. The UN itself invites some of its own subsidiary bodies and Specialized Agencies to work together, which may even lead to the creation of new international actors. For example, UNAIDS was established in 1994 at the recommendation of the Economic and Social Council (ECOSOC) to make the struggle against HIV/AIDS more effective. UNAIDS is made up of eleven agencies.[15] The group is assisted by its own Secretariat and executive machinery including a Program Coordinating Board made up of the eleven agencies, UNAIDS Secretariat, twenty-two UN member states, and NGO representatives, including associations of people living with HIV.[16]

Mobilization of Resources

International organizations have been particularly useful for collecting the means for implementing their projects. For example, UNICEF's total financial resources amounted to $6.5 billion in 2013,[17] and the UNDP about $13 billion for 2012–2013.[18] Some organizations are created outside the UN to mobilize resources, for example, the Global Fund to Fight AIDS, Tuberculosis and Malaria.

Coordination Diplomacy

With the proliferation of independent international organizations involved in global governance, coordination acquires special importance. Some collective projects lead to the creation of joint decision-making structures. The UN has established several bodies, particularly the ECOSOC, to play this role with a multiplicity of agencies. In this regard, the ECOSOC requested the UN secretary-general in 1946 to create a high-level body to foster orderly cooperation between institutions. This was the origin of the UN System Chief Executives Board for Coordination (CEB), originally called the Administrative Committee on Coordination. This body brings together, on a regular basis, the executive heads of the funds, programs, agencies, and offices of the UN system under the chairmanship of the UN Secretary-General. It performs its functions through three committees: (1) The High-Level Committee on Programs, which promotes policy cohesion, cooperation, and program coordination. It develops common strategies to address challenges facing the UN system. (2) The High-Level Committee on Management, which seeks to improve efficiency and to simplify operations. It addresses financial issues and human resources. (3) The third committee (called UN Development Group), which is responsible for coordinating and improving the effectiveness of operational activities at the country level. A Resident Coordinator System helps attain this objective.[19]

Another level of coordination has proven useful in the huge UN humanitarian field. The UN Secretariat has had a large role in it, which has evolved over time. In 1992, the General Assembly created the Emergency Relief

Coordinator, with the rank of an under-secretary-general. This officer is concerned with the relief activities of international organizations, state agencies, and NGOs and is in charge of the Office for the Coordination of Humanitarian Affairs (OCHA) and its Inter-Agency Standing Committee (IASC). OCHA plays a key role in operational coordination in crisis situations. This includes assessing the situation and needs, setting priorities, developing common strategies, mobilizing resources, and monitoring progress. In-country coordinators may be appointed and humanitarian country teams organized. These help humanitarian organizations be more systematic in their work.[20] OCHA promotes preparedness in disaster-prone countries (e.g., by means of contingency planning and early warning). OCHA's IASC is responsible for coordination, policy development, and decision making. It brings together nine UN agencies and a number of standing invitees including non-UN organizations and NGOs.

Special Features of Some Organizations

A number of international organizations offer unconventional characteristics as international actors. Not only do these special features affect their contribution to governance diplomacy, but they also show that international actors can be led away from deeply engrained traditional ways. Equally significant, after the different practices prove useful, other international actors may use them in other settings. What was once unusual becomes more generally acceptable, although there is no guarantee that this will happen, but evolution and change are important elements of global governance.

The Use of Courts in International Organizations

Until the First World War, states viewed the idea of an international court making binding decisions as an invasion of their sovereignty. In 1899 and 1907, when the Hague Peace Conferences were convened to address the growing risk of war, they could not accept the creation of a world court. It took the trauma of the world war to get the League of Nations to create such a court. It did not produce miracles, but states discovered its practicality. In 1945, the San Francisco Conference made this court a part of the UN and, in the years that followed, some thirty international courts (many of them regional) were created. See Textbox 5.1. The European Court of Human Rights lets private individuals sue member states, even their own.[21] How things can change! At the global level, the World Trade Organization (WTO) provides for compulsory court decisions in international trade disputes, with remarkable provision for an appellate jurisdiction and WTO sanctions for violations.

New Forms of International Representation

In 1919, states remained cautious toward international organizations. But labor was globally in a revolutionary mood. Karl Marx was making converts and the Russian Revolution had taken place. Could it happen elsewhere? In 1919, the Treaty of Versailles created the ILO, unique in its mode of nation-state representation. Each member state is to send four delegates: two government representatives, one employer delegate, and one to represent workers. Employer and worker delegates have independent voting rights. They do not have to consult their government. Worker delegates can join other worker representatives and vote against their own governments (the same applies to employer representatives). They are formally independent. ILO has been successful in improving the condition of labor. It became a UN Specialized Agency. By 2011, it had adopted 189 international conventions setting out global labor standards. But few international organizations have accepted independent individual participants such as employers and laborers. Civil society, however, is now beginning to achieve some representation, but not on ILO's scale. Some NGOs are full members of a limited number of international organizations.

Law-making Power

The International Civil Aviation Organization (ICAO), established in 1944 and eventually included as a UN Specialized Agency, was given the unprecedented right to enact binding international air standards. Normally, international regulations are created by treaty (requiring state ratification) and international organizations are usually denied legislative authority. ICAO, however, was given special power to address the spectacular transformation of aviation during the Second World War, which promised to revolutionize civil air transportation. Existing international rules of the air were now inadequate. Air safety required new law. Moreover, aviation technology promised to continue transforming global air transportation, thus requiring continuing adjustments in international air law.

For that purpose, the ICAO Air Navigation Commission drafts standards for the safety and efficiency of international civil aviation. This body is composed of nineteen persons who have suitable qualifications and experience in the science and practice of aeronautics. They act in their personal expert capacity rather than as state representatives. Their proposals are submitted to the ICAO executive (the thirty-six-nation state Council—ICAO has 191 member states). What the council approves is binding on all member states, even those that voted against them. In 1944, this was a radical proposition. No veto either. Today, however, countries finding it impossible to comply with the standards must notify the Council so that the matter may be discussed to find a solution.[22] In a related innovation, ICAO was given the power to enforce the international standards and to apply sanctions, such as grounding specific airlines or blocking air transportation to and from given countries.[23] These remain unusual powers. The EU is the only international organization given more extensive authority. But, aviation technology can present problems, and air safety is critical. Air transportation, on the other hand, is a lucrative business. Keeping it safe and organized is in the interest of all states.

Interparliamentary Bodies in International Organizations

Members of national parliaments normally do not take part in the work of international organizations. However, a number of regional organizations have added parliamentary bodies to their structure. See Textbox 3.1. Most of them are kept out of the organizations' effective decision-making process, although some may offer recommendations. These parliamentary bodies are essentially advisory and permit interparliamentary dialogue, but there are exceptions, for example, the EU. Some are given tasks to perform;

Textbox 3.1   Inter-Parliamentary Bodies in International Organizations

Council of Europe Parliamentary Assembly, 1949. 47 states.
Nordic Council, 1952. 5 states and 3 territories.
European Parliament (European Union), 1952. 28 states.
NATO Parliamentary Assembly, 1955. 28 member states, 14 associate countries plus European Parliament, and 4 regional partners.
Latin American Parliament (Parlatino), 1964. 23 states.
Arab Inter-Parliamentary Union (outside the Arab League), 1974. 22 states.
Andean Parliament, 1979. 4 states.
Central American Parliament. 1987. 6 states.
Pan African Parliament of the African Union, 1991. 47 states.
Baltic Assembly, 1994. 3 states.
Parliamentary Assembly of the Organization for Security and Cooperation in Europe. 1995. 56 states.
Inter-Parliamentary Assembly of the Commonwealth of Independent States, 1995. 9 states.
Parliamentary Forum of the Southern African Development Community, 1997. 15 states.
African, Caribbean, and Pacific States with European Union Joint Parliamentary Assembly. 2000. 79 states plus European Union.
East African Legislative Assembly of the East African Community, 2001. 5 states.
Parliament of the Economic Community of West African States. 2002. 15 states.
MERCOSUR Parliament (Southern Common Market). 2005. 5 states.
Arab Parliament of the League of Arab States. 2005. 22 states.
Parliament of the Economic and Monetary Community of Central Africa. 2010. 6 states.

for example the Parliamentary Assembly of the Council of Europe elects the judges of the European Court of Human Rights. Most of these parliamentary bodies have their members selected by member states from the membership of their national parliaments. Some have them directly chosen in national elections. The size of each member state is usually taken into account to determine the number of its representatives and the number of votes. These parliamentarians are a link to national opinion inviting political dialogue and even policy guidance.[24]

REGIONAL ORGANIZATIONS

Regional organizations, too, play an important role in global governance diplomacy. Many of them contribute to the management of global problems. Some regions are indeed major global players. Like their global counterparts, they serve as forums for the diplomatic interaction of their member states. But they are also independent actors. Following the Second World War, states have created an increasing number of limited membership organizations to serve a variety of purposes such as economic cooperation, integration, collective defense, banking, water management, and much more. There are now more than fifty of them plus their related agencies. See Textbox 3.2. Regional affinity, common interests, and the success of organizations in other regions can explain this drive to organize.

Textbox 3.2   Regional Organizations and Partnerships

Year created
1945   Arab League. 22 member states.
1948   Organization of American States (OAS). 35 member states.
1949   The Commonwealth (Formerly the British Commonwealth of Nations). 54 member states.
1949   Council of Europe. 47 member states.
1949   North Atlantic Treaty Organization (NATO). 28 member states.
1951   European Coal and Steel Community (ECSC). 6 member states. Eventually the European Union (EU). 28 member states.
1951   Organization of Central American States (ODECA). 5 member states.
1952   Nordic Council. 5 member states and 3 autonomous territories.
1960   Latin American Free Trade Association (LAFTA). 7 member states.
1960   Organization of Petroleum Exporting Countries (OPEC). 12 member states.
1961   Caribbean Free Trade Association (CARIFTA). 11 member states.
1961   Organization for Economic Cooperation and Development (OECD). 34 member states.
1963   Organization of African Unity (OAU). Became the African Union (AU) in 2002, 54 member states.

1963 Associated African and Malagasy Countries–EU. Became the African, Caribbean, and Pacific Partnership (ACP Countries) in 2000. European Union plus 79 countries.

1963 African Development Bank Group (includes the African Development Fund). 78 member states (53 African, plus 25 American, European, and Asian member states).

1964 Customs and Economic Union of Central Africa (UDEAC), 6 member states. Became the Economic and Monetary Community of Central Africa (CEMAC) in 1994.

1967 Association of Southeast Asian Nations (ASEAN). 10 member states.

1968 Organization of Arab Petroleum Exporting Countries (OAPEC). 10 member states.

1969 Andean Community. 4 member states.

1969 Organization of the Islamic Conference (OIC). Became the Organization of Islamic Cooperation in 2001. 57 member states.

1969 Southern African Customs Union (SACU). 5 member states.

1970 Liptako–Gourma Authority (LGA). 3 member states.

1973 Mano River Union (MRU). 3 member states.

1974 Northern Forum. 24 subregional or regional governments from 10 countries near the Arctic Circle.

1975 Latin American and Caribbean Economic System (SELA). 28 member states.

1975 Economic Community of West African States (ECOWAS). 15 member states. Includes the West African Economic and Monetary Union (UEMOA) and the West African Monetary Zone (WAMZ).

1976 Economic Community of the Great Lakes Countries (ECGLC). 3 member states.

1980 Southern African Development Coordination Conference. Became the Southern African Development Community (SADC) in 1992. 15 member states.

1980 Latin American Integration Association (ALADI). 13 member states.

1981 Gulf Cooperation Council (GCC). 6 member states.

1981 Organization of Eastern Caribbean States (OECS). 6 member states, 1 member territory.

1984 Indian Ocean Commission (COI). 4 member states.

1985 Economic Community of Central African States (ECCAS/CEEAC). 10 member states.

1985 South Asian Association for Regional Cooperation (SAARC). 7 member states.

1986 Intergovernmental Authority on Drought and Development. Became the Intergovernmental Authority on Development in Eastern Africa (IGAD) in 1996. 8 member states.

1989 Arab Maghreb Union (AMU). 5 member states.

1989 Central European Initiative (CEI). 18 member states.

1989 Asia-Pacific Economic Cooperation Project (APEC). 21 member states.

1991 African Economic Community (AEC). 53 member states.

1991 Common Market of the South (MERCOSUR). 4 member states.

1991 Central American Integration System (SICA). 8 member states.

1991	Commonwealth of Independent States (CIS). 9 member states.
1992	Southern African Development Community (SADC). 15 member states.
1993	Organization for the Harmonization of Business Law in Africa (OHADA). 16 member states.
1994	Common Market for Eastern and Southern Africa (COMESA). 19 member states.
1994	Baltic Assembly. 3 member states.
1994	West African Economic and Monetary Union (WAEMU/UEMOA). 8 member states.
1995	Barcelona Process. Became the Union for the Mediterranean in 2008 (EUROMED). European Union plus 16 countries.
1995	Organization for Security and Cooperation in Europe (OSCE). 56 member states.
1995	Amazon Cooperation Treaty Organization (ACTO). 8 member states.
1996	GUUAM Group. 5 member states.
1996	South East European Co-operation Process (SEECP). 12 member states.
1998	Community of Sahel-Saharan States (CEN-SAD). Expanded to 27 member states
1998	Greater Arab Free Trade Area (GAFTA). 17 member states.
2000	Adriatic-Ionian Initiative. 7 member states.
2000	Pacific Island Forum. 16 member states.
2001	East African Community (EAC). 5 member states.
2001	New Partnership for Africa's Development (NEPAD). 53 member states.
2001	Shanghai Cooperation Organization. 6 member states.
2002	Danube Cooperation Process. 13 member states.
2004	Bolivarian Alliance for the Peoples of Our America (ALBA). 9 member states.
2008	Regional Cooperation Council (RCC). 46 countries, organizations, and financial institutions.
2008	African Free Trade Zone (AFTZ). 26 member states.
2008	Union of South American Nations (UNASUR). 12 member states.
2009	Eastern Partnership. European Union plus 6 member states
2011	Community of Latin American and Caribbean States (CELAC). 33 member states.

Source: Individual organization websites.

The UN itself is attentive to regional interests and concerns and, early on, created five Regional Commissions under the ECOSOC. Each commission is composed of the states of the region. It is assisted by a Secretariat. These commissions also engage in regional projects. For example, in July 2013, the Economic Commission for Africa organized a meeting of regional experts on international migration and development, in cooperation with a number of global and regional organizations. The commissions are the outposts of the UN in these regions. They maintain a New York office serving as liaison with all UN agencies, funds, and programs at the headquarters, including the General Assembly, the ECOSOC, and their subsidiary bodies. The commissions' executive secretaries meet in New York and ensure coordination in their activities.

As expected, regional organizations are very diverse. They have different levels of development and different political motivation. Their desire to work together varies. Some have shown remarkable willingness to innovate and, when successful, serve as an example to other regions. Outlooks evolve. The willingness of some organizations to experiment has made a contribution to global governance. One of the most challenging departures from traditional sovereign practices has been the Council of Europe's judicial enforcement of its own human rights convention. The system is truly revolutionary in that the citizens of the member states (currently 47 of them with a population of more than 820 million[25]) may bring cases even against their own governments for violating the convention. The system has been so popular that it had to be expanded to enable the court to handle its exploding caseload. The Organization of American States (OAS—35 member states) developed its own human rights convention with enforcement institutions patterned after the Council of Europe model.[26]

The political and military decision making of NATO were an important factor in meeting the threat of Soviet expansion. It remains a factor of international security and has contributed to a number of peacekeeping operations along with other regional organizations such as the EU and its African counterpart. This is discussed in further detail in chapter 5. The contribution of the EU in the realm of global governance is more complex. Its story is still evolving, and it teaches global diplomacy the importance of moving one step at a time and accepting that what is not feasible today may be fulfilled with further efforts. The EU has demonstrated that supranational institutions with binding, enforceable decision making are compatible with independent nationhood and present advantages for political and economic integration. Creating a common currency, the euro, has been another innovation. Of 28 EU members, 19 have adopted it, plus 6 nonmembers.[27]

The EU is an important international actor. It maintains its own extensive diplomatic relations. Acting for 28 states gives its participation additional weight. For instance, it launched its partnership with 79 African, Caribbean, and Pacific countries (with a Secretariat in Brussels) contributing significantly to economic and social development and fostering South-South interaction. A number of current regional organizations acknowledge that they are using the EU as a model of integration, for example, by planning to create their own common currency. In the meantime, they create customs unions, and a variety of economic communities. They contribute to economic development. A significant number of regional organizations in all regions foster extensive dialogue not only pertaining to the region itself but to their role in global governance. Their meetings and conferences provide access to members of civil society and NGOs and contribute to the exploration of strategies to address current issues.

It must be acknowledged, however, that the proficiency of international organizations, global and regional, varies. States are not equally eager or capable to contribute to their effectiveness. But international organizations are now an essential part of international society both as instruments of multilateral diplomacy among member states and as international actors wielding their own diplomacy. It is remarkable how many international organizations contribute to the management of international problems working in close cooperation or creating official partnerships as will be seen in part II of this book. International organizations have become effective instruments of global governance and the process is expanding.

NOTES

1. For example, the UN General Assembly has 55 subsidiary bodies (boards, commissions, committees, councils, working groups) and 20 funds and programs. www.un.org/en/aboutun/structure (Accessed May 4, 2015).

2. See Seymour Maxwell Finger, *American Ambassadors at the UN: People, Politics and Bureaucracy in Making Foreign Policy* (2nd ed. New York: Holmes and Meier, 1988), particularly chapter 2, "USUN: The US Mission to the United Nations and the General Assembly," pp. 12–40.

3. See for example Finger, *American Ambassador*, p. 16; see also the experience of Ambassador Melissa Wells in the Economic and Social Council in Ann Miller, *Her Excellency: An Oral History of American Women Ambassadors* (New York: Twayne, 1995).

4. See for example the rules of procedure for the UN Security Council in Bailey and Daws, pp. 441–454. See also Robbie Sabel, *Procedure at International Conferences: A Study of the Rules of Procedure of Conferences and Assemblies of Inter-Governmental Organizations* (New York: Cambridge University Press, 1997).

5. UN Charter, Article 18, paragraph 2.

6. With the exception that "a party to a dispute shall abstain from voting." Article 27, paragraph 3.

7. www.imf.org/external/np/sec/memdir/member (Accessed October 18, 2010), and www.imf.org/external/np/fin/data/rms_sdrv.aspx (Accessed October 25, 2010).

8. See G. R. Berridge and A. Jennings, eds. *Diplomacy at the UN* (New York: St. Martin's, 1985), pp. 173–221, particularly, "Old Diplomacy in New York," pp. 175–190.

9. See Ivor Richard (UK Permanent Representative to the UN, 1974–1979), "The Council President as a Politician," in *Paths to Peace: The UN Security Council and Its Presidency,* edited by Davidson Nicol (New York: Pergamon, 1981), pp. 242–254.

10. With regard to the issue of seeking too many clarifications, see Dag Hammarskjöld's comments in the 1956 Suez Crisis (see chapter 5), Brian E. Urquhart *Hammarskjold* (New York: Norton, 1972), p. 189.

11. Jonas Talberg, Thomas Sommerer, Theresa Squatrito, and Christa Jönsson, *The Opening up of International Organizations: Transnational Access in Global Governance* (New York: Cambridge University Press, 2013).

12. cms.iucn.org/about/union/members (Accessed May 1, 2014).

13. Founded in 1971. www.cgiar.org/who-we-are (Accessed October 22, 2013).

14. CGIAR is governed by the Consortium Board and its Secretariat. www.cgiar.org/who-are-we (Accessed October 22, 2013). See also www.agropolis.org/cooperation/headquarters-cgiar-consortium (Accessed September 17, 2013).

15. The eleven are: UN High Commissioner for Refugees, UNICEF, World Food Program, UN Development Program, UN Population Fund, UN Office on Drugs and Crime, UN Women, and four Specialized Agencies—International Labour Organization, UN Educational, Scientific and Cultural Organization, World Health Organization, and World Bank.

16. www.unaids.org/en/aboutunaids (Accessed October 6, 2013).

17. www.unicef.org/about/execboard/files/financial_management_orientation_session-15Jan2015 (Accessed May 20, 2015).

18. www.undp.org (Accessed January 9, 2014).

19. www.unsceb.org (Accessed November 18, 2013).

20. www.unocha.org/what-we-do/coordination/overview (Accessed November 19, 2013).

21. http://hub.coe.int (Accessed November 20, 2013).

22. www.icao. int/about-icao (Accessed November 7, 2013).

23. www.uu.se/digitalAssets (Accessed November 7, 2013).

24. Andrés Malamud and Luis de Sousa, "Regional Parliaments in Europe and Latin America: Between Empowerment and Irrelevance." Chapter 5 of *Closing or Widening the Gap? Legitimacy and Democracy in Regional International Organizations.* Edited by Andrea Ribeiro Hoffmann and Anna van der Vleuten (Aldershot: Ashgate, 2007), pp. 85–102. www.eui.eu/Personal/Researchers/Malamud (Accessed October 24, 2013).

25. www.coe.int (Accessed May 7, 2015).

26. www.oas.org/en/iachr/mandate/Basics (Accessed May 7, 2015).

27. Europa.eu/about-eu/basic-information (Accessed May 8, 2015). The euro is used by 338.6 million people.

Chapter 4

The Role of NGOs in Global Governance Diplomacy

NGOs are now playing a larger role in global governance. They are a part of civil society[1] and independent from any government. The availability of information about world affairs has greatly increased the number of civil society people who want to be involved in international advocacy and in efforts to shape the course of international events. A large number of NGOs are aggressively seeking participation in the diplomatic process of global governance (e.g., by means of involvement in the work of international organizations and conferences addressing international problems). Greater consciousness of interdependence has undoubtedly contributed to this increased drive.

Personal involvement in the NGO movement has been uneven. Some issues have been very attractive, such as environmental protection, human rights, and a variety of humanitarian pursuits like the struggle against poverty and hunger in less-developed nations. The degree of openness and democracy in a given society is, of course, making a difference in NGO activity and individual participation. And so does local culture since some societies are more interested than others in activism and in joining volunteer organizations. And there are differences also in the degree of people's international interests. But NGOs are spreading around the world, even in the poorest countries. From a global number of 832 in 1951, the NGO aggregate has climbed to 21,026 in 2006.[2] But caution is needed in using these figures. Many NGOs do not engage in international political advocacy, for example, professional or academic associations focused on scholarly research. Another large group of NGOs, although eager to change the way the system works, focuses exclusively on the domestic level. Admittedly, some organizations will be involved at all levels as the circumstances and their facilities permit. NGOs are very diverse.

In terms of international effectiveness, the private sector cannot compare with state institutions. However, some NGOs have become powerful; some are specialized and know their field well. Their expertise can be extremely useful in global governance. Furthermore, spectacular advances in communication technology have greatly increased NGO capability. They can network globally with like-minded groups, receive information instantly, mobilize their followers and associated movements, and launch international campaigns. A growing number of NGOs have shown their determination to be heard by international decision makers and to play a part in global governance.[3] They are now widely recognized as international actors and play a greater role in international affairs. NGOs are involved in the process of global governance in a wide variety of ways that need to be examined.

CONSULTATIVE ASSOCIATION WITH THE UN

NGOs were prominent and vocal enough when the UN was created in 1945 to be acknowledged in the UN Charter. Article 71 specifies that "the Economic and Social Council may make suitable arrangements for consultation with non-governmental organizations which are concerned with matters within its competence. Such arrangements may be made with international organizations and, where appropriate, with national organizations after consultation with the Member of the United Nations concerned."[4] In the following years, NGOs applied for consultative status in growing numbers and pressed for greater participation. Three major revisions of NGO status were carried out in 1950, 1968, and 1996, and the number of accepted organizations grew steadily to 3,287 in 2010.[5]

These NGOs are invited to attend UN conferences and UN meetings; however, participation is governed by the rules of procedures of those bodies. NGOs are authorized to propose items for the ECOSOC agenda, speak at the ECOSOC meetings and meetings of its subsidiary bodies, and circulate statements at these meetings. NGOs have sought to participate in the work of the UN General Assembly, widely perceived as more important than the ECOSOC. A substantial number of states, however, have voiced their opposition. Nevertheless, since the 1970s, select NGOs have been invited to take part in the committee work of Special Sessions of the General Assembly concerned with disarmament, economic and social development, drugs, and apartheid.

Virtually all of the UN Specialized Agencies have entered into working agreements with NGOs, ranging from 15 for the World Meteorological Organization to 580 for UNESCO.[6] Each agency cooperates with NGOs according to its own needs. Participation of NGOs in the UN system is thus very diverse and every agency has its own way of interacting with them. The UN

Non-Governmental Liaison Service, established in 1975 as an interagency program to promote relations between the UN and civil society organizations, acknowledges that UN-NGO relations changed profoundly in the 1990s both quantitatively and qualitatively. This agency today even speaks of a "second generation" of UN-NGO relations essentially political in nature showing NGO involvement throughout the UN system and actively contributing to global governance.[7]

NGOs having "consultative status" at the UN have created their own association, the Conference of NGOs in Consultative Relationship with the United Nations (CONGO), whose function is to facilitate the participation of civil society in the activities of the UN. It is governed by its own General Assembly (meeting every three years), and elects a president and a twenty-member Board of Directors. CONGO has forty-three committees helping NGOs in their activities related to the work of the UN, for example, the CONGO Committee on Human Rights, which held information briefings at the 19th session of the UN Human Rights Council (March 2012) in Geneva. It also organized three NGO panels on human rights education parallel to the Council session. CONGO also launched its first Regional Committee (CONGO-Asia) in 2009.

The importance of stronger UN-NGO relations has been underlined in several UN documents, particularly in the Millennium Declaration of September 2000. Secretary-General Kofi Annan promoted the idea of UN-NGO partnerships. In 2004 he created a panel of experts to formulate recommendations to strengthen UN-civil society interaction. UN member commitment to give greater opportunities to NGOs was reaffirmed in the 2005 World Summit Outcome Document.[8] The expansion of the role of NGOs in the UN system can also be seen in the fact that there are 93 NGO offices throughout the UN, intended to facilitate UN-NGO cooperation, some at the UN headquarters in New York, Geneva, and Vienna, others at the seats of the UN Regional Commission and at the headquarters of the Specialized Agencies.[9]

The Department of Economic and Social Affairs of the UN Secretariat (DESA) has developed an Integrated Civil Society Organizations System to facilitate its interaction with these organizations. DESA has also developed the Civil Society Network (CSO Net), a web portal for NGOs and UN agencies. This portal provides the opportunity to publish news and to engage in discussion. It also permits the submission of NGO statements to the ECOSOC. DESA has a large database enabling registered organizations to share their profile with more than 13,000 civil society organizations, specify their areas of activity, the scope of their work, and their involvement in development issues.[10] The UN has thus expanded its administrative structure and machinery to keep up with the growing role of civil society organizations in global governance and in its own operations.[11]

LOBBYING DIPLOMATS

Many NGOs are anxious to participate in the diplomatic process when issues of international politics are considered in UN organs and in international conferences. In the absence of an invitation to join the proceedings, they seek informal access to national delegates wherever feasible—in hallways, dining areas, hotel lobbies, and even in restrooms.[12] Some lobbyists endeavor to establish a working relationship with official delegates. Better organized NGOs coordinate their lobbying activities, holding frequent strategy meetings and sharing information. As more NGOs seek to play a role, lobbying can become disruptive. Organizers of large diplomatic events as well as the participating states have tried to control this assault by making diplomatic representatives less accessible which, of course, adds logistical complications. It is true that some delegates, usually a small minority, find contact with some NGO people a useful link to public opinion and a source of information. The same is true of contact with the media. In the end, NGOs prefer more effective ways of becoming involved in the diplomatic process and seek official means of access to the diplomatic interaction. As NGOs become more accepted as international actors, international organizations devise procedures to involve them in their deliberations—as will be seen in the following sections—but increasing numbers of NGOs seeking participation can become a problem.

ACCESS TO INTERNATIONAL CONFERENCES

The large number of global conferences sponsored by the UN, many of them media events involving lengthy, well-publicized preparation, have generated massive NGO interest, the more so as the themes of these conferences—for example, social development, women's rights, and the environment—are often of great concern to large segments of civil society. Unprecedented numbers of NGOs are pressing for participation making it more difficult to devise meaningful involvement for them. In the 1960s and 1970s, the part of NGOs in international conferences was limited to those having observer status. But, slowly, NGO involvement and influence increased, from a single, token speaker on the last day of a conference, representing the whole NGO community, to diversified forms of involvement, still varying with the conference, its preparatory committee, and the subject matter of the debate.[13]

Parallel Forums

On the occasion of the first global conference on the environment (Stockholm, 1972), the large influx of civil society representatives led to the opening of a parallel NGO forum to accommodate them, some distance away from the official conference hall, thus keeping them from the diplomatic representatives. This arrangement was also used at other large international conferences, and the number of NGO people in attendance grew considerably.[14] Early NGO forums involved distribution of conference documents, numerous NGO presentations, and workshops on a large variety of issues, including alternative proposals of their own, and the preparation of a formal forum statement. There were also regular briefings on the conference proceedings and what was being accomplished there. NGOs networked and formed alliances—for example, environmentalists and women's movement activists agreed to work together and industrialized societies' NGOs dialogued with their counterparts from developing countries and compared their different emphases. These expanding forums became instruments of cross-fertilization.

Later efforts to increase NGO participation, particularly by the World Bank (as will be seen later), led to NGO forums preceding diplomatic gatherings, in which NGO representatives could prepare proposals of their own to be presented to the diplomatic representatives. This procedure was used also for the observance of the millennium at the UN. In December 1998, as the General Assembly was looking for a fitting way to celebrate this momentous occasion, it designated its fifty-fifth session as a Millennium Assembly, with a segment devoted to a Millennium Summit, and requested the Secretary-General to consult with member states, Specialized Agencies, observers, and NGOs, and submit proposals for this event. In response, Secretary-General Kofi Annan expressed the view that "if the United Nations were to continue to play a vital role in the century ahead it would be imperative that it benefit from the imagination, and engage the support, of the world's people,"[15] and proposed that NGOs and other civil society actors organize a Millennium Forum in connection with the Millennium Assembly. Thus, civil society organizations convened the Millennium Forum in May 2000, bringing to the UN headquarters in New York 1,350 representatives of more than 1,000 NGOs, from over 100 countries.[16] Techeste Ahderom, cochair of the Forum, then addressed the Millennium Summit and presented the substance of the Forum Declaration.

Participation in Preparatory Committee Negotiations

Preparatory committees are usually given the task of organizing large global conferences, a lengthy process taking up to four years, with three or four plenary meetings, and working groups addressing a variety of issues in between. Preparatory committees are established by conference conveners, for example, the UN General Assembly. Preparatory committees are normally open to any state interested in participating in the task and are also open to NGOs, particularly in subcommittees and diverse working groups. Preparatory committees

are important as they are responsible for organizational details, rules of procedure, modalities of participation, but also frequently matters of substance,
the agenda, and drafting conference documents. Even substantive conference
negotiations often start in preparatory committees. Substantive regional meetings in preparation for conference negotiations have also been open to NGOs.
All of these give NGOs a genuine opportunity to contribute to the substance
of international conferences. But representatives of states are still wary of
NGOs and, toward the end of the preparatory process, may meet in closed
informal sessions, leaving them out of the negotiations.

Participation in the Conference Itself

Conference organizers are now giving some limited functions to NGOs (or
coalitions of NGOs) to be carried out during certain conferences, for example
the right to make presentations in plenary sessions, or participation in the
work of conference committees. The specialized or expert knowledge of some
NGOs is particularly useful to a variety of conference committees on which
they will often be equal participants with state delegates. In an unusual move,
the executive heads of four UN agencies (UNICEF, the UNDP, UNESCO,
and the World Bank) went so far as to invite governments, other international organizations, and NGOs to participate in the 1990 World Conference
on Education for All on the basis of complete equality of status and decision making.[17] But this remains very unconventional. There is no firm rule
on the scope of NGO participation in international conferences, but greater
flexibility is noticeable. At the 1995 World Summit for Social Development
(Copenhagen), 29 NGOs and NGO coalitions were allowed to make oral statements during the general debate.[18] Other conferences have devised imaginative
ways of getting official input from civil society. The UN Habitat II Conference
(Istanbul, Turkey, 1996), because of its focus on urban environmental issues,
was anxious to hear from local experts, business leaders, foundations, academics, trade unions, parliamentarians, a variety of NGOs, and UN Secretariat
representatives.[19] Instead of counting their presentations as unofficial input,
the Conference received them as the contribution of Conference Committee
II, while government representative participation was counted as coming from
Conference Committee I, and the output of committees I and II was recognized as an integral part of official conference proceedings.

PARTICIPATION IN CONFERENCE FOLLOW-UP ACTIVITIES

NGOs play an important role in mobilizing public opinion in support of
the work of international conferences and their outcomes, especially for the

ratification of treaties. They are also significant for monitoring how governments carry out their conference commitments and publicizing their findings (comparing official pronouncements and actual performance). For example, after the 1995 Beijing Women's Conference, the Women's Environment and Development Organization drew up progress reports from information provided by governments and NGOs on the implementation of the Beijing Platform for Action, and it marked the first anniversary of the conference with a workshop in New York on "Holding Governments and International Agencies Accountable to Their Promises."[20] Given how governments handle their commitments, this NGO function is invaluable.

Some of the NGO follow-up functions are invited or even mandated in conference documents. Following the UN Conference on Environment and Development (Rio, 1992, "Earth Summit"), the UN General Assembly established (as recommended by Agenda 21) the Commission on Sustainable Development, to ensure effective follow-up activities, specifying that the Commission is "to receive relevant input from competent non-governmental organizations, including the scientific and the private sector and to enhance the dialogue . . . with non-governmental organizations and the independent sector."[21] Chapter 27 of Agenda 21 is titled: "Strengthening the Role of Non-Governmental Organizations: Partners for Sustainable Development." Habitat II, the 1996 UN Conference on Human Settlements, broke new ground in emphasizing the importance of civil society organizations in the implementation of its Global Plan of Action. The Conference's final document specified that the implementation of the Habitat Agenda requires, in the first place, strengthening local authorities, community organizations including NGOs, and, second, developing policymaking procedures that facilitate partnership between governments and civil society in human settlement development.[22]

PARTICIPATION IN UN POLICYMAKING

NGOs are becoming more involved in policymaking activities of UN bodies. This practice has become more pronounced over the last ten to fifteen years. Some of this involvement remains *informal but reaches the highest political level of the world organization*, for example, in regular consultations between the rotating president of the UN Security Council and the New York delegate of the ICRC. Antonio Donini notes that these informal and confidential conversations take place monthly and that both sides have given considerable importance to these meetings for a number of years.[23] The importance of NGOs in shaping policy is recognized by the UN Secretary-General himself as seen not only in his public presentations but also in his schedule of appointments. The heads of prominent NGOs have become frequent visitors to his office on the 38th floor of the UN headquarters. This is also an indication of how active NGOs have become in areas that were previously considered the near-exclusive preserve of state representatives and other high officials.[24] UN Secretariat units at all levels have also developed regular contacts with NGOs, often involving policymaking.

The work of the IASC is particularly significant in this respect. It was created in 1992 for coordination, policy formulation, and decision making involving the major humanitarian organizations (UN and non-UN). It is the primary mechanism for coordination of humanitarian assistance. It is composed of nine UN organizations as full members and nine other organizations as Standing Invitees, among them, *six NGOs*. In practice, no distinction is made between "members" and "standing invitees."[25] The IASC develops humanitarian policies and agrees on a division of responsibility for the various aspects of humanitarian assistance. It also identifies and addresses gaps in international response. Weekly meetings take place at UN headquarters in both New York and Geneva and serve as a forum for communication between UN agencies and NGO members. IASC subsidiary bodies, such as the Task Force on HIV in Humanitarian Situations, assist in developing policy for humanitarian assistance. NGOs fully participate in their work, for example, by cochairing the HIV Task Force.[26]

A current trend is the *extensive involvement of NGOs in the decision-making process of the IMF and the World Bank*, especially for the planning of field projects (these two Specialized Agencies are related and work in close cooperation). Greater NGO participation in policymaking of these bodies is the result of bitter attacks by members of civil society accusing IMF and the Bank of flawed priorities and misguided decisions.[27] The two are perceived as instruments of the rich, as affluent nations have overwhelming control over them. To make matters more difficult, IMF and the Bank have been rigorous in their attempts to enforce fiscal responsibility in the developing world. They impose conditions (such as fiscal reforms) that borrowers must meet to receive financial assistance, and these are often seen as harsh, with severe social and political consequences, for instance with cutting subsidies on basic consumer goods.

As a result, many civil society organizations have risen against them, staging protests and mass demonstrations. In 1982, the World Bank decided to create the NGO-World Bank Committee for the purpose of involving civil society in some of its policymaking.[28] This committee brought together senior Bank management executives and, initially, sixteen major NGO leaders (more were eventually added). Regular meetings permitted extensive policy discussion; but the small NGO group involved was soon accused of not acting independently. Many NGOs have long been suspicious of such NGOs working with the establishment, seeing them as co-opted. In response, the NGOs on the NGO-World Bank Committee created what they called the Bank Working Group composed of five NGO members from each of four regions (Africa, Asia, Latin America and the Caribbean, and Europe), plus four from North America and the Pacific, and two international liaison officers/NGO specialists. The Bank Working Group meets separately to identify NGO priorities before the annual meeting with World Bank leadership in the Committee. It organizes its own program of research to strengthen its policy dialogue with the Bank.

In another development, the NGO-World Bank Committee members were assigned to many of the Bank's resident missions around the world (the Bank's own diplomatic representation with client governments). At the end of 1998, 71 Bank resident missions had staff members specifically assigned to work on civil society issues.[29] In 1995, the Working Group of the NGO-World Bank Committee began holding regional meetings in Africa, Asia, and Latin America and the Caribbean. In 1997, the Working Group's annual meeting decided to support regional versions of the NGO-World Bank Committee. This permitted a wider range of NGOs from developing countries to participate and add to what the developing world grassroots could contribute to the global agenda. Seven Regional Committees were eventually functioning.[30] The Working Group of the NGO-World Bank Committee remained important at the global level as a North-South network and as the focus for advocacy on broad policy issues common to all the regions. Progress had been made.

Nevertheless, as the century came to an end, civil society became more restive, showing increased opposition to globalization, developing nation debt, and poverty, as could be witnessed in the 1999 Seattle riots on the occasion of WTO negotiations and the 2000 Washington protests during IMF/World Bank meetings. To increase civil society participation in World Bank policymaking, a new World Bank Civil Society Policy Forum was created in 2000.[31] As a result, a dramatic increase took place in the level of collaboration between the World Bank and a broad range of civil society organizations worldwide. Two Civil Society Policy Forums are now organized each year, one on the occasion of the IMF/World Bank annual meeting in the fall and one in the spring. These forums explore issues related to international economic development and assess the work programs of both financial institutions. The number of civil society participants has kept increasing. 400 civil society representatives from over 60 countries attended the Forum in October 2010. In order to increase participation from the developing world, the Bank is now providing grants to between 25 and 40 of its NGO representatives. IMF and World Bank executives point out that civil society organizations can bring innovative ideas and new cooperative approaches to finding solutions for local problems.[32] UNAIDS is another significant example of the inclusion of NGOs in policymaking. In fact, it was the first UN program to have formal civil society representation on its governing body.[33] (See next section.)

PARTICIPATION IN THE IMPLEMENTATION
OF FIELD PROJECTS

Many international agencies and UN programs maintain a close working relationship with a variety of NGOs for the implementation of their field projects. This was UN Secretary-General Kofi Annan's vision of partnership. Local NGOs have intimate knowledge of the communities in which many projects are to be carried out and provide valuable assistance on the ground (at times beyond the capacity of the international agencies trying to address the problems at hand). The Office of the UN High Commissioner for Refugees (UNHCR) depends on its cooperation with NGOs to carry out its vast mission. By the end of 2014, nearly 60 million people had been driven from their homes by war and persecution. Some 14 million people were newly displaced in 2014.[34] In 1994, the UNHCR created the Partnership in Action program to facilitate its relationship with more than 800 NGOs involved in its humanitarian mission around the world. The UNHCR acknowledges that this is a huge undertaking that has, at times, proved difficult to manage. From the outset, the perceptions of NGOs and the UNHCR often differed and there were communication problems even between the NGOs themselves. There were also difficulties in achieving effective cooperation between local governments, NGOs, and the UNHCR. However, they have worked together to improve their relationship. For example, the UNHCR and NGOs jointly produced a field guide for NGOs, which increased cooperation between local and other NGOs. The number of partnerships has tripled since 1994. National and international NGOs have been brought together and have raised the capability of local organizations.

More recent but more extensive is now the role of civil society in implementing the UNAIDS programs. It may be even more critical (aside from the scale of the crisis) because UN's relationship with civil society developed at a time when many governments were reluctant (or even opposed) to acknowledge the existence of the HIV/AIDS problem. Early partnership started with HIV/AIDS activists and gradually developed into cooperation on a global scale, with the UN launching UNAIDS in 1994. Tackling the stigma and discrimination experienced by so many of the people living with HIV and their afflicted communities is critical in creating the kind of environment in which people with HIV may live in a meaningful way. Universal access to treatment is a priority along with prevention.

Partnerships have been created between HIV/AIDS NGOs and NGO networks to carry out advocacy campaigns. The number of NGOs involved is now growing rapidly and generating more awareness and support. UNAIDS has enlisted the assistance of international celebrities from the world of arts, science, literature, entertainment, and sport as international goodwill ambassadors. UNAIDS works with the UN Special Envoys on AIDS appointed by the UN Secretary-General to represent him and contribute to the global effort. The World AIDS Campaign was founded by UNAIDS and is now an independent NGO enlisting the support of international trade unions through the organization Global Union and parliamentarians through the International Parliamentary Union.[35] The vast international NGO effort has led to an increase in the funds made available to combat HIV/AIDS from governmental sources as well as from foundations and individuals. In 2008, donor agencies and governments earmarked $13.8 billion to support the HIV/AIDS response, an increase of nearly 40 percent from 2007.

The World Bank itself has increasingly involved NGOs in the implementation of Bank-funded projects. The participation of NGOs in such projects has increased from 21 percent of the total number of newly funded projects in 1990 to an estimated 86 percent in fiscal 2010.[36] Other agencies have field projects involving NGOs. The ECOSOC is now encouraging local NGOs, particularly from developing countries, to join the ranks of NGOs already affiliated with it, particularly for the implementation of UN programs in the field.[37]

NGO contribution to the implementation of field projects has another dimension: helping donor countries and international organizations to *channel development and humanitarian funds* into less-developed countries. The funds are made available to NGOs to carry out local projects. With the spread of failed states and of governments whose administration is ineffective in parts of the country because of unrest or corruption, NGOs are given the means to provide social services, which these governments cannot offer. Thus, NGOs' share of public financing has increased. They become the instruments for projects that donors would like to fund; NGOs implement the humanitarian policies of the funding agencies. The World Bank itself funds NGOs directly through headquarters-based mechanism. The total flow of financial assistance channeled through NGOs in transfers of bilateral and multilateral funds for projects in the developing world was estimated by the OECD at $8.3 billion in 1992, representing the second largest amount of development and relief assistance. Public grants accounted for 1.5 percent of NGO income in 1970 and 35 percent in 1988.[38]

ASSOCIATION WITH NATIONAL GOVERNMENTS

NGOs have tended to be suspicious of governments and have therefore been hesitant (if not opposed) to become associated with them, even when partnerships seem possible.[39] And a large number of national governments do not like dealing with NGOs in the course of their international transactions. Nonetheless, a growing number of state-NGO associations have been found practical by both sides, which is not all that surprising given the fact that NGOs have aggressively expanded their participation in global diplomacy and have become parties in many international transactions. Association has simply been useful in a variety of circumstances, and many NGOs have found that working with states has increased their role in international affairs. Diplomacy is changing—and may well be changing faster with the growth of interdependence in global society.[40]

A number of states have found a negotiating advantage in adding NGO representatives to their diplomatic delegations to a number of international conferences, and the NGOs invited have welcomed this opportunity to participate in the diplomatic process. For example, in the global climate treaty signed at the Rio Earth Summit in 1992, more NGO representatives served on national delegations than ever before.[41] The tiny Pacific Island of Vanuatu went one step further and used an NGO with expertise in international regulation to staff its entire official delegation. All NGO representatives in national delegations were involved in the Climate Action Network and were able to bridge North-South differences among governments that many had expected would prevent an agreement. NGOs fought out contentious issues among themselves, then took an agreed position to the national delegations on which they served. When NGO representatives could not reach agreement, they would communicate to their national delegations what the problem was and where a compromise might be found. This process led to a climate treaty.[42]

The Landmines Campaign

The most remarkable partnership between states and NGOs led to the creation of the global treaty to ban antipersonnel landmines, which the UN itself had failed to do.[43] These mines are particularly inhumane. They have been used by the million. They are small, inexpensive, and easily spread out. However, when a conflict comes to an end, they tend to be abandoned in the field and, perhaps years later, people living in the area—farmers, children—get maimed or killed.[44] A 1980 UN treaty produced some international regulation but did not solve the problem.

In the early 1990s, six NGOs[45] met in New York and agreed to seek a comprehensive ban of these mines. They launched the ICBL and started recruiting other NGOs. In 1993, fifty of them met in London and appointed a coordinator, Jody Williams.[46] In 1995, the UN convened a conference to strengthen the 1980 treaty. ICBL, the NGO coalition, decided to support this effort, lobbying governments and mobilizing media support. ICBL was allowed to address a plenary session of the UN conference and recruited more NGOs for its effort. The UN conference failed but the NGOs associated with ICBL grew to more than 350. A Dutch group decided to bring together the governments that had supported a total ban at the UN conference. Seven states responded to the Dutch invitation. A second NGO-government gathering was called. This time 14 governments participated and the Canadian government decided to convene a joint government-NGO strategy conference in 1996. 50 states attended as full participants, and 24 as observers. Jody Williams, the ICBL coordinator, sat at the main conference table with government representatives.

At the end of the 1996 strategy meeting, the Canadian foreign minister announced that Canada planned to work for a total landmine ban in open partnership with ICBL and daringly declared that Canada would host the signing ceremony for a treaty banning all antipersonnel landmines in December 1997. The UN General Assembly, impressed by this initiative, passed a resolution urging states to support this project (the vote was 155 for, none against).[47] A core group of states took the lead in participating with Canada and ICBL. They held joint meetings and agreed that they needed to involve a greater number of states, particularly from the developing world, to avoid a North-South split. Much diplomacy was involved. Intense telephone and fax communication followed. Leaders traveled around the world seeking allies. NGOs used the media extensively to promote a total landmine ban. Prominent personalities, among them Princess Diana of Britain, Archbishop Desmond Tutu, Jimmy Carter, and the UN Secretary-General, used their stature to support a total ban.

ICBL and its own legal experts drafted the kind of treaty they thought negotiators should seek. State diplomats sought ICBL's advice on treaty language. And more NGOs joined ICBL (more than 1200 by the end of the campaign). The Organization of African Unity, in consultation with Canada, agreed to host an Africa-wide landmine conference. In the meantime, three conferences were held to draft proposals for the treaty itself. Remarkably, during the third drafting conference (Belgium, June 1997), 97 states signed a declaration banning antipersonnel landmines. Jody Williams, the ICBL coordinator gave one of the keynote addresses in which she coined the refrain that ICBL members would use in all diplomatic gatherings: "No exceptions, no reservations, no loopholes!"[48]

All of this led to the final treaty negotiations in Oslo (September 1997) bringing together 87 participating countries and 33 observer states. During this official phase, the interaction of state diplomats and NGO representatives continued. ICBL members and government missions worked in the conference hall itself. NGOs pressed government delegates to incorporate into the treaty what they deemed essential. Many governments were anxious to get the United States to become a party to the final treaty despite its many reservations, and there was a serious danger that the negotiators might make concessions and create exceptions to meet US objections—something the Jody Williams and ICBL had fought hard to avoid. The US delegation circulated a package of amendments, but made a fundamental error by making its proposals non-negotiable. It was all or nothing! This proved unacceptable and the United States pulled out. The following day, the conference adopted the antipersonnel mine ban without exceptions or loopholes and the bulk of the negotiators rose for a prolonged standing ovation. The treaty was ready for signature at the Ottawa ceremony in December 1997, just as the Canadian foreign minister had proposed in the fall of 1996. This was a monumental achievement for the ICBL and the states it worked with.[49] Jody Williams and the ICBL were awarded the 1997 Nobel Peace Prize.

INSTRUMENTS OF OPPOSITION

On occasion, NGOs prefer to campaign against what governments are doing and seek radical change. They have done that by convening conferences of their own (*"counter conferences"*) simultaneously or prior to state meetings. In the process, they get the attention of the media and present what they believe should be done. NGOs have also created counteraction coalitions, for example, in the mid-1990s, the OECD undertook the task of concluding an agreement to provide greater enforceable protection to international investors. This was widely perceived as intended to protect the rich at the expense of the poor. In 1997–1998, a protest movement of more than 600 very diverse NGOs in seventy countries was formed to fight the project. The proposed treaty was denounced on the Internet and in letter-writing campaigns, petitions, and public demonstrations. The OECD negotiations foundered and the project collapsed.[50]

In more severe cases of alienation, civil society groups have resorted to violent disorder, as in their opposition to globalization and to the work of the IMF, the World Bank, and the WTO. Violent demonstrations took place on the occasion of the 2001 G8 summit in Genoa, Italy ("the Battle of Genoa"), which led the Canadian government to take extraordinary precautions when it hosted the G8 summit in 2002. The meeting was held at the small, remote resort village of Kananaskis in Western Canada, in the shadow of Mount Kidd, sixty miles from Calgary, Alberta, accessible by only one road. This location made it easier to keep away uninvited guests. And, as added precaution, the Canadian government deployed 4,500 police officers and 6,000 troops guarding a fifteen-mile perimeter around the village. Journalists were kept in Calgary at a media center around which a barrier was erected. All of this cost in excess of $200 million.[51]

Another example of global protest is provided by the World Social Forum, the annual meeting of an antiglobalization movement held since 2001 (initially in Brazil) at the same time as the meeting of the World Economic Forum in Davos, Switzerland. The World Social Forum is organized by an international council representing a global network of civil society organizations. The Forum also sponsors many local, regional, and national social gatherings. The seventh World Social Forum held in Nairobi, Kenya, in January 2007, attracted 66,000 registered participants and 1,400 organizations from 110 countries.[52]

AGENTS OF CONFLICT RESOLUTION

Civil society people and NGOs are well suited to engage in conflict resolution. They can be more impartial and more focused on the preservation of peace than states that are perennially concerned with their national interests (and even international organizations with their conflicting member states). A number of NGOs and church-related institutions engage in a variety of conflict resolution and mediation efforts, particularly the ICRC in humanitarian situations,[53] and a number of others, such as the Community of Sant'Egidio, the Carter Center, and the World Council of Churches.

RECONCILIATION AND PEACE BUILDING

Related to conflict resolution but going beyond such efforts, civil society members and NGOs engage in a variety of activities to promote stability and harmony in a number of countries. Extensive involvement in grassroots activities, networking, and mobilization of public opinion give certain civil society institutions and NGOs opportunities to build or rebuild the sociopolitical foundations of peace.[54]

A wide variety of NGOs now participates in the international political process and contributes to global governance. They are not normally major decision makers and often add a degree of complexity to global diplomacy—not necessarily constructive. Some NGOs, too, are out of touch with reality (but so are a number of other international actors, including states). NGOs give a voice to many people, which many decision makers are unwilling to hear. Different perspectives and imaginative approaches (perhaps unconventional) are important elements in human progress. Global governance needs the benefit of their contribution.

The international political process is now adjusting to the new reality. Do NGOs improve global governance? Undoubtedly, but the involvement of civil society adds a degree of complexity to global diplomacy. It gives a voice to a variety of people, which other actors are often unwilling or unable to hear. But many NGOs are special interest groups not always tolerant of other interests or views. Some are themselves out of touch with reality. However, with the information revolution and complex global interdependence, more NGOs are likely to participate in global diplomacy. International conferences and UN agencies will help many of them play a role. NGOs may not be major decision makers in global governance, but they have much to contribute. Different perspectives, imaginations, and drives are important elements in human progress. Possibilities remain open-ended. Circumstances, skill, and the kind of political systems involved are important variables. But past experience indicates that these new kinds of actors can make a difference and their growing participation will help global governance diplomacy.

NOTES

1. Anthony Judge, "NGO and Civil Society: Some Realities and Distortions. The Challenge of 'Necessary-to-Governance Organizations' (NGOs)," *Transnational Associations* Vol. 47, No. 3 (1995), pp. 156–180. See also James N. Rosenau, "Governance in the Twenty-first Century," *Global Governance* Vol. 1, No. 1 (1995), pp. 13–43.

2. Union of International Associations, *Yearbook of International Organizations 2006–2007* (43rd ed. Munich: K. G. Saur, 2006) Vol. 1B, p. 3,024.

3. P. J. Spiro, "New Global Communities: Nongovernmental Organizations in International Decision-Making Institutions," *Washington Quarterly* Vol. 18, No. 1 (1995), pp. 45–56.

4. UN Charter, Chapter X, The Economic and Social Council, Article 71.

5. www.un.org/esa/coordination/ngo (Accessed November 12, 2010).

6. A. LeRoy Bennett and James K. Oliver, *International Organizations: Principles and Issues* (7th ed. Upper Saddle River, NJ: Prentice-Hall, 2002), p. 291.

7. www.un-ngls.org (Accessed November 20, 2010).

8. Paragraphs 172–174, www.un-ngls.org (Accessed November 21, 2010).

9. UN, Office of the UN Under-Secretary-General. See discussion by Alger, pp. 103–110.

10. http://esango.un.org/civilsociety/login.do (Accessed July 14, 2011).

11. www.un.org/esa/coordination/ngo/documents; also www.un.org/dpi/ngosection (Accessed October 10, 2012).

12. Felix Dodds, with Michael Strauss, *How to Lobby at Intergovernmental Meetings* (London: Earthscan, 2004).

13. Willetts (2000), "From 'Consultative Arrangements,'" pp. 192–193.

14. About 300 NGOs came to the 1972 Stockholm Conference, 1,400 NGOs registered for the 1992 Rio Conference, and some 17,000 people attended the Parallel Forum. www.un.org/geninfo/bp/enviro (Accessed November 30, 2010). See also Ann Marie Clark. Elizabeth J. Friedman and Kathryn Hochstetler, "The Sovereign Limits

of Global Civil Society: A Comparison of NGO Participation in UN World Conferences on Environment, Human Rights, and Women," *World Politics* Vol. 51, No. 1 (1998), pp. 1–35.

15. General Assembly, document A/52/850.

16. UN General Assembly, A/54/959. www.un.org/millennium/declaration (Accessed November 19, 2010).

17. Cyril Ritchie, "Coordinate? Cooperate? Harmonize? NGO Policy and Operational Coalitions," in *NGOs, the UN, and Global Governance*, edited by Thomas G. Weiss, and Leon Gordenker (Boulder, CO: Lynne Rienner, 1996), pp. 177–188.

18. www.un.org/ga/president/55/speech/civilsociety1 (Accessed November 24, 2010).

19. www.un.org/Conferences/habitat (Accessed December 3, 2010).

20. Aviel, p. 162.

21. General Assembly resolution A/RES/47/191 of December 1992, Article 3(f) and (g). www.un.org/documents/ga/res/47/ares47-191 (Accessed December 6, 2010).

22. www.un.documents.net/ha-4f (Accessed December 7, 2010).

23. Antonio Donini, Office of the UN Secretary-General, "The Bureaucracy and the Free Spirits: Stagnation and Innovation in the Relationship Between the UN and NGOs," in *NGOs, the UN, and Global Governance*, edited by Thomas G. Weiss, and Leon Gordenker (Boulder, CO: Lynne Rienner, 1996), p. 86. The ICRC was given Observer status in the UN in 1990, a promotion from its earlier NGO status under UN Charter Article 71.

24. Donini, p. 87.

25. www.humanitarianinfo.org/iasc/pageloader (Accessed November 19, 2010).

26. www.humanitarianinfo.org/iasc/pageloader.aspx?page=content-about-default (Accessed November 19, 2010).

27. See Richard Peet, Unholy Trinity: The IMF, World Bank, and WTO (2nd ed. London: Zed Books, 2009).

28. World Bank, Social Development, the NGO Unit, *The Bank's Relations with NGOs: Issues and Directions* (Social Development Paper No 28. Washington, DC: World Bank, August 1998).

29. World Bank Group, "Overview: NGO-World Bank Collaboration," online at www.worldbank.org (1999).

30. www.staff.city.ac.uk/p.willetts/NGOWG/INDEX (Accessed November 23, 2010).

31. www.staff.city.ac.uk/p.willetts/NGOWG/INT-RES (Accessed November 23, 2010).

32. http://web.worldbank.org/WBSITE/EXTERNAL/TOPICS/CSO/O/ contentMDK:22745676~page (Accessed November 24, 2010).

33. www.unaids/org/en/Partnerships/Civil+society/default (Accessed December 19, 2010).

34. Annual Report of the Office of the UN High Commissioner for Refugees. *New York Times*, June 18, 2015, pp. A1 and A4.

35. www.unaids.org/en/Partnerships/Advocacy+partners/default (Accessed December 10, 2010).

36. See *World Bank-Civil Society Engagement: Review of Fiscal Years 2007–2009.* http://web.worldbank.org/WBSITE/EXTERNAL/NEWS (Accessed July 14, 2011).

37. www.un.org/esa/coordination/ngo (Accessed November 12, 2010).

38. Donini, pp. 88–90.

39. See R. Tandon, *NGO-Government Relations: A Source of Life or the Kiss of Death?* (New Delhi: Society for Participatory Research in Asia, 1989).

40. See Jessica T. Mathews, "Power Shift," *Foreign Affairs* Vol. 76, No. 1 (January–February 1997), pp. 50–66.

41. See Thomas Princen, "NGOs Creating a Niche in Environmental Diplomacy," in *Environmental NGOs in World Politics: Linking the Global and the Local*, edited by Thomas Princen and Matthias Finger (London: Routledge, 1994).

42. Mathews, pp. 55–56.

43. Metoko Mekata, "Building Partnerships Toward a Common Goal: Experiences of the International Campaign to Ban Landmines," in *The Third Force: The Rise of Transnational Civil Society*, edited by Ann M. Florini (Washington, DC: Carnegie Endowment for International Peace, 2000), pp. 143–176.

44. Ibid.

45. Three in the United States, one in France, one in Germany, and one in the United Kingdom. Ibid.

46. Jody Williams and Stephen Goose, "The International Campaign to Ban Land Mines," in *To Walk Without Fear: The Global Movement to Ban Landmines,* edited by Maxwell A Cameron, Robert J. Lawson and Brian W. Tomlin (New York: Oxford University Press, 1998), pp. 23–25.

47. Metoko Mekata, "Building Partnerships Toward a Common Goal: Experiences of the International Campaign to Ban Landmines," in Florini, ed. *(op. cit)*, pp. 143–176.

48. Williams and Goose *(op. cit)*, p. 36.

49. Robert J. Lawson, Mark Gwozdecky, Jill Sinclair and Ralph Lysychyn, "The Ottawa Process and the International Movement to Ban Anti-Personnel Mines," in Cameron, Lawson, and Tomlin, eds. *(op. cit.)*, p. 180. As of December 21, 2010, 156 governments have ratified the treaty. www.icbl.org/treaty/members (Accessed December 21, 2010).

50. Craig Warkentin and Karen Mingst, "International Institutions, the State, and Global Civil Society in the Age of the World Wide Web," *Global Governance* Vol. 6, No. 2 (April–June 2000), pp. 240–242.

51. Clifford Kraus, "Security Tight for G-8 Talks at Idyllic Spot in Canada," *New York Times* (June 26, 2002), p. A6.

52. www.ngocongo.org/index.

53. David P. Forsythe, "Humanitarian Mediation by the International Committee of the Red Cross," in *International Mediation in Theory and Practice*, edited by Sandia Touval and I. William Zartman (Boulder, CO: Westview, 1985), pp. 233–249.

54. See Nadim N. Rouhana, "Unofficial Intervention: Potential Contributions to Resolving Ethno-National Conflicts," in *Innovation in Diplomatic Practice*, edited by Jan Melissen (New York: St. Martin's, 1999), pp. 111–132.

Part II

GLOBAL CHALLENGES AND THE ROLE OF DIPLOMACY

Chapter 5

Global Governance Diplomacy for Peace and Security

The maintenance of peace and security remains the greatest challenge confronting international society. As the world changes, new threats materialize. The concerns that led to the creation of the League of Nations in 1919 are now so different. There are more states pursuing conflicting objectives. Even nonstates such as the al-Qaeda and the Islamic State of Iraq and Syria (ISIS) create major threats. Technology makes international violence more threatening and more lethal. Some internal wars lead to genocide. Can anything be done to ensure the maintenance of peace and security? Even if the problem must remain symptomatic of the "human condition," an enormous amount of diplomacy is devoted to keeping it from getting worse.

THE RULE OF LAW

Legal order is one of the foundations of international peace—perhaps maligned because of the many violations endured by the global legal system with seemingly no hope for international enforcement. The rule of law is nevertheless indispensable to the functioning of international society. It can be strengthened. Legal norms need to be kept relevant to global needs as they evolve. Through much of the nineteenth century, the greater part of international law was customary, that is, unwritten—the result of international state practice recognized by courts. With the rapidly increasing pace of international relations, and the growing complexity of world affairs, treaty law became indispensable. Customary law still plays an important role but treaty law acquires greater significance. Treaty law is of course the result of diplomatic negotiations among nation states. The UN has become a major instrument in its development. In 1945, the UN Charter stipulated that "the General

Assembly shall initiate studies and make recommendations for the purpose of
. . . encouraging the progressive development of international law and its codification" (Art. 13). To carry out this mandate, the General Assembly created
the International Law Commission, a body of 34 independent international
law experts sitting in their individual capacity and not as representatives of
state governments. The statute of the Commission specifies that "in the Commission as a whole, representation of the main forms of civilization and of the
principal legal systems of the world should be assured" (Art. 8). The General
Assembly guarantees the observance of this rule in selecting the experts.

The Commission considers proposals for new rules of international law
submitted by the UN General Assembly, and also by individual members of
the UN, other UN organs, the Specialized Agencies, or other international
organizations. The Commission itself may take the initiative to draft new
law, but it generally seeks the endorsement of the General Assembly before
doing so. It may also recommend to the General Assembly the codification
of the law pertaining to a particular field.[1] In developing proposals for new
law, the Commission freely seeks the input of states and the General Assembly. National concerns, therefore, enter the discussion of the Commission's
proposals. The Commission also consults a variety of bodies, both official
and unofficial, such as NGOs, independent legal experts, and the academic
community.

A Commission draft is submitted to the General Assembly, which may
submit modifications. Once a draft is endorsed by the General Assembly, that
body usually convenes a diplomatic conference to engage in formal negotiations for a new convention. Some negotiations may be complex, depending
upon the subject matter and scope of the project. Then comes ratification,
the process of acceptance by individual governments, each state determining
its own procedure. In the United States, the process involves a decision by
the president following approval by two-thirds of the Senate. A treaty is not
binding on a state failing to ratify it. Many multilateral treaties are open to
accession by states that did not participate in the negotiations.

In 1966, the UN General Assembly created the UN Commission on
International Trade Law (UNCITRAL), a body reminiscent of the UN International Law Commission, but more specialized. Its mandate is to remove
legal obstacles to international trade by progressively modernizing and
harmonizing trade law. It drafts legal texts in a number of key international
trade areas in preparation for the negotiation of new trade law conventions.
Other international organizations are instrumental in the creation of new
international law in their areas of specialization, mostly by convening international conferences to negotiate new conventions. Some organizations were
granted quasi-legislative authority by the treaties creating them. An example
of this is the ICAO, created in 1944 to permit the safe expansion of civil air

transportation in the wake of the revolutionary transformation of aviation during the Second World War. The ICAO Council (36 member states elected by the ICAO Assembly for three-year terms) was given the power to create the international standards necessary for the safety of international air navigation. These standards are revised regularly to keep up with the evolution of aviation technology.[2]

International norms are occasionally created by declaration, for example, by the UN General Assembly.[3] Although formally nonbinding, repeated pronouncements formulating international norms, when supported by a large cross section of the political systems of the world, can acquire legal power. The *Codex Alimentarius* developed jointly by the Food and Agriculture Organization (FAO) and the WHO (starting in 1963), represents another way to create international norms. It was created to protect public health and to facilitate fair trade practices in the food area. It is a collection of some 200 standards dealing with maximum limits on pesticides, food additives, and even labeling observed by some 190 states members of FAO and WHO.[4]

The standards of the *Codex Alimentarius* are created and continually revised and expanded under the authority of the Codex Alimentarius Commission, a body open to all member nations and associate members of FAO and WHO. The development, revision, and administration of standards are done by some 42 intergovernmental task forces and committees, each of which focuses on a category of food or issue. This work brings together scientists, technical experts, and government regulators, as well as international consumer and industrial organizations, altogether involving 47 intergovernmental organizations, 16 UN bodies, and 138 NGOs. The standards need to be accepted by the Codex Alimentarius Commission but do not require national ratification. As the standards are developed, national governments are consulted at several stages of the drafting process. The large-scale involvement of the scientific community, civil society, and international organizations in the development of standards undoubtedly contributes to their authority. The *Codex Alimentarius* is recognized by the WTO as an international reference standard for the resolution of disputes concerning food safety and consumer protection. It can thus be said that international rules of this kind, although created outside the international treaty-making process, have the same force as international law.[5] Participation in the creation of international legal norms has truly expanded—and without making the headlines.

PEACEFUL SETTLEMENT OF DISPUTES

From the dawn of history, some rulers or governments have tried, with more or less vigor or skill, to find alternatives to armed conflict. It must be noted however, that "alternatives to conflict" do not necessarily amount to a settlement. *Settling* the problem, that is, solving it, is of course preferable. But peace may be preserved (even in deep-rooted conflicts) if the parties learn to live with their differences. In practice, the terms "*conflict resolution*" and "*peaceful settlement*" are often used to identify dispute *management* helping the maintenance of peace. There are two basic types of peaceful means in use today: political and judicial.

Political Means of Peaceful Settlement

Political means involve essentially *negotiations* and agreement between the disputants. This can be the result of the parties' own initiative to negotiate their differences. It happens routinely. Disagreement does not necessarily imply enmity. States having the closest of relations have their own differences, and they have a full range of diplomatic means to address them, for example, by using their embassy personnel, special missions, ad hoc meetings, and even negotiations at the summit level.

When negotiations are unsuccessful, a settlement may be sought with the help of a third party, either because the disputants seek such assistance, or because the third party intervenes and offers its services. Such assistance can take a variety of diplomatic forms, depending upon the identity of the third party, its relationship with the disputants, the nature of their differences, and the circumstances, among other factors. A fairly minimal intervention on the part of a government or foreign head of state is called *good offices* and may consist in an offer of a neutral venue to be used by the disputing parties to conduct their own negotiations—usually a face-saving device avoiding one party having to travel to the other country. The party offering such good offices does not participate in the discussion. The idea is to make the negotiations easier. But good offices do not have hard and fast boundaries. In the Oslo process between the Israeli government and the Palestinian leadership in 1992–1993, the Norwegian government offered to facilitate the conversations by making some secluded estates available in Norway where secret talks could take place. However, the Norwegian foreign minister attended the negotiations. In fact, some of the meetings took place in his own home and he was reported to have helped the two sides continue their conversations.

Facilitation in some form of good offices may easily lead to *mediation* in which the third party becomes involved in the negotiations, even proposing terms of settlement.[6] Whatever the mediator contributes is intended to enable the conflicting parties reach an agreement. The parties are not bound by what the mediator proposes. Such proposals may in fact become the object of further negotiations between the conflicting parties.

Mediation is extremely versatile and a widely used instrument of global governance. It is particularly useful when the parties in conflict refuse to talk to each other. This is often the case when ideology or matters of principle are involved. The situation may be so polarized that the parties cannot politically afford to meet. Cultural differences may also complicate the initiation of negotiations, and perhaps also pride and notions of national honor. A mediator then becomes the only means of communication between the contending parties, seeing each of them separately, exploring the situation, suggesting terms, looking for alternatives to what separates them, and communicating counterproposals to the other side, until some common ground may be found or the parties accept to engage in face-to-face negotiations. This is what the media have called "shuttle diplomacy" as the mediator travels from one capital to the other.

Mediators are occasionally in a better position to lead the parties to make concessions when these are seen as granted, however implausibly, to the mediator rather than to the other side (perhaps a matter of saving face). In a similar vein, proposals are more acceptable when they are seen as coming from the mediator rather than from the opposite side. The final agreement or document settling the dispute may also be more acceptable if presented in a declaration by the mediator rather than as an agreement between the disputants (no deal made with the enemy). For example, the final (1981) agreement in the Iran hostage negotiations took the form of a declaration by the Algerian government (the mediator).[7] A prestigious mediator (actual negotiator or an international actor in whose name the mediation is carried out) is more likely to succeed in getting the parties to reach an agreement.

A variety of international actors provide mediation, including NGOs and prominent individuals acting on their own authority, for example, former US president Jimmy Carter. The Community of Sant'Egidio, a church lay association established in Rome in 1968, has engaged in a variety of mediation efforts in times of armed conflict[8] (and so has the ICRC). Their humanitarian motivation may foster greater trust among the conflicting parties in trying to find some common ground. States, however, have tended to be more proficient as mediators, since they have more diplomatic resources and can make use of their power and authority in coaxing the disputants or even in providing positive inducements (as in the 1977 Camp David negotiations, in the course of which the United States offered several billion dollars in the form of "assistance" to Israel and Egypt to reach an agreement, eventually leading to a peace treaty). Some states can also offer some forms of guarantee for the implementation of the settlement they brokered. In any case, mediation usually requires excellent diplomatic skills.

International organizations (the UN as well as regional institutions) are involved in mediation. An important reason is that when a serious dispute occurs that the parties are unable to deal with, other states are not always anxious to mediate, unless their national interests are at stake. The UN (and most regional organizations), on the other hand, have the responsibility to ensure the maintenance of peace. Chapter VI of the UN Charter is devoted to "The Pacific Settlement of Disputes," and under Article 33, the parties to any dispute, "the continuation of which is likely to endanger the maintenance of peace and security," undertake to seek a solution by any of the means available.

Any state may bring disputes likely to endanger international peace to the attention of the Security Council or of the General Assembly (Art. 35). This may be easier than for a state to take on the role of mediator. The Security Council itself may, *at any stage* of situations likely to endanger the maintenance of peace, recommend "appropriate procedures or methods of adjustment" or "terms of settlement" (Arts. 36 and 37). All of this usually entails sending a high-ranking UN diplomat to engage in some form of mediation. This procedure carries the weight of being mandated by the Security Council, and may also constitute some form of pressure. Failure to cooperate may entail the use of international sanctions under Chapter VII of the UN Charter, as happened in the case of Libya's involvement in the 1988 bombing of Pam Am flight 103.[9]

The UN Secretary-General has been significantly involved in various forms of mediation. The UN Secretariat's Department of Political Affairs has strengthened its mediation-support capability. In 2006, it created a Mediation Support Unit to serve as a central repository for peacemaking experience and as a clearing house for lessons learned and best practices. The unit also coordinates training for mediators and provides them with advice on UN standards and operating procedures. A UN Peacemaker website was launched in 2006 providing UN mediators and their staff with online tools including a comprehensive database of peace agreements and insight into peacemaking strategy. In 2008, a Mediation Support Standby Team was added to the Department of Political Affairs. This is a five-person expert team that can be deployed on short notice to assist UN and non-UN mediation efforts around the world.[10]

UN conflict resolution facilities have been extensively used. Between 1946 and 1998, more than 180 disputes were brought to the Security Council or to the General Assembly; 48 were brought to both organs. Some of the disputes were protracted; 59 of them were under consideration for more than five years. Regional organizations too, offer mediation services.[11] A political means of peaceful settlement mentioned in the UN Charter is conciliation. It consists of a panel selected by the parties to examine their dispute, hear their arguments, and propose terms of settlement. These are nonbinding and the settlement, as in the case of mediation, is dependent upon the parties at the dispute accepting what the panel is offering. They may also try to negotiate a settlement on the basis of what the panel has proposed. Conciliation is less versatile than mediation, which may explain why this instrument is receiving less attention.

Enquiry or fact finding is also used as a means of peaceful settlement. It is true that an unbiased and authoritative examination of the situation may facilitate reaching a settlement. This procedure is frequently used by international organizations before deciding on a course of action. Article 34 of the UN Charter specifies that the Security Council may, on its own authority, without the need of any state requesting it, "investigate any dispute, or any situation which might lead to international friction or give rise to a dispute, in order to determine whether the continuation of the dispute or situation is likely to endanger the maintenance of international peace and security." This may be particularly useful in conjunction with any system of early warning.

Judicial Means of Peaceful Settlement

This method is essentially characterized by the binding nature of the decision reached by a court or arbitral body. Judicial means normally base their settlements on international law. Note that many courts have the option of deciding in equity (*ex aequo et bono*) if the parties prefer it. Arbitral bodies usually leave it to the parties to choose the basis on which a decision is to be reached. In contrast to the political means of peaceful settlement, in judicial settlement, a decision is handed down by the court or judicial body rather than negotiated among the disputants. One party is usually seen as having won the case, thus making the other the loser. The procedure tends to be perceived as a zero-sum game, although some cases are not that clear cut, with neither party getting all that it was trying to get, and the court deciding how the benefits are to be shared. A legal approach does not normally make allowances for face-saving considerations. The decision is not subject to further negotiations and international cases still offer few appeal possibilities (although this is beginning to change). Nonobservance or departure from the terms of the decision is a violation under international law.

In other words, judicial procedure is less flexible than its political counterpart—and law tends to be conservative. If one of the parties is seeking anything beyond what the law offers (and the law may not cover the field comprehensively), then, invoking the law is unlikely to provide a solution. But a legal solution has its advantages. When two parties value their relationship but cannot find a negotiated solution to what is now dividing them, an impartial determination of what they are entitled to under the law can be a way out. In the name of their cordial relations, they pledge to accept whatever the law offers—not that they necessarily consider it right or desirable, but an impartial decision under the law can be accepted for the sake of their valued relationship. This is a friendly submission to a judicial settlement. In the case of a dispute between hostile states, a legal decision may be sought for vindication. It will not remove the hostility, but it will help one of the antagonists to show the rest of the world that it has the law on its side (as happened when Iran and the United States went to the World Court over the seizure of the American Embassy in Tehran. The hostages were not released. The conflict endured. But the United States used the decision as vindication, a politically desirable outcome).

International arbitration is the oldest judicial procedure, dating back to Ancient Greece. The arbitration body is established ad hoc by means of negotiations among the parties to the dispute and spelled out in a treaty often called *compromis d'arbitrage*. They select the judges (and in technical cases, they may choose experts in the field rather than jurists). They choose the rules to be applied (normally, international law—but other rules may be selected by the parties). The parties also determine the procedures to be followed, and whatever else is needed to decide the case. The decision is called an *award*. Pairs of states may establish arbitral bodies *before* being involved in a dispute. This is usually done in so-called *treaties of friendship*. Arbitration provisions are also included (in whatever detail the parties are inclined to specify) for the purpose of the application of a given treaty (e.g., a trade agreement), that is, only disputes pertaining to the application of the treaty may be submitted. States may also create one arbitral body to decide an entire collection of cases accumulated over the years, for example, at the end of a war, to decide the war claims of the two parties. Such arbitral bodies are often referred to in the literature as *mixed claims commissions*. They remain in session until all the claims are settled. The US-German mixed claims commission set up after the First World War decided claims virtually until the outbreak of the Second World War.[12]

And then there is the Permanent Court of Arbitration (PCA) established by the Convention for the Pacific Settlement of Disputes during the first Hague Peace Conference of 1899. Currently, the PCA has 109 member states. The purpose of this arbitral body is to create a standard arbitral institution saving future disputants the task of negotiating its composition and terms, thus facilitating resort to arbitration. Each party to the treaty is to select, in advance, a maximum of four potential arbitrators. When the signatories decide to submit a dispute to the "Court" (a misnomer as it is not a standing court), each party selects two arbitrators from the collective list (only one to be a national of the selecting state). Then the four of them will select an umpire who will prevent ties. The Convention spells out all the rules of procedure to be applied by the PCA. In addition to arbitration, the PCA administers conciliation and fact finding in disputes involving various combinations of states, state institutions, international organizations, and private parties. International commercial arbitration can also be conducted under PCA auspices. As of 2009, the case-load totals 33 pending cases including 21 bilateral or multilateral investment treaties.[13]

International commercial arbitration has experienced a vast expansion as a result of the tremendous growth of international trade. The leading nongovernmental institution is the International Court of Arbitration of the International Chamber of Commerce of Paris, France, hearing cases between business enterprises. It currently receives some 350 cases per year.[14] Other prominent private commercial arbitration bodies include the London Court of International Arbitration, the International Center for Dispute Resolution of the American Arbitration Association, and the Arbitration Institute of the Stockholm Chamber of Commerce. There are more than 100 forums for private arbitration.[15]

The UN Commission on International Trade Law (UNCITRAL) has developed a Model Law on International Commercial Arbitration which has been adopted by a number of states. In addition, the 1958 New York Convention on the Recognition and Enforcement of Foreign Arbitral Awards has been ratified by more than 120 states including nearly all major commercial nations. Thus, an arbitration clause in a contract with a foreign state ensures that any dispute in connection with this contract will be arbitrated and that any award in such a dispute will be enforceable virtually anywhere in the world. The International Center for the Settlement of Investment Disputes (ICSID), a subsidiary organ of the World Bank, is a prominent center for international arbitration. It enables individuals or corporations to arbitrate disputes with foreign states. And another UN agency, the World Intellectual Property Organization sets up panels for resolving disputes involving patent, copyright, and trademark infringement claims.[16]

International Courts. There is now a variety of international courts available for international dispute settlement (see Textbox 5.1), but states have been slow in turning to this form of international adjudication. As late as the second Hague Peace Conference (1907), 44 states trying to create more effective means of peaceful settlement were unable to establish a world court. It took the First World War and the League of Nations to establish the World Court (simply continued under the UN), but it came with restrictions. States did not accept to be sued without their consent. A case can be heard only if both contending parties accept the jurisdiction of the court, normally to be done when a case is brought to the court. If the state being sued refuses to give its consent, the case cannot be heard. Consent may be given in advance. As in the case of arbitration, World Court jurisdiction can be accepted in a treaty of friendship before any dispute arises between the two states. Or jurisdiction may be accepted in a treaty for the purpose of the application of that specific treaty. About 250 treaties currently in force have provisions to that effect. The United States is a party to more than 70 of them.[17] Another way to accept World Court jurisdiction in advance is for states to adhere to the optional clause found in the Statute of the Court (Art. 36). This may be done unconditionally, or on condition of reciprocity or for a certain time. 70 states have accepted the optional clause (some with reservations).[18]

Textbox 5.1   International Courts

African Court of Justice
African Union Court of Human and Peoples' Rights
Arab Maghreb Union Court of Justice
Caribbean Court of Justice
Central American Court of Justice
Common Court of Justice and Arbitration of the Organization
for the Harmonization of African Business Law
Court of Justice of the Andean Community
Court of Justice of the Benelux Union
Court of Justice of the Common Market for Eastern and Southern Africa
Court of Justice of the East African Community
Court of Justice of the Economic Community of Central African States
Court of Justice of the Economic Community of West African States
Court of Justice of the Economic and Monetary Community of Central Africa
Court of Justice of the European Free Trade Association
Court of Justice of the European Union
Court of Justice of the West African Economic and Monetary Union
European Civil Service Tribunal (EU)
European Court of First Instance (EU)
European Court of Human Rights
Inter-American Court of Human Rights
International Court of Justice (UN's World Court)
International Criminal Court
International Criminal Tribunal for the Former Yugoslavia
International Criminal Tribunal for Rwanda
International Labor Organization Administrative Tribunal
International Tribunal for the Law of the Sea
Judicial Board of the Organization of Arab Petroleum Exporting Countries
Special Court for Sierra Leone
Special Tribunal for Lebanon
Tribunal of the Southern African Development Community
Tribunal of the International Center for the Settlement of Investment Disputes
UN Administrative Tribunal
World Bank Administrative Tribunal
World Trade Organization Dispute Settlement Body
World Trade Organization Appellate Body

-o-

Only states may be parties to cases before the World Court except with regard to its advisory jurisdiction in which the Court may give an opinion on any legal question when requested by the General Assembly, the Security Council, or other UN organs authorized to do so by the General Assembly. To date, four UN organs and 16 UN Specialized Agencies have been authorized to request advisory opinions. The Court has rendered 25 advisory opinions. Advisory opinions are not legally binding. In practice, however, the Court has given its advisory opinions the same high level of professional attention as it does when deciding contentious cases. As a result, advisory opinions are highly authoritative and have been cited in contentious cases just as Court decisions are.

It must be noted, too, that some international agreements provide that disputes pertaining to the interpretation and application of such agreements are to be submitted to the World Court for an opinion that will be accepted as binding by the parties to the dispute.[19] In addition, the Court may exercise appellate jurisdiction when specified in international conventions. For example, the 1944 Convention on International Civil Aviation provides for appeals to the World Court for decisions of the ICAO Council.[20] Since 1946, more than 100 cases have been presented to the World Court, more than 75 of them under its contentious jurisdiction and 25 for advisory opinions. This may be viewed as fairly modest activity in this highly conflictual international society. In 1989, the UN established the Secretary-General's Trust Fund to assist states in the settlement of disputes through the World Court.[21]

Nation states have slowly come to accept the usefulness of international adjudication, particularly before specialized courts and courts created by regional organizations. Of particular interest is the 1994 agreement creating the World Trade Organization (WTO), going a long way toward compulsory dispute settlement among more than 140 member states. Its Dispute Settlement Body even makes provision for an Appellate Body.[22] Even more revolutionary (i.e., in the context of the nation-state system), is the judicial enforcement system of the European Convention for the Protection of Human Rights and Fundamental Freedoms (1950), created by the Council of Europe (not related to the European Union), an organization of 47 member states. What is so different about it is not only that it involves the enforcement of human rights, a subject matter much more politically sensitive than trade, but that its judicial system is open to private individuals who may even bring complaints against their own governments before the European Court of Human Rights. Court redress has been so widely sought that the court procedure had to be revised to meet the overwhelming caseload. In 2007 alone, the Court delivered 1,503 judgments.[23] As the caseload keeps growing, it is likely that the Court structure will be revised again.

The Court of Justice of the European Union is of course different as it is part of a supranational system. It settles legal disputes between EU governments and EU institutions. Individuals, corporations, and other organizations can bring cases before the Court when their rights have been infringed by any EU institution.[24] Because of the heavy caseload, the EU added a Court of First Instance in 1988. The EU also maintains a Civil Service Tribunal.

The number of international courts has grown in the last two or three decades.[25] By contrast, in the criminal field, international courts were initially conflict-specific, and temporary in nature, established by the Security Council—for example, the International Criminal Tribunal for the Former Yugoslavia, which tried President Milošević. But in 1998, 120 states adopted a treaty establishing the International Criminal Court. In addition, a number of international bodies have judicial and other peaceful settlement functions. An example of this is the Executive Council of the ICAO.

PREVENTIVE DIPLOMACY

Diplomatic efforts to maintain international peace are more likely to achieve success when undertaken before problems get out of hand. Some forms of mediation qualify as methods of preventive diplomacy. International organization intervention is now becoming more routine. But it must be acknowledged that discussing international differences in the Security Council or the General Assembly can easily escalate confrontations. Much depends upon how the issue is approached, and diplomacy is the critical element in or outside the UN. In the course of the first meeting held by the Security Council at the summit level in 1992, UN Secretary-General Boutros Boutros-Ghali was requested to prepare a document proposing ways of strengthening the capacity of the United Nations for preventive diplomacy. In so doing, the Secretary-General took a broader view of preventive diplomacy. Not only did he see it as the use of diplomacy to prevent disputes from arising and to ease tensions before they result in conflict, but also, "if conflict breaks out, to act swiftly to contain it and resolve its underlying causes."[26]

He suggested starting with *confidence-building* measures including periodic consultations with parties to potential, current, or past disputes. He also suggested arrangements for the free flow of information, including the monitoring of regional arms agreements, that is, greater transparency. Avoiding what may be seen as threatening is another confidence-building strategy. The international climate can also be improved by getting states to work together on projects in which they have a common interest, for example, economic partnerships. To be more effective in preventive diplomacy, Boutros-Ghali saw the need for more timely and accurate information and an understanding of global trends, certainly pertaining to political developments but also economic and social matters as these are also factors of international tension—leading him to recommend the use of *fact-finding* missions as problems arise. In addition, he stressed the importance of interaction between member states and the Secretary-General to gain insight into situations requiring greater attention for the maintenance of peace.

Boutros-Ghali pointed out that the UN has developed a valuable network of early warning systems with regard to environmental threats, the risk of nuclear accident, natural disasters, mass movements of populations, the threat of famine, and the spread of disease. He emphasized the need to build upon these arrangements by developing *political indicators* to assess the existence of threats to international peace. Secretary-General Javier Pérez de Cuéllar, his predecessor, had himself seen the need for early warning in political crisis and had created, in 1987, a small unit in the Political Section of the Office of the Secretary-General, called the Office for Research and the Collection of Information.[27] This office was designed to begin the development of a database combining quantitative and qualitative data for the purpose of giving the Secretary-General's analysts up-to-date information about problems in specific countries, regions, or the world at large. Boutros-Ghali stressed the continuing need to strengthen this early warning capability.

The question remains: Can early warning lead decision makers to take preventive action? In the early stages of a problem, taking preventive action may trigger the crisis it is trying to prevent. Early on, the UN found an alternative: international observation. This could take the form of international civilian or military observer groups to report what is happening. Keeping the situation under continuing observation can reveal the nature of the danger and how to respond. Over the years, the UN has deployed many of these missions. Some have been given additional tasks to perform.[28] See Textbox 5.2. The changing nature of these UN missions is discussed in the peacekeeping section of this chapter.

Textbox 5.2   Currently Deployed UN Missions

Part I. Peacekeeping Forces
UN Peacekeeping Force in Cyprus (UNFICYP). Since 1964. 860 troops; 68 police.
UN Disengagement Observer Force, Syria (UNDOF). Since 1974. 1,000 troops.
UN Interim Force in Lebanon (UNIFIL). Since 1978. 11,500 troops.
UN Organization Mission in the Democratic Republic of the Congo (MONUC).
   Since 1999. Renamed UN Stabilization Mission in the Democratic Republic of the Congo (MONUSCO) in 2010. 20,000 troops; 760 military observers; 1,400 police.
UN Operation in Côte d'Ivoire (UNOCI). Since 2004. 19,000 troops; 700 military observers; 1,300 police.

UN Stabilization Mission in Haiti (MINUSTAH). Since 2004. 7,300 troops; 2,800 police.

UN Mission in the Sudan (UNMIS). Since. 2005. Replaced in July 2011, following the independence of South Sudan, by the UN Mission in the Republic of South Sudan (UNMISS). 5,500 troops; 480 police.

African Unity-UN Hybrid Operation in Darfur, Sudan (UNAMID). Since 2007. Currently 23,000 uniformed personnel.

UN Interim Security Force for Abyei, Sudan (UNISFA). Since 2011. 3,800 troops; 135 military observers.

UN Multi-dimensional Integrated Stabilization Mission in Mali (MINUSMA). Since 2013. 11,200 troops; 1,400 police.

UN Multi-dimensional Integrated Stabilization Mission in the Central African Republic (MINUSCA). Since 2014. 10,000 military personnel; 2,000 police.

Note: All missions are assisted by international and local civilian personnel.

Part II. Military or Civilian Observers, and Other Missions

(These are often listed with Part I missions as they are led by the Department of Peacekeeping Operations).

UN Truce Supervision Organization (UNTSO), in the Middle East. Since 1948. 150 military observers.

UN Military Observer Group in India and Pakistan (UNMOGIP). Since 1949. 41 military observers.

UN Mission for the Referendum in Western Sahara (MINURSO). Since 1991. 30 troops; 185 military observers; 6 police.

UN Interim Administration Mission in Kosovo (UNMIK). Since 1999. 7 liaison officers; 6 police.

UN Mission in Liberia (UNMIL). Since 2003. 7,500 troops; 130 military observers; 1,300 police.

Note: All missions are assisted by international and local civilian personnel.

Part III. Political and Peacebuilding Missions

(Most of these are directed by the Department of Political Affairs)

UN Political Office for Somalia (UNPOS). Since April 1995. 37 international civilians; 19 local civilians.

UN Peacebuilding Support Office in Guinea-Bissau (UNOGBIS). Since March 1999. 12 international civilians; 14 local civilians; 2 military advisers; 1 police adviser

Office of the UN Special Coordinator for the Middle East (UNSCO). Since October 1999.28 international civilians; 29 local civilians.

UN Peacebuilding Office in the Central African Republic (BONUCA). Since February. 2000. 23 international civilians; 59 local civilians; 5 military advisers; 6 police; 4 UN volunteers.

Office of the Special Representative of the Secretary-General for West Africa (UNOWA). Since November 2001. 2 international civilians; 14 local civilians.

UN Assistance Mission in Afghanistan (UNAMA). Since March 2002. 291 international civilians; 1,169 local civilians; 16 military observers; 7 police; 32 UN volunteers. (Directed by the Department of Peacekeeping Operations).

UN Assistance Mission for Iraq (UNAMI). Since August 2003.323 international
civilians; 452 local civilians; 223 troops; 10 military observers. Staff is based in
Iraq, Jordan, and Kuwait.

UN Integrated Office in Burundi (BINUB). Since January 2007. 130 international
civilians; 246 local civilians; 8 military observers; 7 police; 43 UN volunteers.
(Directed by the Department of Peacekeeping Operations).

UN Mission in Nepal (UNMIN). Since January 2007. 64 international civilians; 164
local civilians; 59 military observers; 19 UN volunteers.

Office of the UN Special Coordinator for Lebanon (UNSCOL). Since February 2007.
16 international civilians; 42 local civilians.

UN Regional Center for Preventive Diplomacy for Central Asia (UNRCCA). Since
December 2007. 5 international civilians.

UN Integrated Peacebuilding Office in Sierra Leone (UNIPSIL). Since October 2008.
29 international civilians; 15 local civilians.

Sources: www.un.org/Depts/dpko/dpko/bnote (Accessed June 12, 2009), www.un.org/
Depts/dpko/dpko/ppbm.pdf (Accessed June 17, 2009), and www.un.org/en/peacekeep-
ing (Accessed October 29, 2014).

RESPONDING TO THE OUTBREAK OF WAR

Preventive diplomacy may not prevent the outbreak of war. How can organized society respond to armed conflict? The League of Nations launched a
novel approach: *collective security*. The member states would unite against
whoever went to war in violation of the League Covenant. But nineteenth-
century concepts of state sovereignty prevailed: the League could only recommend what the member states should contribute to a military response to
an act of aggression. In any case, in the interwar period, the major powers did
not even try to use the League in response to the blatant aggression of Japan,
Italy, and Germany. The failure had less to do with the League than with the
spineless response of its members.

United Nations Collective Security

The UN Charter endeavored to strengthen collective security and ensure protection against the unprovoked use of armed force. It gave the Security Council the authority to use force: "[The Security Council] may take such action
by air, sea, or land forces as may be necessary to maintain or restore international peace and security" (Art. 42). It was unprecedented that nine members
of the organization (with the concurrence of the five permanent members
of the Security Council) could make such a decision, an indication of how
state attitude toward sovereignty had evolved since the nineteenth century.

Was it realistic? Could it be implemented? The Security Council does not have any military forces of its own. The Charter provides that "all members of the United Nations, in order to contribute to the maintenance of international peace and security, undertake to make available to the Security Council, on its call and in accordance with a special agreement or agreements, armed forces" (Art. 43).

Of course, no organization can guarantee that its members will be willing to act when necessary. International organizations must still rely upon the decisions of their member states and their will to act (as was the case in the League's days). The Cold War soon precluded Security Council decisions (by means of the veto). Nevertheless, with luck and plenty of diplomatic skill, the system made it possible to stop North Korean aggression in 1950–1951—and to devise new rules to circumvent deadlock in the Security Council. On June 25, 1950, when North Korea invaded South Korea, the Security Council met at the request of the United States and was able to act because of the absence of the Soviet Union. The USSR had been boycotting the Security Council since January in protest against the UN's refusal to seat Communist China. The absence of a permanent member was not foreseen in UN rules, and the Security Council decided that it should not be counted as a veto (as a literal interpretation of the Charter would). As a result, the Council was able to act against the North Korean aggression—an imaginative diplomatic use of circumstances and of enemy error (not to mention the United States' readiness to provide the necessary armed forces).

The Soviet Union swiftly came back. Although it could not repair its grievous blunder, it proceeded to prevent any further Council action pertaining to the UN operation now underway against North Korea—and more decisions were obviously needed to conduct the first UN response to an act of aggression. This was accomplished by means of an unconventional change in the rules (a de facto change in the UN Charter without going through the process of amendment). The UN General Assembly, angered by communist aggression in Korea and by Soviet efforts to undermine UN collective security efforts, overwhelmingly approved the *Uniting for Peace Resolution* on November 3, 1950, according to which, upon the impossibility of Council action in times of crisis due to the use of the veto power, the General Assembly will meet within 24 hours in an *emergency special session* to address the issue, thus expanding the authority of this body. The Soviet Union, as expected, claimed blatant illegality, but used the resolution in June 1967 during the Six-Day War between Israel and its neighbors. Emergency special sessions of the General Assembly have now been convened ten times.[29] The practice must therefore be considered as well established. A Security Council deadlock need not prevent the UN from addressing a threat to international peace.

Informal Security Council Consultations

The Security Council has devised diplomatic means of its own to avoid the crippling use of veto power. When a controversial issue needs to be considered, instead of calling a Council meeting (the normal way of proceeding), the Council president assembles Council members *informally* in the consultation room adjacent to the Council chamber. The matter is discussed off the record and various courses of action can be explored away from the limelight until an agreement is reached. The Council president plays an important role in guiding the negotiations in search of some common ground but success is never guaranteed.[30] When an agreement is reached or opposition mitigated, the Security Council is brought into session and a vote is taken. At this point there is no debate; a decision is already in place. Some members may want to comment on their positions for the record but the give and take of the negotiation process has already taken place off the record.

This way of proceeding has increased the usefulness of the Security Council.[31] It must be noted that this approach skirting the use of the veto was developed during the Cold War when East and West were still clashing. There were times when one of the antagonists insisted on publicizing its opposition and vetoed what the other members were proposing. But the informal negotiations frequently led Council members to find a compromise or an alternative position they could support. In the process, the Council regained its usefulness. It is small, which helps constructive diplomatic dialogue and facilitates the search for accommodation, however imperfect. And the major players are involved in the negotiations, which gives it authority. It is true that other major players deserve to participate in the deliberations. This remains a weakness in the Council's structure. Another issue is that it takes forever for the other members of the UN to be elected as nonpermanent members of the Council.[32] But after all these years, no agreement has been found to reform the Council and still keep it small—and even less agreement as to what to do about the veto. Abolish it? Undoubtedly a sensible alternative but one that the current holders of the privilege are not about to accept. In the meantime, the Council plays a useful role, particularly in *peacekeeping* efforts going beyond what the UN Charter envisioned.

PEACEKEEPING AND OTHER OPERATIONS

As seen earlier, Secretary-General Boutros-Ghali included keeping conflict from escalating in his view of preventive diplomacy.[33] The negotiated deployment of peacekeeping forces became an instrument for reaching this goal. It was first used in an attempt to achieve a cease-fire and troop disengagement in the rapidly escalating Suez Crisis.

The Suez Crisis

It all started with Egypt's nationalization of the Franco-British Suez Canal Company in July 1956 after the United States cancelled its offer to provide funding for the construction of the Aswan Dam. The Egyptian masses were jubilant. Negotiations started at the UN, but the French and British governments secretly planned military operations to retake the canal and enlisted the support of the Israeli government. The United States was opposed to any aggravation of the situation (likely to increase Egyptian alignment with the Soviet Union).

With the nationalization negotiations still in progress at the UN, the Franco-British-Israeli force attacked. Lester Pearson of Canada told his friend Secretary-General Dag Hammarskjöld that he thought a United Nations force might become necessary. Hammarskjöld doubted the feasibility of this idea. Nevertheless, Pearson, with the support of his government, presented the idea to the UN General Assembly in the early hours of the morning of November 2, suggesting that the Secretary-General be authorized to make arrangements with member states for a truly international peace force large enough to maintain peace, and introduced a resolution to that effect, adopted in the early morning hours of Sunday, November 4. No one was sleeping much. The resolution requested the Secretary-General to submit, within forty-eight hours, a plan for the setting up, with the consent of the nations concerned, of an emergency UN force to secure and supervise the cessation of hostilities. President Nasser of Egypt approved in principle the idea of a UN force.[34]

And then came a Soviet bombshell: on the evening of Monday, November 5, the Security Council met to consider a Soviet proposal that France, Britain, and Israel withdraw their troops within three days and that the Soviet Union, the United States, and other UN Members give armed assistance to Egypt. This should be an enforcement action under Article 42 of Chapter VII of the Charter. The Soviet Union offered to send Egypt the air and naval forces necessary. This threatened to transform the situation into a major war. It may well be that the Soviet move was only to add pressure on the invaders; but it was taken seriously and many saw it as an aggravation of the crisis. It hastened UN efforts to create an international force. The Security Council refused to adopt the Soviet agenda item as the United States pointed out that the proposal would convert Egypt into a still larger battlefield. But the Soviets might have still come to the help of Egypt even without UN endorsement— and who knows what the United States would have done. It was critical to bring the conflict to an end—fast.

By 2:00 a.m., on Tuesday, November 6, Hammarskjöld's plan was ready for the negotiated deployment of a neutral force excluding great power participation. It laid the foundation for this entirely new kind of UN action that would become a precedent for future UN peacekeeping operations. Before lunch the same day, France and Britain announced that a ceasefire by their forces would begin by midnight. Now it was critical to bring a UN force to Egypt without delay and get the attacking forces to withdraw. This meant having neural countries accept to provide the force, and getting Nasser to accept its deployment and determine what the troops could do while in Egypt. On the evening of Wednesday, November 7, the General Assembly accepted Hammarskjöld's plan. It also established an Advisory Committee for the peacekeeping mission under Hammarskjöld's direction. Interestingly, France and Britain voted for this Assembly resolution; the entire Soviet Bloc, Egypt, Israel, and South Africa abstained. Israel announced that it would never agree to the stationing of the UN force on its own territory or in territories that it occupied. Hammarskjöld asked the US representative at the UN to request President Eisenhower to send a personal message to the Israeli prime minister urging immediate Israeli withdrawal from Egyptian territory and accepting deployment of the UN force there. The next day the Israeli government announced its intention to comply.

The rapid deployment of the UN force was now the condition for belligerent troop withdrawal. Obtaining Egyptian agreement on the composition of the force and the terms of its operation in Egypt were the most difficult issues left by the General Assembly to Dag Hammarskjöld. There was no precedent for such a mission. And it was even more difficult in Egypt because of the history of colonial occupation and the current invasion. The Secretary-General invited the representatives of about a dozen UN member states to meet with him to explore the availability of troops for this mission. As early as November 9, Hammarskjöld announced that arrangements were nearly complete for sending the first units of the force. United States aircraft would fly the troops from their home countries to a staging area near Naples. From there, Hammarskjöld had made arrangements with the Swiss government for Swissair to fly the troops to Egypt because the permanent members of the Security Council were not allowed there.[35] Hammarskjöld wanted to go to Egypt with the first UN troops and negotiate with Nasser the details of the operation. But more Egyptian objections delayed this move. An agreement was finally reached and the first contingent arrived on November 15. By then, 21 states had offered troops, and 650 officers and men were waiting in Naples.

Hammarskjöld spent three days in Cairo in intense negotiations with Nasser and his foreign minister. In the end, many aspects of the operation were left unsettled. For example, no agreement could be reached on a formula for the withdrawal of the UN force. Nasser could not agree that it be subject to General Assembly approval. Each side made its own declaration on the subject and let the troops deploy without agreement on withdrawal.

Dag Hammarskjöld admitted to his Advisory Committee that he had to accept "a certain lack of clarity."[36] He later told the same committee "If, from the beginning of this operation we had attempted to be specific, we would not have had an operation at all."[37] This is not unusual in difficult negotiations and the parties learn to live with ambiguity. Furthermore, diplomatic practice shows that states are often willing to do more *in fact* than they can formally accept on paper. This was the case in the Suez Crisis. The conflict did not escalate and Hammarskjöld could conclude: "The operation has simply suc-ceeded."[38] The UN Emergency Force (UNEF) remained in place, and contrib-uted stability in the area, for close to eleven years.

This success generated international enthusiasm for peacekeeping—which Dag Hammarskjöld tried to tone down as he knew how difficult the deploy-ment negotiations had been. But as new conflicts arose, peacekeeping came to be more frequently resorted to. However, what made it a success in the Suez Crisis was that the states involved saw how this conflict could escalate out of control, and the UNEF enabled the invaders to back down. It did not *force* them to do so. In some of the later conflicts, such as the Congo (ONUC, 1960–1964), the conflicting parties were not willing to back down, and the peacekeeping force was given an *enforcement* mission, a different kind of operation, costlier, and requiring combat. This was no longer the kind of peacekeeping involved in the Suez Crisis.

New tasks have been given to many of the missions subsequently deployed, beyond facilitating disengagement and keeping the adversaries apart. Among the new functions are the negotiation of political settlements, monitoring the implementation of some conflict resolution agreements, and even some "civilian" functions such as building the foundations for future stability[39] (see Textbox 5.2). This has been labeled *"complex peacekeeping."* The new mis-sions include international civilian personnel, international police, and local civilians. These missions vary enormously in their structure and mandates. One UN document refers to them as UN Peace Support Operations.[40] Each mission is really ad hoc, created to address the problem at hand, and the official label is not always helpful in understanding the mission.[41] Politics may color the name chosen. When Secretary-General Boutros Boutros-Ghali responded to the 1992 Security Council request for suggestions for future UN missions, he added a category—Post-Conflict Peacebuilding—usually a difficult and complex endeavor. Instability and the threat of conflict are often rooted in poverty and dysfunctional sociopolitical structures. The UN now has a number of Political and Peacebuilding Missions in the field (see Textbox 5.2, Part III). These are under the control of the UN Department of Political Affairs and usually smaller than peacekeeping missions.

In 2005, the UN General Assembly and the Security Council established the Peacebuilding Commission, upon the recommendation of the 2005

World Summit.[42] In a report of March 2005, Kofi Annan observed that 50 percent of all conflict settlements collapse back into violence within five years of reaching a peace agreement.[43] In an attempt to remedy this situation after a conflict, the new Commission is to contribute to building the foundations for a viable society. Its mandate is threefold: (1) bring together all of the relevant actors, including international donors, the international financial institutions, national governments, and troop-contributing countries; (2) assemble needed resources; and (3) propose strategies for postconflict peacebuilding, reconstruction, and, where appropriate, identify what threatens to undermine peace.[44] The Commission is composed of seven members of the Security Council, including the five permanent members, thus acknowledging the highly political nature of its work. Also included in the Commission are seven members of the General Assembly; five states selected among the top providers of military personnel and civilian police to UN missions; seven members of the ECOSOC; and seven states chosen among the main providers of contributions to UN budgets, program funds, and agencies. A good deal of diplomacy is therefore indispensable for the Commission to address its peacebuilding issues.

The UN resolutions establishing the Peacebuilding Commission created a Peacebuilding Fund and a Peacebuilding Support Office. The Fund seeks to provide resources at a time when other funding mechanisms may not be available and thereby reduce the risk of a relapse into conflict. It is to support countries even before the Peacebuilding Commission launches its recovery program. It is also available to countries in similar circumstances as designated by the Secretary-General. The Fund has a special emergency procedure (the "Emergency Window"). The Peacebuilding Support Office services the Peacebuilding Commission, administers the Fund, and helps the UN Secretary-General in coordinating UN agencies in their peacebuilding efforts. It also helps mobilize international support for peacebuilding work undertaken by individual states.[45] The initial funding target for this UN peacebuilding program was $250 million. In 2015, total deposits from donor countries amounted to $650 million.[46] The Fund is currently supporting 200 projects in 25 countries with a wide range of focus, for example, security, disarmament, demobilization and reintegration, youth employment, national reconciliation, good governance, and the rule of law. No one has any illusion about the difficulty of peacebuilding, but there is no doubt about its vital importance.

UN Peacekeeping and Peacebuilding Records

To date, the UN has deployed about 25 military peacekeeping forces and more than 75 of the observer, and more complex, multipurpose political and peacebuilding missions.[47] Some of them are not included in the UN

Department of Peacekeeping Operations (DPKO) statistics because of the special nature of their missions, particularly in the area of politics (e.g., election monitoring). Humanitarian missions are not included in this count, for example, missions under the OCHA or under the UNHCR. It must be noted, however, that some of these missions contribute to the de-escalation of tensions and peacebuilding.

Some missions are hard to categorize. They see their role evolve as the situation changes. The total number of personnel currently serving in these operations is about 130,000, among them:

Troops	more than	80,000
Military observers		2,200
Police		13,500
International civilian personnel		5,500
Local civilian personnel		12,600
UN volunteers		2,200

What is remarkable is that the UN membership would contribute this kind of resources. 119 nations are reported providing the personnel involved in the current missions, supported by a budget of some $7 billion.[48]

The size of these operations varies enormously with the nature of the mission. Some observer missions are under 100, but a few operations in chaotic situations have been large; for example, United Nations Operation in the Congo (ONUC) (1960–1964) 20,000; United Nations Transitional Authority in Cambodia (UNTAC) (1992–1993), 22,000; United Nations Operation in Somalia (UNOSOM II) (1993–1995), 30,000; and United Nations Protection Force (UNPROFOR) (former Yugoslavia, 1992–1995), 38,600. Currently, United Nations Organization Stabilization Mission (MONUSCO), the UN mission in the chaotic Democratic Republic of the Congo, has almost 20,000 peacekeepers. Large forces are usually needed in enforcement operations where the local parties to the conflict do not accept UN peacekeeping efforts.

The proliferation of instability has led to a growing demand for peacekeeping missions with increasingly complex mandates. These forces are becoming more effective thanks to the use of unarmed drones vastly increasing their knowledge of what is happening on the ground. The UN is in the process of reorganizing its peacekeeping administrative structure to be in a better position to support this vast peacekeeping effort.[49] The DPKO has now added a Department of Field Support under the direction of an Under-Secretary-General. More administrative changes are likely to take place. On January 23, 2009, the Security Council held a meeting to explore ways to strengthen peacekeeping, importantly noting that peacekeeping remains essentially a political rather than a military instrument.[50] Although military force has had to be used in some operations, peacekeeping is not an enforcement mechanism.

UN Secretary-General Boutros Boutros-Ghali himself, in his response to the Security Council on how to strengthen UN practices wisely pointed out that, in the largest sense of this work, the UN must "address the deepest causes of conflict: economic despair, social injustice and political oppression."[51] Current peacebuilding work is conscious of this part of the problem.

Peacekeeping by Regional Organizations

The peacekeeping work of the UN has led some regional organizations to get involved in peacekeeping (see Textbox 5.3). Approval of these operations, their strength, and mandates is the result of negotiations by the member states of the organizations concerned. Most of these missions have been sent to areas of profound controversy. They are costly and promise to be hard to carry out.

NATO participated in several missions in Bosnia and Herzegovina. In December 1995, the UN Security Council authorized (under Chapter VII of the UN Charter) a NATO-led Implementation Force of some 60,000 until December 1996. It was replaced by NATO's Stabilization Force (SFOR) initially 31,000 strong, under a follow-up mandate by the Security Council. By 2004, it was reduced to 7,000 and was replaced in 2005 by a European Union Force.[52] In June1999 NATO led another force under a UN Security Council mandate, this time in Kosovo (KFOR) to deter renewed hostilities by Yugoslav and Serb forces. Following Kosovo's declaration of independence in February 2008, NATO still had over 14,000 troops in the country. It agreed to take on new tasks to support the development of professional, democratic, and multiethnic security structures.[53] NATO became even more extensively involved in Afghanistan. It took command of the International Security Assistance Force (ISAF) in August 2003 when requested by the United Nations and the government of Afghanistan.[54] Nine Security Council resolutions pertain to ISAF.[55] Some 50 countries have contributed troops, including all 28 NATO members. NATO calls these multinational forces "peace support operations," and considers them enforcement missions in the sense of Chapter VII of the UN Charter.

The EU, too, has conducted a number of military operations. In 2003, it organized an International Emergency Multilateral Force in Eastern Congo (Operation Artemis) with 1,500 troops, and, since 2005, an Advisory and Assistance Mission for Security Reform in the Democratic Republic of the Congo (EUSEC DR Congo), with 50 agents. It also led a police mission in Kinshasa (EUPOL Kinshasa), between 2005 and 2007. Since July 2005, it has provided civilian-military support to the African Union (AU) mission deployed in Darfur. The EU launched Operation Althea, taking over from NATO's SFOR mission in Bosnia and Herzegovina (2005–present) then with about 6,200 troops, now reduced to about 2,000, in Liaison and

Textbox 5.3   Peacekeeping Operations by Regional Organizations

NATO

NATO Implementation Force in Bosnia-Herzegovina (IFOR). 1995–1996. 60,000 troops.

NATO Stabilization Force in Bosnia-Herzegovina (SFOR). 1997–2004. Initially 31,000 troops.

NATO Force in Kosovo (KFOR). 1999–present. Initially 50,000 troops.

NATO International Security Assistance Force in Afghanistan (ISAF), 2003–present. 50 countries are contributing troops. The total number of troops is decreasing. The operation came to an end in 2015.

European Union

International Emergency Multilateral Force in Eastern Congo (Operation Artemis). 2003. 1,500 troops.

EU Advisory and Assistance Mission for Security Reform in the Democratic Republic of the Congo (EUSEC DR Congo). 2005–present. 50 agents.

EU Police Operation in Kinshasa (EUPOL Kinshasa), 2005–2007.

EU civilian-military support to the African Union in Darfur. From July 2005–present.

EU Operation Althea in Bosnia-Herzegovina (EUFOR). 2005–present. Initially 6,200 troops.

EU Rule of Law Mission in Kosovo (EULEX), 2008–present. 1,800 judicial officers.

EU Peacekeeping Mission in Chad and the Central African Republic, 2008. 3,700 troops. Expanded in 2014.

African Union

African Mission in Burundi (AMIB). 2003–2004. 3,300 troops.

African Mission in Sudan (AMIS). 2004–2011. 15,300 troops.

AU-UN Hybrid Force in Darfur (UNAMID). 2006–present. 23,000 troops, 4,400 civilian staff

AU Peacekeeping Operation in the Central African Republic (MISCA), 2013–2014. UN MINUSCA took over in September 2014.

Economic Community of Central African States (ECCAS)

ECCAS Peacekeeping Force in the Central African Republic. 2013. 2,500 troops.

Source: See websites of individual operations.

-o-

Observation Teams.[56] In Kosovo, the EU launched its Rule of Law Mission (EULEX) in February 2008, a technical mission of about 1,800 judicial officers currently working under UN Security Council Resolution 1244, mentoring and advising for the purpose of strengthening the rule of law in Kosovo.[57] In 2008, the EU started to deploy 3,700 troops in Chad and the Central

African Republic and, in 2014, it prepared to send another 1,000 troops to the Central African Republic.[58]

The AU has also become involved in peacekeeping operations. Its initial effort was an attempt to curb violence in Burundi (2003–2004), just before the power transfer to the Burundian Transitional Government, when the strongest Hutu rebel movement in the country threatened to step up its offensive. On February 3, 2003, at the AU summit meeting in Addis Ababa, the African Mission in Burundi was approved, and a force of about 3,300 was deployed to provide security and contribute to the disarmament and demobilization process.[59] But broader peacekeeping involvement was occasioned by the Darfur crisis. As the plight of the Darfur people increased, the AU, at its July 2004 summit meeting agreed to deploy 300 troops to provide protection to the AU observers in Darfur. Later that month, the AU indicated its willingness to transform this force into a peacekeeping mission, the African Mission in Sudan (AMIS), and expand it. Its mandate was to protect civilians. By the end of May 2005, AMIS had over 2,500 personnel on the ground. (It was brought to an end with the independence of South Sudan.) On July 31, 2006, the UN Security Council decided to join the AU in a hybrid force. It approved the first joint AU-UN Peacekeeping Force in Darfur (UNAMID), with a total of 23,000 uniformed personnel and some 4,400 civilian staff as of June 2011.[60] And in 2013, the AU sent a peacekeeping force—the International Support Mission to the Central African Republic, established by the UN's Security Council decision.[61] The same year, the Economic Community of Central African States decided to send 2,500 troops to the Central African Republic, and by 2014, the UN was to have its own United Nations Organization Stabilization Mission – Central African Republic (MINUSCA-CAR) in the country. Peacekeeping is becoming a very practical instrument.

RESPONDING TO INTERNATIONAL TERRORISM

Terrorism is as old as human society. But with modern technology and complex interdependence it poses new problems for the maintenance of global security and new challenges for global governance. Governments cannot agree on a common definition of terrorism as some of them manipulate the term to serve their political ends. Terrorists attack innocents to apply pressure on governments or societies. Some of their actions are revolting, even when they are not on the scale of the September 11, 2001, attack on the World Trade Center and the Pentagon. Many governments do not want the revolutionary groups they support castigated as terrorists; conversely, they find it beneficial to characterize some of their enemies as terrorists. Someone's terrorist is someone else's freedom fighter.

Terrorism is now an international phenomenon. Granted, many revolutionary movements have a domestic orientation; but terrorists network; they seek refuge abroad; they may receive support from foreign states, and they may strike abroad to attract international attention and make global opinion aware of their cause or their plight—another dimension of interdependence reinforced by modern technology. Revolutions (and the terrorist activities frequently resorted to) are now rarely circumscribed by national boundaries. The international proliferation of terrorism started in 1968 when aircraft hijacking became a favorite tool of Middle East movements. The ICAO responded quickly. It had already addressed part of the problem when a small number of hijackings took place in the 1950s and was instrumental in the negotiation of the 1963 Tokyo Convention that was primarily concerned with the rapid return of the aircraft and passengers (rather than the arrest of the hijackers). The 1970 Hague Convention and the 1971 Montreal Convention addressed the prosecution of the perpetrators and made an important contribution to the field.

To understand what these conventions did, one needs to know the issue of the criminal prosecution of fugitives located in foreign states. Under international law, no state has a right to obtain custody from a state in which the fugitive is found. In the absence of a treaty of extradition, the host state is free to decide whether to return the individual or not. And most states are very cautious in helping foreign states exercise their criminal jurisdiction (because of different outlooks as to what a crime is and what punishment to apply). Accordingly, states conclude bilateral extradition treaties specifying what conditions need to be fulfilled for the extradition of fugitives.[62] The United States has extradition treaties with more than 100 countries. However, most states exclude extradition for offenses of a political nature (the criminal offense exception clause found in most extradition treaties)—which means that normally, people involved in international terrorism escape extradition even when the states involved are parties to an extradition treaty. Britain, for example, could not obtain custody of IRA fugitives by means of its treaty of extradition with the United States until President Ronald Reagan and Prime Minister Margaret Thatcher agreed to negotiate a Supplementary Extradition Treaty (1985) to remedy the situation.[63] ICAO devised a new way to address this issue in its 1970 and 1971 hijacking treaties with the formula *aut dedere aut judicare*: the parties to these treaties must extradite or prosecute the accused—no exception. This formula has been used in other UN treaties pertaining to international offenses.

International measures against terrorists have tended to be difficult because of ideological considerations, as can be seen in the wake of the September 1972 spectacular capture of Israeli athletes at the Munich Olympics by the Palestinian Black September movement. This attack took place two weeks before the opening of the twenty-seventh session of the UN General Assembly (which was of course expected to address the issue). UN Secretary-General Kurt Waldheim consulted with a number of Middle Eastern states in the hope that they would place international terrorism on the Assembly agenda (if only to show their concern). They refused. Waldheim himself therefore decided to propose it as an agenda item, to read as follows:

> Measures to prevent terrorism and other forms of violence which endanger or take innocent lives or jeopardize fundamental freedoms.[64]

In discussing his proposal before the General Committee, the Secretary-General pointed out the increasing violence directed at national leaders, diplomats, or innocent civilians creating a climate of fear from which no one was immune. But Saudi Arabia, after consultation with other Arab states proposed adding the following to Waldheim's text:

> and study the underlying causes of those forms of terrorism and acts of violence which lie in misery, frustration, grievance and despair and which cause some people to sacrifice human lives, including their own, in an attempt to affect radical change.[65]

There was a message in this amendment, which was approved by a vote of 81 to 18 with 27 abstentions. Action in the General Assembly on this agenda item was just as controversial. The United States introduced a draft Convention for the Prevention and Punishment of Certain Acts of International Terrorism. But the African-Asian Bloc and the Arab states opposed it. When no action proved possible the Assembly appointed an Ad Hoc Committee on International Terrorism that was just as unable to agree on any course of action.[66]

Another approach proved more feasible, that is, focusing on specific acts of violence that the UN membership was willing to condemn. At the very same time as the General Assembly was unable to take any action against terrorism, the UN International Law Commission was drafting a Convention on the Prevention and Punishment of Crimes against Internationally Protected Persons, Including Diplomatic Agents[67]—that is, people who were increasingly attacked by terrorists. Many states were concerned about the security of their diplomats (and the proposed Convention did not try to condemn terrorism in general). The draft Convention was endorsed at the next meeting of the General Assembly (December 1973) and became international law upon ratification. In 1976, following the same approach, Germany introduced a draft convention against the taking of hostages. This was a little closer to generic terrorism and therefore more controversial. But it became an international convention in 1979. In fact, as terrorism spread, and more countries suffered the consequences, counterterrorism began to lose its Western/colonialist antirevolutionary aura in the eyes of newly independent nations. It became more widely recognized as a global problem, and in 1985, on the occasion of the fortieth anniversary of the UN, the General Assembly, in a historic decision reached by consensus of the entire membership, passed a resolution condemning terrorism. In 1994, it went one step further and issued a Declaration on Measures to Eliminate International Terrorism.[68]

In another sign of greater international readiness to combat terrorism, more international conventions on the issue were endorsed by the UN membership (see Textbox 5.4).

Regional organizations, too, used their diplomatic process to negotiate instruments of their own in response to the special concerns of their membership.[69] Between 1971 and 2007, sixteen regional counterterrorism treaties were negotiated by eleven organizations or ad hoc regional groupings (see Textbox 5.5).

NATO, in fact, identified combating terrorism as a core element of its mission and created, toward the end of 2003, a Terrorist Threat Intelligence Unit. In 2004, a Partnership Action Plan against Terrorism was launched, according to which the 28 NATO members and 22 partner states (including Russia) cooperate by means of political consultation, information sharing and a range of practical measures such as border security.[70] In 2009, NATO and Russia created an Explosive Detection Program based on research carried out since 2003, to respond to threats presented by suicide bombers and attacks against mass transit systems. Another example of practical cooperation is found in the March 2012 NATO-Russia joint exercise to test the participants' response to a simulated terrorist attack. In a different realm of counterterrorism, following major cyber attacks against Estonia in 2007, the 2010 NATO summit placed cybersecurity at the forefront of its agenda.[71]

The EU deserves special recognition for its remarkable contribution to the international campaign against terrorism. Immediately after 9/11, it adopted a European Plan of Action as a roadmap for EU counterterrorism. Then, for the purpose of guiding member states in coherent efforts to implement the Action Plan, the EU appointed a Security Coordinator (quickly nicknamed the "European Terrorism Czar") and managed to arrive at a comprehensive definition of terrorism binding on all EU members.[72] The EU created Europol for law-enforcement cooperation and intelligence sharing and established a 24-hour alert counterterrorism unit and joint investigation teams. Eurojust was launched to increase judicial cooperation The EU also created a European Arrest Warrant. As early as 2004, this warrant began to replace extradition procedures among EU members. It abolishes the criteria of political offense and nationality for refusing extradition, thus facilitating the prosecution of terrorists among EU members.[73] The high level of European

Textbox 5.4   UN Conventions Dealing with Terrorism

1. 1963 Convention on Offenses and Certain Other Acts Committed on Board Aircraft (Tokyo). 184 parties.
2. 1970 Convention for the Suppression of Unlawful Seizure of Aircraft (The Hague). 183 parties.
3. 1971 Convention for the Suppression of Unlawful Acts against the Safety of Civil Aviation (Montreal). 187 parties.
4. 1973 Convention on the Prevention and Punishment of Crimes against Internationally Protected Persons Including Diplomatic Agents (adopted by the UN General Assembly). 171 parties.
5. 1979 International Convention against the Taking of Hostages (adopted by the General Assembly). 166 parties.
6. 1980 Convention on the Physical Protection of Nuclear Material (Vienna). 138 parties.
7. 1988 Protocol for the Suppression of Unlawful Acts of Violence at Airports Serving International Civil Aviation. Supplementary to the Convention for the Suppression of Unlawful Acts against the Safety of Civil Aviation (Extends and supplements the Montreal Convention on Air Safety). 166 parties.
8. 1988 Convention for the Suppression of Unlawful Acts against the Safety of Maritime Navigation (Rome). 151 parties.
9. 1988 Protocol for the Suppression of Unlawful Acts against the Safety of Fixed Platforms Located on the Continental Shelf (Rome). 139 parties.
10. 1991 Convention on the Markings of Plastic Explosives for the Purpose of Detection (Montreal). 139 parties.
11. 1997 International Convention for the Suppression of Terrorist Bombings (adopted by the UN General Assembly). 161 parties.
12. 1999 International Convention for the Suppression of the Financing of Terrorism (adopted by the UN General Assembly). 167 parties.
13. 2005 (April) International Convention for the Suppression of Acts of Nuclear Terrorism (adopted by the UN General Assembly). 47 parties.
14. 2005 (July) Amendment to the Convention on the Physical Protection of Nuclear Material (Vienna). 20 parties.
15. 2005 Protocol to the Convention for the Suppression of Unlawful Acts against the Safety of Maritime Navigation (London). 8 parties.
16. 2005 Protocol to the Protocol for the Suppression of Unlawful Acts against the Safety of Fixed Platforms Located on the Continental Shelf (London). 6 parties.

Source: www.unodc.org/documents/terrorism/TPB_brochure_English_final_printed_copy.pdf (Accessed June 29, 2009). Number of parties as of December 31, 2008. Full texts available in *United Nations Treaty Collection, Conventions on Terrorism.* www.un.org/terrorism/instruments.shml (Accessed June 25, 2009).

-0-

Textbox 5.5   Regional Counterterrorism Instruments

1. 1971 Organization of American States Convention to Prevent and Punish the Acts of Terrorism Taking the Form of Crimes against Persons and Related Extortion That Are of International Significance.
2. 1977 European Convention (Council of Europe) on the Suppression of Terrorism, as Amended by Its Protocol.
3. 1987 South Asian Association for Regional Cooperation (SAARC) Regional Convention on Suppression of Terrorism.
4. 1998 Arab Convention on the Suppression of Terrorism (Arab League).
5. 1999 Treaty on Cooperation among the Members of the Commonwealth of Independent States in Combating Terrorism.
6. 1999 Convention of the Organization of the Islamic Conference on Combating International Terrorism.
7. 1999 Organization of African Unity (OAU) Convention on the Prevention and Combating of Terrorism.
8. 2001 Shanghai Convention against Terrorism, Separatism, and Extremism
9. 2002 Inter-American Convention against Terrorism.
10. 2004 Additional Protocol to the SAARC Regional Convention on Suppression of Terrorism.
11. 2004 Convention of the Cooperation Council for the Arab States of the Gulf on Combating Terrorism.
12. 2004 Protocol to the OAU Convention on the Prevention and Combating of Terrorism.
13. 2004 Additional Protocol on Combating Terrorism to the Agreement among the Governments of the Black Sea Economic Cooperation Organization Participating States on Cooperation in Combating Crime, in Particular in Its Organized Forms.
14. 2005 Council of Europe Convention on the Prevention of Terrorism.
15. 2005 Council of Europe Convention on Laundering, Search, Seizure and Confiscation of the Proceeds from Crime and on the Financing of Terrorism.
16. 2007 Association of Southeast Asian Nations (ASEAN) Convention on Counter-Terrorism.

Source: United Nations, *International Instruments Related to the Prevention and Suppression of International Terrorism* (New York: United Nations, 2008), pp. 159–348.

integration developed over the years and supranational decision making are of course critical factors enabling the EU to achieve this unprecedented level of cooperation in combating terrorism.

At the global level, the International Criminal Police Organization (INTERPOL) has developed extremely useful counterterrorism functions. Created in 1923, this institution facilitates cross-border police operations and provides assistance in preventing and combating international crime.[74] It has currently 190 member states. However, Article 3 of its constitution prohibits any involvement in operations of a political, military, religious, or racial character. Thus, in the early 1970s, when international terrorism was entering its new phase, INTERPOL could not assist law-enforcement authorities in curbing this form of criminal activity. This was changed in September 1984 when it asked all its units "to cooperate as fully as possible to combat terrorism."[75] It has helped states strengthen their preventive measures. INTERPOL has also concluded cooperation agreements with the UN, its Specialized Agencies, and other international organizations. In November 2004 INTERPOL decided to have a Special Representative at the UN.[76]

An important concern has been to cut off the financial resources of terrorist organizations. At the G7 Paris summit in1989, it was decided to establish the Financial Action Task Force on Money-Laundering (FATF) and in 1990 the group issued a comprehensive plan of action to combat money laundering. In 1999, the UN General Assembly itself adopted its own International Convention for the Suppression of the Financing of Terrorism (currently endorsed by 167 parties). In October 2001, following the 9/11 attack, FATF issued new recommendations to address the financing of terrorism (eventually revised and expanded). Diplomatic outreach has enabled the FATF and its recommendations to have an impact far beyond its membership with the creation of eight regional task forces against money laundering and the financing of terrorism.[77]

The UN too began organizing structurally for its own counterterrorism work. In 1997, it combined its Drug Control Program and Center for International Crime Prevention and established a UN Office on Drug and Crime (UNODC) in Vienna operating an extensive network of field offices around the world.[78] This new agency has a Law Enforcement, Organized Crime and Anti-Money-Laundering Unit that is responsible for carrying out the Global Program against Money-Laundering, Proceeds of Crime, and the Financing of Terrorism, which was also established in 1997. The Unit's mandate was strengthened in 1998 by the General Assembly. Al-Qaeda's global threat had a catalytic effect on UN counterterrorism efforts. In 1999, almost two years before the 9/11 attack, UNODC opened a Terrorism Prevention Branch.[79] On October 15, 1999, the Security Council established the Al-Qaeda and Taliban Sanctions Committee. This was done under Chapter VII of the UN Charter,[80] an indication of how seriously the UN viewed the threat. The sanctions included assets freeze, a travel ban, and arms embargo.[81] In response to the 9/11 attack, the Security Council established the Counter-Terrorism Committee (CTC), which became the leading UN body to promote collective action against international terrorism. This committee is supported by an Executive Directorate (CTED), which carries out the policy decisions of CTC.[82]

In March 2005, Secretary-General Kofi Annan, proposed a comprehensive UN counterterrorism strategy and in July, established the UN Counter-Terrorism Implementation Task Force (CTITF).[83] In September of the same year the World Summit gathered on the occasion of the sixtieth anniversary of the organization and identified terrorism as a major threat to international peace and security. In May 2006, the Secretary-General issued recommendations for a Global Counter-Terrorism Strategy and launched diplomatic consultations to produce such a strategy. This led to a unique consensus in September on a plan of action covering four types of measures:[84]

1. Measures to address the conditions conducive to the spread of terrorism. They involve strengthening the fabric of society, fostering conflict resolution, and peacebuilding. The plan of action specifies reducing poverty, marginalization, and the attendant sense of victimization.
2. Measures to prevent and combat terrorism. Among them, denying terrorists the means to carry out their attacks, improving border controls, and airport security.
3. Measures to build states' capacity to prevent and combat terrorism. This group of measures also includes encouraging the UN to reach out to the private sector for what it can do to improve security.
4. Measures to ensure respect for human rights and the rule of law. States need to resist the urge to curtail fundamental freedoms in their drive to defeat terrorists.

Getting UN member states to carry out this Action Plan will, as usual, remain a challenge. The CTITF is to ensure coherence of efforts in the UN system.[85]

The UN Interregional Crime and Justice Research Institute established in 1968 to assist intergovernmental, governmental, and nongovernmental organizations in crime prevention and criminal justice, created, in June 2010, a Center on Policies to Counter the Appeal of Terrorism, intended to focus on early intervention efforts against terrorist recruitment as well as rehabilitation initiatives.[86] In September 2008, the UN General Assembly held its first review of the implementation of the 2006 comprehensive counterterrorism strategy and examined progress in its implementation. It adopted a resolution reaffirming its commitment to the global strategy and its implementation.[87] UN diplomacy can be credited with having generated a global consensus on combating terrorism, no small accomplishment if we remember the confrontations of the early 1970s.

On September 9, 2008, UN Secretary-General Ban Ki-moon convened the first-ever global symposium on supporting victims of terrorism, all too often forgotten in all the political struggles involved in this problem. A report summarizing the key themes and recommendations of the symposium was released at a discussion with victims, UN member states, and NGOs on March 18, 2009.[88] Dialogue in the General Assembly, Security Council, and outside the UN, has led more states to overcome their ideological reluctance to cooperate. Combating terrorism will remain difficult; acts of terrorism can be committed in so many different ways even by totally untrained insurgents and for reasons practically unlimited. But global cooperation will help reduce its impact.

ARMS CONTROL

In the global efforts to achieve peace and international security, arms control has attracted a good deal of attention, particularly under the label of disarmament. But it must be realized that, given international insecurity, the prospects of actual disarmament are not promising. It is true that a reduction of tensions may lead to a lessening of the arms race. Some states, such as Costa Rica, because of regional and other circumstances, have no army. A few arms control agreements have occasioned the destruction of some types of armament. But general comprehensive disarmament remains essentially unfeasible.

Controlling arms races, on the other hand, is a worthwhile, practical endeavor—if within certain limits. It has obvious economic benefits. And, in a number of instances, for example, during the Cold War, arms control agreements contributed to the reduction of international tensions. However, because of the pervasive struggle for power and aggressive tendencies, not to mention the profound distrust existing between states, and a variety of vested interests,[89] achieving genuine arms control is no simple endeavor. Much diplomacy is needed to create effective controls. Conversely, successful arms negotiations contribute to the creation of a climate in which other negotiations can be engaged in. Arms control arrangements play a part in international confidence building.

States need to look for what can be controlled. This endeavor will vary with the states concerned, regional conditions, and the international political climate, and it will require delicate diplomatic negotiations. Some weapons are extremely hard to regulate, for example, small arms. Another difficulty is that security needs are not symmetrical (i.e., states have different military requirements). Security, too, has a highly subjective dimension. Reciprocity is necessary, but it may have to involve asymmetrical terms (e.g., trading missiles for long-range bombers) and there is no set formula to guarantee equivalence. Because of the varying nature of security risks, some negotiations will need to be multilateral and others bilateral. Keeping the matter of arms control on the international agenda—for example, in UN General Assembly debates and diplomatic conversations—is useful to identify areas in which some realistic efforts can be made.

Effective arms control is dependent upon reliable verification (an important element in confidence building). But monitoring certain forms of arms production (e.g., in the chemical and biological weapons categories) is too intrusive to be politically feasible. On the other hand, the practical verification of many weapon systems need not be 100 percent foolproof to insure security. A certain margin of error will be acceptable (the amount of possible cheating that will not destabilize the military balance). This will of course vary with the weapons concerned. But a measure of cooperation and transparency will be required. Normative arms agreements (e.g., developing norms against certain weapons) are of a different type. They are (politically) extremely difficult to enforce, often because inspection would be too intrusive, as in the case of chemical weapons. Their effectiveness is based on the strength of the norms (e.g., against the resort to environmental warfare), or because of the prospect of retaliation (a form of deterrence).

The suffering caused by the use of chemical weapons during the First World War, as well as its relative military ineffectiveness, led to the adoption of the 1925 Geneva Protocol prohibiting them.[90] Although such weapons were used by Italy in its conquest of Ethiopia (1935–1936), none of the belligerents used them in the Second World War. It is true that all sides were prepared to retaliate with far more lethal agents than available in the First World War. But the 1925 norm may have played a role. President Truman refused to accede to his commanders' request to use chemical means to defeat the Japanese forces resisting in the caves of Okinawa (March–June 1945), which US forces had to clear in a costly hand-to-hand combat. At the time, the United States was not a party to the 1925 Protocol, and there was no risk of retaliation. But Truman declared that he refused to be the first to violate the poison gas ban in the Second World War. Norms influence behavior when they are widely accepted. Other normative treaties have been concluded in the post–Second World War era, for example, against the use of biological weapons (see Appendix).

The UN Charter did not provide for arms control. But the dangers and the costs of the East-West arms race led to serious arms negotiations. These, in turn contributed to coexistence and, eventually, détente. The UN became a useful forum to keep governments and global opinion focused on the need to control armaments. Interest in this issue was such that the General Assembly held three Special Sessions (1978, 1982, and 1988) on disarmament. It also convened a global conference on Disarmament and Development (1987).[91] The UN experimented with the creation of a permanent body concerned with armament issues. In 1952, a twelve-member Disarmament Commission was created, eventually enlarged, and replaced by a new Disarmament Commission of the entire UN membership. It meets annually for three weeks in plenary meetings and uses a number of working groups.[92] In addition, a succession of smaller bodies were created, replaced in 1979 by the Conference on Disarmament, the main UN forum for all multilateral arms negotiations.

It is now composed of 65 participants[93] and reports to the UN General Assembly. The UN maintains three Regional Centers for Peace and Disarmament in Africa (Lomé, Togo), in Latin America and the Caribbean (Lima, Peru), and in Asia and the Pacific (Kathmandu, Nepal). The extensive involvement of the UN in the arms dialogue and diplomatic process has produced more than twenty multilateral arms conventions and protocols as well as a number of institutional arrangements for their supervision and periodic review (see Appendix).

The UN has created the UN Institute for Disarmament Research in Geneva. This UN Institute is the result of a proposal by the government of France at the first Special Session on Disarmament of the General Assembly (1978). It began its operations in 1980 and works in close cooperation with the UN Secretariat in New York, as well as with governments, research organizations, universities, and NGOs. It is funded by voluntary donations from governments, private foundations, and a small subsidy from the UN regular budget to cover part of the Institute's administrative costs. It engages in research on the various aspects of arms control and disarmament, current and future security issues, publishes in these areas (including a quarterly journal, *Disarmament Forum*), assists diplomatic negotiations and disarmament efforts, organizes conferences, and contributes to the discussion series of its Geneva Forum.[94] Its board of trustees is the UN Secretary-General's Advisory Board on Disarmament Matters, a fifteen-member body made up of experts in arms control, disarmament, and security issues, selected by the Secretary-General.[95]

Another form of control is found in the work of the International Atomic Energy Agency (IAEA). Established in 1957 as an independent organization, it became affiliated with the UN and reports to the General Assembly and the Security Council. As of September 2013, it had 162 member states. IAEA promotes the peaceful use of nuclear power, fosters scientific and technical cooperation in its field, safety in the use of nuclear technology, and the establishment of safeguards to ensure that nuclear power will not be used for military purposes.[96]

Important as UN diplomacy is in the promotion of arms control, bilateral and regional initiatives have produced some 34 agreements and arrangements pertaining to armaments and military activity since the end of the Second World War (see Appendix). Five Nuclear-Weapon-Free Zones have been created in Latin America (1967 Tlatelolco Treaty), the South Pacific (1985 Rarotonga Treaty), Southeast Asia (1995 Bangkok Treaty), Africa (Pelindaba Treaty), and Central Asia (2006 Semipalatinsk Treaty).[97]

The Organization for Security and Cooperation in Europe which began as the *Conference* on Security and Cooperation in Europe, has been particularly involved in fostering diplomatic dialogue on military activities and arms control (eight agreements concluded). Other arms agreements were negoti-ated outside the framework of international organizations, for example, the 1997 landmines treaty, which was spearheaded by an NGO diplomatic cam-paign and strong Canadian participation.[98]

Arms control efforts are also promoted by groups of states, for example, the Missile Technology Control Regime (MTCR) negotiated in 1987 by Canada, France, Germany, Italy, Japan, Britain, and the United States shar-ing the goal of preventing the proliferation of unmanned systems capable of delivering weapons of mass destruction. To this end, these states seek to coor-dinate export licensing procedures in these technologies. In 2002, MTCR was supplemented by the International Code of Conduct against Ballistic Missile Proliferation (ICOC), also known as the Hague Code of Conduct, which has 119 members.

What have all these arms control initiatives done for the maintenance of peace and security? More than 100 armed conflicts have occurred since the end of the Second World War, many of them subregional or local, fed by a continuous stream of arms and munitions. Al-Qaeda, ISIS, and other funda-mentalist movements remain a serious threat. Obviously, much needs to be done for global security. But arms control agreements have created useful limitations even if international security requires much more, including vigi-lance and international cooperation.

NOTES

1. United Nations, *The Work of the International Law Commission* (2 volumes, 7th edition, New York: United Nations, 2007) Vol. 1, pp. 32–44.

2. www.icao.int/Pages/governance (Accessed August 7, 2012).

3. Joe Sills, "The Role of the United Nations in Forming Global Norms," *International Relations Studies and the United Nations* (American Council on the United Nations System, ACUNS, 2002).

4. www.fao.org/docrep/v7700/v7700t09 (Accessed July 29, 2011).

5. See, for example, *Filartiga v. Pena-Irala*, United States Court of Appeals, Second Circuit, 1980. Lori F. Damrosch, Louis Henkin, Richard Crawford Pugh, Oscar Schachter, and Jans Smit, *International Law, Cases and Materials* (4th ed. St.Paul, MN: West Group, 2001), pp. 143–145.

6. See chapter 1, negotiation section.

7. Randa M. Slim, "Small-State Mediation in International Relations: The Algerian Mediation of the Iranian Hostage Crisis," in Bercovitch and Rubin, *Mediation*, pp. 206–231.

8. www.santegidio.org (Accessed May 21, 2009).

9. http://history1900s.about.com/od/1980s/a/flight103 (Accessed May 21, 2009).

10. www.un.org/Depts/dpa/peace (Accessed July 1, 2009).

11. A. LeRoy Bennett and James K. Olilver, *International Organizations: Principles and Issues* (7th ed. Upper Saddle River, NJ: Prentice-Hall, 2002), pp. 236–273.

12. L. Oppenheim, *International Law: A Treatise* (7th ed. by H.Lauterpacht. New York: Longmans, Green, 1952), pp. 328–329.

13. www.pca-cpa.org/showpage.asp?pag_id=1029 (Accessed May 22, 2009).

14. William R. Slomanson, *Fundamental Perspectives on International Law* (5th ed. Belmont, CA: Thomson/Wadsworth, 2007), p. 397.

15. See Karns and Mingst, pp. 95–96.

16. Slomanson, p. 398.

17. Damrosch, p. 858.

18. www.icj.org (Accessed October 28, 2014).

19. Ibid.

20. www.pict-pcti.org/courts/ICJ (Accessed November 14, 2012).

21. www.un.orglaw/trustfund/trustfund (Accessed May 25, 2014).

22. William R. Slomanson. *Fundamental Perspectives in International Law* (5th ed. Belmont, CA: Thomson/Wadsworth, 2007), pp. 631–645.

23. www.echr.coe.int/ECHR/EN/Header/Reports+and+Statistics (Accessed May 27, 2009).

24. Europa.eu/about.eu/institutions-bodies/court-justice/index_en (Accessed May 26, 2014).

25. See Cesare P. R. Romano, "The Proliferation of International Judicial Bodies: The Pieces of the Puzzle," *New York University Journal of International Law and Politics* Vol. 31 (1998–1999), pp. 709–751.

26. Boutros Boutros-Ghali. www.un.org/Docs/SG/agpeace (Accessed April 14, 2009).

27. B. G. Ramcharan, *The International Law and Practice of Early-Warning and Preventive Diplomacy: The Emerging Global Watch* (Dordrecht: Nijhoff, 1991), pp. 44–45.

28. www.ciaonet.org/book/schmeidl/schmeidl09 (Accessed June 3, 2009).

29. Karns and Mingst, p. 103.

30. Ivor Richard, "The Council President as a Politician," in *Paths to Peace: The UN Security Council and Its President*, edited by Davidson Nicol (New York: Pergamon, 1981), pp. 242–254.

31. Nicol, *Paths to Peace.*

32. Karns and Mingst (2010), p. 110.

33. Boutros-Ghali, *An Agenda for Peace.*

34. Urquhart, *Hammarskjold*, pp. 175–179.

35. Urquhart, *Hammarskjöld*, pp. 181–187.

36. Ibid., p. 189.

37. Ibid., p. 192.

38. Ibid., p. 227

39. Ramesh Thakur and Albrecht Schnabel, eds. *United Nations Peacekeeping Operations* (Tokyo: United Nations University Press, 2001).

40. www.pkops.net/unops (Accessed June 15, 2009).

41. Laura Zanotti, *Governing Disorder: UN Peace Operations, International Security, and Democratization in the Post-Cold War Era* (University Park, PA: Penn State University Press, 2011).

42. www.centerforunreform.org/node/24 (Accessed August 9, 2011).

43. www.centerforunreform/node/24 (Accessed August 9, 2011).

44. www.un.org/peace/peacebuilding/mandate (Accessed July 20, 2009).

45. www.un.org/peace/peacebuilding/pbso (Accessed July 20, 2009).

46. www.mptf.undp.org/factsheet/fund (Accessed May 14, 2015).

47. Bennett and Oliver, 7th ed., pp. 157–160, supplemented by www.pkops.net/unops (Accessed on June 15, 2009), www.un.org/Depts/dpko/dpko/bnote (Accessed on Jume 12, 2009), and www.un.org/Depts/dpko/dpko/ppbm.pdf (Accessed on June 17, 2009).

48. www.un.org/en/peacekeeping/resources/statistics/factsheet   (Accessed September 11, 2012).

49. Timo Pelz and Volker Lehmann, *The Evolution of UN Peacekeeping (2): Reforming DPKO.* FESNY Fact Sheet (November 2007). http://library.fes.de/pdf-files/bueros/usa/04977 (Accessed June 17, 2009).

50. www.un.org/News/Press/docs/2009/sc9583.doc (Accessed on April 6, 2009).

51. Boutros Boutros-Ghali, *An Agenda for Peace.* www.un.org/Docs/SG/agpeace (Accessed April 14, 2009).

52. www.nato.int/issues/sfor/index (Accessed June 22, 2009).

53. www.nato.int/cps/en/natolive/topics_48818 (Accessed June 19, 2009).

54. www.nato.int/issues/Afghanistan/index (Accessed June 22, 2009).

55. www.nato.int/issues/Afghanistan/index (Accessed June 22, 2009).

56. www.euforbih.org/eufor/index (Accessed June 19, 2009).

57. Council of the European Union. Homepage >> Policies >> Security and Defense >> EU Operations >> EULEX KOSOVO (Accessed June 22, 2009).

58. www.reuters.com/article/2014/1/17 (Accessed May 27, 2014).

59. www.iss.co.za/AF/current/burundijun03 (Accessed June 22, 2009).

60. www.un.org/en/peacekeeping/missions/unamid/facts (Accessed August 16, 2011).

61. www.reuters.com/article/2013/07/19 (Accessed May 27, 2014).

62. Many states, including the United States, specify that they never extradite their own nationals. Louis Henkin, Richard Crawford Pugh, Oscar Schachter, and Hans Smit, *International Law, Cases and Materials* (3rd ed. St. Paul, MN: West, 1993), pp. 1111–1125.

63. Henkin and others, 3rd ed., p. 1114.

64. *1972 UN Year Book* (New York: United Nations, 1976), p. 639.

65. Ibid., p. 640.

66. Grant Wardlaw, *Political Terrorism: Theory, Tactics, and Counter-Measures* (2nd ed. New York: Cambridge University Press, 1989), pp. 105–110.

67. untreaty.un.org/ilc/texts/instruments/.../conventions/9_4_73.pdf (Accessed June 25, 2009).

68. www.un.org/documents/ga/res/49/a49r060 (Accessed June 30, 2009).

69. United Nations, *International Instruments Related to the Prevention and Suppression of International Terrorism* (New York: United Nations, 2008), pp. 159–348.

70. www.nato.int/cps/en/natolive/76706 (Accessed November 22, 2012).

71. www.nato.int/cps/natolive/official_texts_87905 (Accessed November 22, 2012).

72. Eugenia Dumitriu, "The EU's Definition of Terrorism: The Council Framework Decision on Combating Terrorism," *German Law Journal* Vol. 5, No. 5, Special Issue (2004), pp. 585–602.

73. See Oldrich and Ahern, pp. 192–196.

74. www.interpol.int/Public/ICPO/default.asp (Accessed July 14, 2009).

75. Ibid.

76. Ibid.

77. www.fatf-gaft.org/pages (Accessed July 14, 2009).

78. www.unodc.org/unodc/en/about-unodc/index (Accessed June 29, 2009).

79. www.uncjin.org/ (Accessed June 29, 2009).

80. Chapter VII, "Action with Respect to Threats to the Peace, Breaches of the Peace, and Acts of Aggression."

81. www.un.org/sc/committees/1267 (Accessed June 29, 2009).

82. www.un.org/sc/ctc (Accessed June 30, 2009).

83. www.un.org/terrorism/cttaskforce (Accessed June 25, 2009).

84. www.un.org/terrorism/strategy-counter-terrorism (Accessed June 26, 2009).

85. www.un.org/terrorism/cttaskforce (Accessed June 25, 2009).

86. www.un.org/terrorism/UNICRI-Counter-Terrorism (Accessed July 1, 2009).

87. *Implementing the Global Counter-Terrorism Strategy: Fact Sheet* (March 2009). UN Department of Public Information. www.un.org/terrorism/cttaskforce (Accessed June 26, 2009).

88. www.un.org/terrorism/index (Accessed June 26, 2009).

89. For example the "military-industrial complex," in the oft-quoted words of President Dwight D. Eisenhower.

90. Eric A. Croddy and James J. Wirtz, eds. *Weapons of Mass Destruction* (Santa Barbara, CA: ABC-CLIO/Greenwood, 2004), pp. 139–142.

91. www.armscontrol.org/factsheets (Accessed March 10, 2009).

92. www.un.org/disarmament/HomePage/DisarmamentCommission/UNDiscom (Accessed July 8, 2009).

93. www.reachingcriticalwill.org/disarmament-fora/ed (Accessed November 21, 2012).

94. www.unidir.org/html/en/geneva_forum (Accessed August 17, 2011).

95. www.unidir.org/html/en/home (Accessed July 8, 2009).

96. www.iaea.org (Accessed May 29, 2014).

97. www.un.org/disarmament/WMD/nuclear/NWFZ (Accessed December 6, 2012).

98. See diplomacy of this Convention in chapter 4.

Chapter 6

Diplomacy of Economic Governance

Economic issues achieved prominence in the nineteenth century with the rapid advance of technology, the growth of industrial power, and international trade. They led to the creation of many of the early forms of international organizations (the international public unions and bureaus), and first efforts to regulate international markets, for example, sugar (see Textbox 6.1). After the First World War, many of these arrangements were kept in operation and chose to remain independent from the League of Nations (e.g., the International Telegraphic Union and the Universal Postal Union). A number of new transportation and commodity councils and the Bank for International Settlements were created outside the League.

Textbox 6.1 Pre-First World War International Organizations

Transportation:
  Rhine River Commission, 1804.
  Elbe River Commission, 1821.
  Douro River Commission, 1835.
  Po River Commission, 1849.
  European Danube Commission, 1856.
  Pruth River Commission, 1866.
  Permanent International Commission for the Freedom of Trade through the Suez
    Canal, 1885.
  International Union of Railroad Freight Transportation, 1890.
  Permanent Association of Road Congresses, 1908.
Communication:
  International Telegraphic Union, 1865.
  Universal Postal Union, 1874.
Commerce and Banking:
  Permanent International Monetary Bureau, 1878.

International Union for the Protection of Industrial Property, 1883.
International Union for the Protection of Works of Art and Literature, 1886.
Central Council on North Sea Fisheries, 1890.
International Bureau for the Publication of Tariff Statistics, 1890.
International Sugar Union, 1902.

Agriculture:
Permanent Bureau against the Spread of Phylloxera, 1878.
International Institute of Agriculture, 1905.

Science:
International Institute of Statistics, 1853.
Geodetic Union, 1864.
Metric Union, 1864.
International Bureau of Weights and Measures, 1875.
Bureau for the Exchange of Official and Scientific Documents, 1886.
Permanent Council for the Exploration of the Sea, 1899.
International Seismological Union, 1899.
International Hydrographic Bureau, 1902.
Central Bureau of the International Map of the World, 1913.

Health:
First International Sanitary Council in Constantinople, 1838.
International Sanitary Council in Tangier, 1840.
International Sanitary Council in Alexandria, 1881.
International Sanitary Council in Tehran, 1881.
International Sanitary Office in Washington, 1902.
International Office of Public Health in Paris, 1907.

Humanitarian:
Bureau for the Repression of the Slave Trade on the African Coast, 1890.
International Bureau for Enquiries Regarding Relief to Foreigners, 1907.

Other:
International Penal and Penitentiary Commission, 1880.
International Union of American Republics, 1890.
Central American Union, 1895.
Opium Commission, 1909.

Source: Annuaire de la vie internationale, 1905–1907 (Brussels: Office Central des Institutions Internationales, 1910–1911).

Although the League Covenant almost ignored the global economy,[1] as international economic problems arose, particularly the Great Depression, the League tried to get its members to work together. It advocated multilateral remedies and published studies pointing to the benefits of collective approaches. However, League members tended to believe that economic matters were domestic issues rather than international and, in any case, hardly tolerated regulation, domestic or international.[2] The Great Depression did not change this outlook. States resorted to intense protectionism and worked at cross purposes. League officials were aware of the dangers of economic nationalism but had no power to prevent it. The lessons of the interwar period and of the depression helped the architects of a new world order pay attention to economic issues in their diplomatic negotiations. President Roosevelt's struggle to revive the American economy in the 1930s undoubtedly influenced his bold Second World War initiatives, in association with Churchill, for what the Allies should do for the future.

First came the United Nations Relief and Rehabilitation Administration, in 1943, planning for which began barely seven months after Pearl Harbor. Intended to be a temporary endeavor, it would lay the foundations for economic reconstruction. It provided more than $3.5 billion in international assistance, the largest amount ever dispensed by an international institution. The outlook was very different from what prevailed after the First World War.[3] The next move came also in 1943 when the 44 Allied and Associated Powers created the Food and Agriculture Organization (FAO). This was to be a permanent organization, not an emergency stop-gap program. There was support for independent, specialized institutions to address specific economic problems without delay. Among them, created in 1944, were the unprecedented Bretton Woods institutions (International Monetary Fund (IMF) and World Bank) to face the postwar monetary situation and the International Civil Aviation Organization (ICAO), to address the dire need for new air transportation rules as a result of the transformation of aviation technology during the Second World War.

In the meantime, negotiations were under way for a new multipurpose global organization. This time, provision for an economic and social body was made at the Dumbarton Oaks meeting in August 1944 but without elaboration. At the insistence of the smaller countries, much attention was given to this matter at the San Francisco Conference, in 1945, when the UN Charter was written, and the proposed Economic and Social Council (ECOSOC) was raised to the level of a main organ with power to draft international conventions and convene international conferences. Membership was kept small to permit easier diplomatic negotiation of complex economic and social problems (comparable to the approach taken for the Security Council). Initially, the ECOSOC had eighteen members elected by the General Assembly for three-year terms. But as UN membership grew, it was expanded to 27 in 1965, and to 54 in 1973. The size of this body is still seen as a problem with a UN membership of 193. Many UN members see themselves excluded for too long and many economic issues are sent to the General Assembly where the entire UN membership may participate in the diplomatic interaction, thus adding to an already crowded agenda. Eventually, ECOSOC reorganization is likely to take place.

In order to serve the different needs of various parts of the world, the ECOSOC has created five UN Regional Commissions:

1947   The Economic Commission for Europe, which includes the United
       States, Canada, and the Central Asian countries.
1947   The Economic Commission for Asia and the Far East, changed in 1974
       to the Economic and Social Commission for Asia and the Pacific.
1948   The Economic Commission for Latin America, renamed in 1984 as the
       Economic Commission for Latin America and the Caribbean.
1958   The Economic Commission for Africa.
1974   The Economic Commission for Western Asia (i.e., the Middle East),
       whose name was changed in 1985 to the Economic and Social Com-
       mission for Western Asia.

Each Regional Commission is made up of the diplomatic representatives
of the UN members of the region and uses a number of specialized committees, serviced by a large Secretariat. Each commission chooses the nature of
its work program in light of regional needs. The Regional Commissions work
closely with the UN Secretariat in New York, the UN Development Program
(UNDP), the UN Conference on Trade and Development, and with the UN
Specialized Agencies. They cooperate also with non-UN organizations such
as the African Union (AU) and the Organization of American States (OAS).
These commissions are useful diplomatic forums.

A number of *programs and funds under the General Assembly* have economic functions—for example the International Trade Center, a joint agency
of the World Trade Organization (WTO) and the UN, the UNDP, and the UN
World Food Program. A great deal of the UN economic mission is carried out
by a number of *Specialized Agencies*, for example, the World Bank. They are
independent intergovernmental organizations created by separate international
agreements, some of them, as seen earlier, even before the UN was created.
They have their own memberships and their own independent budgets. They
are brought into relationship with the UN by means of agreements between each
Specialized Agency and the ECOSOC subject to the approval of the UN General
Assembly. The ECOSOC coordinates the activities of the Specialized Agencies.

The UN system is thus a major player in global economic governance
diplomacy. Nations are also making unprecedented use of a variety of international organizations they have created outside the UN system. Among them
are regional multipurpose organizations, many of which have significant
economic functions (see Textbox 3.2) and a considerable number of trade
partnerships and economic communities (see Textbox 6.2). In addition, many
international banks are now contributing to economic growth in the developing world[4] (see Textbox 6.3).

The great powers meeting as the Group of 7 (G7) gradually added economic consultations to their global governance diplomatic work. It became
more structured as these conversations proved useful in guiding them in their

Textbox 6.2 Trade Partnerships and Economic Communities

1950	Council for Technical Cooperation in South and Southwest Asia (Colombo Plan). 26 member states.
1951	European Coal and Steel Community (ECSC). Became the European Union in 1992. Currently 28 member states.
1960	European Free Trade Association (EFTA). 4 member states.
1960	Latin American Free Trade Association (LAFTA). 7 member states. Became the Latin American Integration Association (LAIA) in 1980. 12 member states.
1960	Central American Common Market (CACM). 5 member states.
1960	Organization of Petroleum Exporting Countries (OPEC). 12 member states.
1961	Organization for Economic Cooperation and Development (OECD). 24 member states.
1963	Associated African and Malagasy Countries. Became the African, Caribbean and Pacific (ACP) Partnership in 2000. EU and 79 countries.
1964	Council of Arab Economic Unity (AEU). 12 member states.
1964	Arab Common Market. 7 member states.
1964	Customs and Economic Union of Central Africa (UDEAC), 6 member states. Became the Economic and Monetary Community of Central Africa (CEMAC) in 1994.
1965	Caribbean Free Trade Association (CARIFTA). 4 member states.
1967	Association of South East Asian Nations (ASEAN). 10 member states. Became the ASEAN Free Trade Area (AFTA) in 1992. 10 member states.
1968	Organization of Arab Petroleum Exporting Countries (OAPEC). 11 member states.
1969	Andean Group. 5 member states. Became the Andean Community (1997) with 4 member states.
1969	Southern African Customs Union (SACU). 5 member states.
1970	Liptako–Gourma Authority (LGA). 3 member states.
1973	Caribbean Community (CARICOM). 13 member states.
1973	Mano River Union (MRU). 3 member states.
1975	Economic Community of West African States (ECOWAS). 15 member states. *Sub-groups:* West African Economic and Monetary Union (UEMOA) and West African Monetary Zone (WAMZ)
1975	Latin American Economic System (SELA). 27 member states.
1976	Economic Community of the Great Lakes Countries (ECGLC). 3 member states.
1980	Southern African Development Coordination Conference. Became the Southern African Development Community (SADC) in 1992. 15 member states.
1981	Organization of Eastern Caribbean States (OECS). 7 member states. The successor of the West Indies Associated States (1967).
1984	Indian Ocean Commission (COI). 4 member states.
1985	Economic Community of Central African States (ECCAS). 10 member states.
1985	Economic Cooperation Organization (ECO). 10 member states.

1986	Intergovernmental Authority on Drought and Development. Became the Inter-governmental Authority on Development in Eastern Africa (IGAD), in 1996. 7 member states.
1989	Arab Maghreb Union (AMU). 5 member states.
1989	Asia Pacific Economic Cooperation (APEC). 21 member states.
1991	African Economic Community (AEC). 53 member states.
1991	Central American Integration System (SICA). 8 member states.
1991	Common Market of the South (MERCOSUR). 4 member states.
1992	Black Sea Economic Cooperation Business Council (BSEC). 11 member states.
1993	Organization for the Harmonization of Business Law in Africa (OHADA). 16 member states.
1994	Common Market for Eastern and Southern Africa (COMESA). 20 member states.
1994	North American Free Trade Agreement (NAFTA). 3 member states.
1994	West African Economic and Monetary Union (WAEMU). 8 member states.
1995	South Center Organization. 51 member states.
1995	Barcelona Process. Became the Union for the Mediterranean in 2008. EU and 15 countries.
1996	Eurasian Economic Community (EAEL). 5 member states.
1998	Greater Arab Free Trade Area (GAFTA). 17 member states.
1998	Community of Sahel-Saharan States (CEN-SAD). Expanded to 28 member states.
2001	East African Community (EAC). 5 member states.
2001	New Partnership for Africa's Development (NEPAD). 53 member states.
2002	ASEAN-China Free Trade Area. 11 member states.
2003	Gulf Cooperation Council Customs Union. 6 member states.
2003	ASEAN Economic Community. 10 member states.
2003	ASEAN-India Free Trade Area. 11 member states.
2003	ASEAN-Japan Free Trade Area. 11 member states.
2004	Central America Free Trade Agreement (DR-CAFTA). 7 member states.
2005	ASEAN-Republic of Korea Free Trade Area. 11 member states.
2008	Union of South American Nations (UNASUR). 12 member states
2008	Africa Free Trade Zone. 26 member states.
2009	ASEAN-Australia-New Zealand Free Trade Area. 12 member states.

Source: Individual organization websites.

informal cooperation, with premeeting agenda preparation and postmeeting diplomatic follow-up. Then *G7 finance ministers and central bank governors* started meeting in parallel sessions during the annual summits to explore what the major powers could contribute to economic and financial stability. By the late 1990s, a series of financial crises centered largely on Asia, led to the conclusion that emerging economies needed to be included in these global economic management dialogues, and in 1998 and 1999, they experimented

Textbox 6.3   International Financial Institutions

1930	Bank for International Settlements www.bis.org
1944	International Bank for Reconstruction and Development www.world-bank.org
1944	International Monetary Fund www.imf.org
1956	Council of Europe Development Bank www.coebank.org/index
1957	European Development Fund europa.eu/scadplus/glossary/eu_development_fund_en
1958	European Investment Bank www.eib.org
1959	Inter-American Development Bank www.iadb.org
1960	Central American Bank of Economic Integration www.bcie.org/english/bcie/index
1964	African Development Bank www.afdb.org. Includes: African Development Fund and Nigeria Trust Fund
1966	Asian Development Bank www.adb.org
1967	East African Development Bank www.eadb.org
1968	Andean Development Corporation www.caf.com/view/index
1968	Arab Fund for Economic and Social Development www.arabfund.org/ENINDEX
1969	Caribbean Development Bank www.caribank.org
1973	Islamic Development Bank www.isbd.org
1973	West African Development Bank www.boad.org
1976	Arab Monetary Fund www.amf.org.ae/vEnglish
1976	Nordic Investment Bank www.nib.int/home
1976	OPEC Fund for International Development www.ofid.org
1977	Development Bank of the States of the Great Lakes www.diclib.com
1988	Latin American Reserve Fund www.flar.net
1991	European Bank for Reconstruction and Development www.ebrd.org
1992	European Central Bank www.ecb.int/pub
1993	North American Development Bank www.nadb.org
1997	Black Sea Trade and Development Bank www.bstdb.org/bank
2002	African Central Bank www.africa-union.org/root/au/organs/Financial_Institutions_en
2002	African Investment Bank www.africa-union.org/root/au/organs/Financial_Institutions_en
2002	African Monetary Fund www.africa-union.org/root/au/organs/Financial_Institutions_en
Proposed	Bank for Economic Cooperation and Development in the Middle East and North Africa www.jewishvirtuallibrary.org/source/Politics/Amman
Proposed	West African Monetary Zone http://unpan1.un.org/intradoc/groups/public/documents

with enlarged financial consultations involving groups of 22 member states, and then, groups of 33. In December 1999, a group of 20 countries was created bringing together the finance ministers and central bank governors of the G7, and of significant emerging countries including China, India, and Brazil, as well as the EU. Also included (ex officio) were the managing director of the IMF, the president of the World Bank (both UN Specialized Agencies) as well as the chairs of the Development Committee and of the International Monetary and Financial Committee of the IMF and of the World Bank.[5] This group was called G20 although it met at the ministerial level.

The G20 seeks to integrate emerging states into the global economy. Together, its member countries represent around 90 percent of the global gross national product, 80 percent of world trade (including intra-EU trade), and two-thirds of the world's population, giving this institution a high degree of legitimacy and authority in the governance of the global economy, particularly when it comes to the adoption of international standards and the task of reforming the global financial architecture.[6] Unlike other international organizations, the G20 has no permanent staff of its own, which could become a liability as its role expands. The G20 chair rotates between member states and is selected from a different region each year, but within a troika system of past, present, and the next chairs. The incumbent establishes a temporary Secretariat for the duration of his or her term to coordinate the group's work and organize its meetings. The normal work schedule entails one meeting of finance ministers and central bank governors each year, each one of these preceded by two meetings of their deputies and extensive technical work in the form of workshops and studies on specific issues—for example, a workshop on financing for climate change or an analysis of the global economy[7]—to give the ministers and governors up-to-date analyses and relevant data.

The financial crisis led to more numerous meetings of the finance ministers and central bank governors, and a transformation of the G20: for the first time, in 2008, the G20 met at the summit level. The participants found this summit diplomacy effective and convened two G20 summits in 2009 and two more in 2010, each preceded by elaborate diplomatic consultations. Another summit was held in 2011 where it was decided that G20 summits would take place annually. G20 finance ministers and central bank governors are still holding their own separate meetings. G20 summits often invite the participation of non-G20 members, varying with the theme of the summit. Such non-members could include, for example, the heads of a number of international organizations such as the ILO, the WTO, or the UN secretary-general.[8]

Prior to G20 summits, as is often the case with other summits, national governments engage in a good deal of diplomacy to gain support for the policies they favor. For example, in the weeks preceding the April 2009 summit, UK prime minister Gordon Brown himself visited several countries on *three continents*, conducting his own diplomacy in the attempt to secure backing for his goals at the summit. G20 decisions can be noteworthy. For example, the April 2009 summit agreed to provide about $1 trillion to various programs, such as IMF assistance to struggling economies, and programs to boost world trade.[9] It also reached an agreement to expand the global regulation of financial agencies.

Leaders in the private sector are now maintaining a dialogue with governments in a number of organizations, for example, the Pacific Economic Cooperation Council (PECC). Created in 1980, it is a tripartite partnership of senior individuals from business and industry, governments, academic and other intellectual circles, all participating in their private capacity. PECC's regional community-building efforts led to the establishment of the official Asia- Pacific Economic Cooperation (APEC) process in 1989. PECC is one of three official observers of the APEC process.[10] PECC organizes task forces to promote dialogue and economic cooperation in the Asia-Pacific region. These task forces bring together leaders from business, government, the research community, and civil society to consider various options for the region's decision makers.[11] The importance of civil society is increasing even in emerging markets and is likely to have a more significant effect on the diplomacy of economic governance[12] (see chapter 4).

GLOBAL GOVERNANCE AND INTERNATIONAL TRADE

Trade is one of the main engines of economic prosperity. The Great Depression and the Second World War devastated global trade. Resurrecting it was an essential element of global economic reconstruction. The Bretton Woods institutions (IMF and World Bank) were intended to provide the foundations for this rebirth—and they succeeded beyond expectation. Trade barriers, however, were a monumental problem. The UN ECOSOC, in its first session (January 1946), therefore adopted a US-sponsored resolution creating a Preparatory Committee of 19 countries to draft an International Trade Charter in preparation for an International Conference on Trade and Employment. This committee conducted its diplomatic negotiations in London from October to November 1946 and in Geneva from May to August 1947.[13] At the suggestion of the United States, the Committee agreed to sponsor tariffs negotiations in Geneva.

These negotiations took several months and led to the General Agreement on Tariffs and Trade (GATT) in October 1947. This remarkable diplomatic work reduced tariffs on some 45,000 items through 123 sets of bilateral negotiations whose concessions were extended to the other participants by means of the Most Favored Nation Clause incorporated in all agreements, each party agreeing to give its counterpart the benefit of the concessions granted to the most favored nation in its trade relations.[14] The 1947 agreement affected two-thirds of the import trade of the 23 participating countries and about half of overall world imports.[15] GATT was to fit within the framework of an International Trade Organization (ITO) whose charter was to be the object of diplomatic negotiations during the International Conference on Trade and Employment, which met in Havana from November 1947 to March 1948, the first trade conference that was opened to all nations. 56 attended to discuss the draft Charter produced by the ECOSOC's Preparatory Committee.

The Charter was hard fought. Some 800 amendments were proposed, but a document was signed by 53 countries on March 24, 1948. However, protectionist opposition in the United States blocked ratification and the ITO never materialized. GATT, intended to be only a preliminary step in the restructuring of world trade, remained the only achievement in this venture. It was however institutionalized and given an administrative framework to undertake further diplomatic negotiations to reduce trade barriers. GATT became an international organization by default and ended up convening seven additional rounds of trade negotiations. Despite the failure of the International Trade Organization (ITO), the growth of world trade was spectacular. The value of world exports expressed in constant 1970 dollars (excluding the communist countries with the exception of Yugoslavia) soared from $63 billion in 1948 to $107 billion in 1958 and $280 billion in 1970. By 1977, it had climbed to $480 billion and was growing much faster than world production. In 1992 world exports amounted to $3.7 trillion at current prices.[16] Gradually, developing nations joined the GATT.

The eighth round of negotiations (the Uruguay Round) began in 1986 and was concluded in 1993. It was historic in that it brought together 105 state participants. It was hampered by increased protectionism, but it covered new trade items including services (e.g., insurance), intellectual property (e.g., copyrights and patents), and, for the first time, agriculture and textiles. Agriculture was a particularly contentious issue because of US agricultural subsidies and the EU's protectionist Common Agriculture Policy. The agreement prescribed special treatment for developing countries, and required participants to make their trade policies transparent by providing information on the laws in force and the trade measures adopted. The 400-page set of documents was the most comprehensive achieved to date.[17] Even more importantly, the participants revised the entire institutional framework. They rewrote the original GATT articles and negotiated an instrument creating a new organization—the *WTO*—including procedures for the compulsory settlement of disputes. After more than seven years of negotiations, the Final Act of the Uruguay Round was signed on April 15, 1994, at a ministerial meeting in Marrakech, Morocco. The 1947 agreement (GATT) still exists as

WTO's umbrella treaty and is now supplemented by some 60 agreements, annexes, decisions, and undertakings. The WTO began operations in 1995, with headquarters in Geneva, and now has 160 members, including China.[18]

The WTO does not have an agreement of affiliation with the UN. Therefore, it is not a "Specialized Agency," but letters exchanged by the director-general of the WTO and the secretary-general of the United Nations set out a Framework for Cooperation between the two organizations. The WTO was added to the sponsorship of the International Trade Center whose name was changed to the International Trade Center of the UN Conference on Trade and Development/ World Trade Organization. Furthermore, the director-general of WTO is a full participant of the UN System Chief Executives Board (CEB) under the chairmanship of the secretary-general of the UN. This body brings together, on a regular basis, the executive heads of the organizations of the UN system for coordination and cooperation on a whole range of substantive issues facing global society.[19]

The WTO provides stronger administrative machinery than available with GATT. One of its most important contributions is probably the creation of the Dispute Settlement Body that includes an appeals system—a rare facility in international adjudication—with provisions for sanctions for failure to carry out decisions.[20] But there is no magic bullet to solve international problems. To increase world trade—an essential element of global prosperity—more negotiations are needed to remove the barriers that so many states keep inventing. Indeed, nations are still trying to protect some of their domestic markets and the deep recession of the new millennium is increasing their protectionist inclinations. Diplomatic negotiations are the critical tool and special consideration must be given to the needs of destitute countries. Post-Uruguay negotiations were therefore initiated and are still underway, proving to be more difficult than ever. Many of the Uruguay Round agreements required more work (the "Built-in Agenda" involving more than thirty items). In addition, the WTO parties were anxious to start a new round of barrier reduction, the Millennium Round, scheduled to start at the 1999 ministerial meeting. But the antiglobalization riots (the "Battle of Seattle") on the occasion of this meeting contributed to the collapse of this effort.[21]

WTO members continued their diplomatic consultations and launched new negotiations in November 2001, in Doha, Qatar (the Doha Development Round). Some of the "Built-in Agenda" items were merged with the new Doha negotiations. But the rift between developed and developing nations prevented a comprehensive deal to reduce tariffs and other trade barriers. WTO members did not give up. They tried again at meetings in Cancún (2003), Geneva (2004), Hong Kong (2005), Geneva (2006, 2008, 2009, and 2011[22]). In 2013, in Bali, the 159 members reached an agreement, but they had to accept more modest results. They accepted to restructure their customs procedures, reduce corruption at border checkpoints, and let countries like

Chad and Haiti sell more goods duty-free. They also accepted Yemen as a new WTO member.[23] WTO dispute settlement facilities help global trade; their rulings are keeping states from taking unfair measures to protect their economy. Beyond the WTO, the regular and summit meetings of the G20 contribute to the global economic dialogue. China, India, Brazil, and South Africa offer useful insights about the developing world but they cannot speak for all the destitute nations. Much remains to be done to reach the goal of freer global trade.[24]

REGIONAL DIPLOMACY TO FOSTER TRADE AND ECONOMIC INTEGRATION

Regional organizations multiplied following the Second World War. In this process, increased trade rapidly became a major interest leading many states to create separate trade partnerships and common markets amounting to sub-regional associations in Latin America and the Caribbean, Asia, and Africa (see Textbox 6.2). Some of these trade partnerships led to the development of institutions contributing to economic integration. A major experiment was undertaken in Europe, leading slowly, step by step, to a common market and to the *EU*, an unusual supranational venture. The EU has created partnerships with developing countries fostering trade relations as well as economic and social development.

THE DIPLOMACY OF ECONOMIC DEVELOPMENT

Soon after the Second World War, even before recovery was complete, the emergence of new nations raised the issue of large-scale poverty. The UN, to its credit, took the first few steps to address this emerging crisis. In August 1948, the ECOSOC adopted a resolution authorizing the secretary-general to send, upon request, technical assistance teams (e.g., water resource experts to locate sites for new wells) to specific regions. This resolution, however, made no provision for special funding. In January 1949, President Truman proposed, in his inaugural address, a bold new program to accelerate technical assistance to underdeveloped countries (the Point-Four Program). To implement this initiative, the US diplomatic delegation at the UN proposed a resolution that the ECOSOC adopted in March 1949 calling for an expansion of technical assistance. The General Assembly acted on it in November and created the Expanded Program of Technical Assistance (UNEPTA), but only provided $20 million to carry it out. By 1963, its solid accomplishments led 105 states to pledge more than $50 million for this program. By 1965 about 9,000 experts had been sent to developing countries for periods of two to three years and more than 27,000 developing nation citizens had been awarded fellowships for relatively short periods of training abroad.

In 1959, the UN decided to increase its assistance effort and created the Special UN Fund for Economic Development, which initially remained modest. The Fund concentrated on preinvestment projects involving fairly small expenditures for equipment in addition to sending experts for pilot projects. Gradually, contributions increased, becoming larger than what was given to UNEPTA, although still modest. In 1965, the Fund collected $91.6 million as compared to $54 million for UNEPTA. It must be noted that some of the UN Specialized Agencies conducted their own technical assistance programs; others contributed to UNEPTA.

The developing nations became frustrated with the limited amounts of assistance and demanded the creation of more effective development programs. In 1962, the ECOSOC and the General Assembly endorsed the convening of an UNCTAD conference, which met in Geneva in 1964 and generated negotiations spanning twelve weeks. The conference was dominated by a solid coalition of 77 underdeveloped states pressing their demands, with the affluent countries consistently opposed to their proposals. At the end of the negotiations, the underdeveloped nations made clear their intention to keep insisting on greater assistance and came to constitute the Group of 77, whose number eventually exceeded 125. They pledged to reconvene the conference periodically to achieve faster development.

UNCTAD became institutionalized with the creation of a quasi-autonomous UN Secretariat unit in Geneva thus creating an instrument to promote the cause of the underdeveloped world. Raoul Prebisch, the animator of the coalition at the first conference, and an economist and former executive secretary of the UN Economic Commission for Latin America (ECLA), was chosen to be the secretary-general of the new organization. UNCTAD engaged in strident activism for the disadvantaged nations, causing many confrontations with the affluent states, probably hurting its cause in the process. The organization met every four years or so, beginning in 1968 with UNCTAD II in New Delhi. Between sessions, UNCTAD's Trade and Development Board, open to participation by all members, met annually. Radical UNCTAD proposals complicated the task of funding assistance to the developing nations. In 1974, the Group of 77 called for a special session of the UN General Assembly devoted to the issue of development. From these proceedings came the demand for a "New International Economic Order" (NIEO) calling for a radical restructuring of the global economic system and generating more confrontations. By the mid-1990s NIEO had become a dead issue. In fact, during the eighth UNCTAD meeting, in 1992, the final document called for reconciliation in a new partnership for development.

In the meantime, despite the acrimonious confrontations, efforts to help poor countries continued. In 1965, the General Assembly decided to merge the Special Fund and the UNEPTA by creating the UN Development Program (UNDP). This initiative led to better administration and coordination of the assistance. The amount of aid continued to rise. Funding commitments to UNDP in 2009 amounted to about $1 billion. Other resources (including local participation and funding for specific programs) came to $4 billion.[25] It is true that donor governments have provided much more development assistance in direct bilateral aid than through international organizations. During the Cold War, the United States and the Soviet Union competed in the distribution of funds to developing nations to win their support. Some of these grants, however, were not primarily focused on economic development.

UNDP maintains offices in 166 countries, implementing programs, developing the capacity of national and local governments, and working with NGOs and community groups to reduce poverty.[26] Consultation with local decision makers and an understanding of local conditions enables the UNDP to be more realistic and effective in its development assistance. This is comparable to some of the functions served by diplomatic representation, although UNDP representatives are seldom perceived as *diplomatic* agents. This is another example showing how international contacts are now maintained by more diverse means, still essentially involving diplomacy.[27] UNDP works with other UN agencies, for example, UNICEF, the World Bank, or the WHO, in providing assistance. With more than 125 of the 193 UN members ranked among emerging economies, it is hardly surprising that so many UN institutions are extensively involved in development activities, either in their own specialized mission areas, or by cooperating with other agencies. This implies a great deal of extra-diplomatic activity.

New avenues for development work have also been created. In the same year when the UNDP was launched (1965), the General Assembly approved the establishment of the UN Industrial Development Organization (UNIDO). This new venture actually began in 1967 as a UN program (an integral part of the main UN structure), but was authorized to raise additional funding from voluntary contributions and to receive some support from the UNDP. Its Secretariat in Geneva was part of the UN Secretariat. As with UNCTAD, UNIDO enjoyed a high degree of autonomy. In 1975, however, a proposal was made to convert UNIDO into an independent Specialized Agency. Diplomatic negotiations followed and it took ten years to complete the process in 1985—one cannot complain this was a hasty decision. UNIDO now has 171 member states as of January 1, 2014,[28] and 850 technical cooperation projects in 120 countries. Its agenda focuses on private-sector industrial development, the creation of employment, and the development of technical capacity to produce items that can compete on international markets.

In 1997, the UN secretary-general created the UN Development Group (UNDG) bringing together 32 UN units that play a role in development. This body is chaired by the administrator of the UNDP and its function is to deliver more effective UN development assistance, primarily through coordination of assistance at the country level. A Secretariat, the Development Operations Coordination Office, provides administrative services and identifies issues for the UNDG's decision. This Secretariat also supports the UN Resident Coordinators operating in 134 countries.[29]

THE MILLENNIUM DEVELOPMENT GOALS UNDERTAKING

On the occasion of the opening of the new millennium, the UN convened the Millennium Summit in September 2000 at the UN headquarters in New York to address the critical issues of the new era. 147 heads of state or government participated in the meeting with 8,000 other delegates. 5,500 journalists flocked to this gathering. It was the largest summit meeting ever held.[30] As expected, it reaffirmed the mission of the UN in the new millennium but, in its Millennium Declaration, it focused on the widening gap between rich and poor and spelled out what needs to be done. This led to the adoption of eight Millennium Development Goals (MDGs):

Eradicate extreme poverty and hunger
Achieve universal primary education
Promote gender equality and empower women
Reduce child mortality
Improve maternal health
Combat HIV/AIDS, malaria, and other diseases
Ensure environmental sustainability
Develop a global partnership for development

This pledge was even more ambitious as it specified that the Millennium Goals were to be reached by 2015. This global resolution generated a remarkable amount of diplomatic activity and an upsurge of international assistance to economic and social development. Supporting this effort was the first International Conference on Financing for Development, convened by the UN in Monterrey, Mexico, in March 2002. Although separate from the UN Millennium venture, it was an important element in reaching the Millennium Goals and the participants took this into account in their dialogue. The Conference was attended by 50 heads of state or government, over 200 government ministers, senior officials of all the major intergovernmental financial, trade, economic and monetary institutions, as well as leaders from the private sector including the international business community. This conference permitted the first quadripartite exchange of views between governments, intergovernmental institutions, NGOs, and the international business community[31] and led a number of states to announce new development assistance programs. The United States, in a significant departure from past policy, pledged to contribute $5 billion a year to its new Millennium Challenge Account.[32] The EU also agreed to boost its assistance to $5 billion a year by 2006.

Promises by governments often remain only partially fulfilled. In the case of the MDG, however, the UN went out of its way to foster implementation. Numerous high-level meetings and review conferences examined progress toward the 2015 deadline. In 2007, the secretary-general created the MDG Gap Task Force[33] to identify where the international community was falling behind, using more than 60 indicators to measure the problem and recommend remedial action. The high visibility of the Millennium Development Project and intensity of implementation efforts generated massive popular interest. More than 100 million people were mobilized in 2008 under the banner of "Stand Up—Take Action" at events in more than 100 countries, rich and poor, and made the pages of the *Guinness Book of World Records* as the largest ever human mobilization.[34] Some of the targets of the Millennium Development Project were met ahead of schedule: The world achieved equality between boys and girls in primary education. International society cut in half the number of people living in extreme poverty five years before the deadline. Over 2.1 billion people gained access to improved sources of drinking water—reaching the MDG target in 2010—despite significant population growth.[35] It was clear, however, that some of the goals would not be met by 2015. Continuation efforts are still under way.

Beyond 2015. The UN Secretary-General has established a UN System Task Team on the Post-2015 UN Development Agenda bringing together more than 60 UN agencies and international organizations. He has also launched a high-level Panel of Eminent Persons comprising 27 members, including representatives from the private sector and local authorities, to provide guidance and submit recommendations. He has appointed his own Special Advisor on Post-2015 Development and Planning. These steps are supplemented by a set of global and national consultations in over sixty countries facilitated by the UNDG.[36] A global civil society campaign is underway to create a strong successor to the MDGs. It is bringing together for this purpose more than 1,000 civil society organizations from more than 130 countries, rich and poor.[37]

REGIONAL EFFORTS FOR ECONOMIC DEVELOPMENT

The UN Regional Commissions have contributed to development by fostering regional cooperation and creating development projects taking into account local circumstances and opportunities. For example, the ECLA helped to establish the Central American Common Market and the Inter-American Development Bank. Numerous international development banks have themselves made capital available for development projects (see Textbox 6.3), and regional organizations have created development projects of their own. The EU itself has created partnerships in several parts of the developing world, helping the countries involved. Much has also been done by means of regional negotiations to remove trade barriers and attempt to create common markets (see Textbox 6.2).[38] What has happened in Europe over the years has tempted a number of emerging economies to foster economic integration in their own region. This form of self-help and effort to do what has succeeded elsewhere is a potent force for economic and social change and even political transformation.

Regional efforts have generated "South-South" cooperation, a type of activity that the UN has sought to encourage to achieve greater development and regional integration. To this end, in 1974, the UN General Assembly endorsed the creation of a special unit within the UNDP, namely, the UN Office for South-South Cooperation.[39] In 1995, the General Assembly established a fund eventually called the UN Fund for South-South Cooperation used to support development projects. This UN support also led to the creation of the India-Brazil-South Africa Facility for Poverty and Hunger Alleviation. Starting in 2008, an annual South-South Development Expo has been organized, showcasing successful development projects originating in the developing world and leading UN agencies to hold "Solution Forums," for example, Clean Technologies for Green Industry, put together by the UNIDO.[40]

THE MULTINATIONAL CORPORATION ISSUE

Multinational corporations (MNCs), also called transnational corporations at the UN, have long been controversial. They are economically powerful and their number has grown dramatically. They can strengthen the economy of underdeveloped countries, bring badly needed capital, provide technology, employment, training, and increase production and trade. But they often do it without taking into account the special needs of these countries. Increasing their profits is of course their main objective. They do not hesitate to use their enormous power to force host states to do whatever serves their purpose, even exploiting them. They stifle local competition, inhibit local infant industry, and export their profits. Their technology and modus operandi may even be ill-suited to the local economy.[41]

In the 1960s and the early 1970s, many underdeveloped countries bitterly complained that they could not control the multinationals and were being abused. They wanted UN protection. In 1973, the ECOSOC appointed a group of eminent persons to study the problem, and in 1974 a UN Commission on Transnational Corporation was created. The Commission started work on an international code of conduct for MNCs[42] but did not make any progress. Socialist countries and market economies could not reach agreement because of their ideological differences. A number of specialized UN bodies, however, were led to address the MNC issue in the course of their own activities. In 1977, the ILO adopted the Tripartite Declaration of Principles concerning Multinational Enterprises and Social Policy,[43] the key tool for promoting labor standards in the corporate world. The ILO Multinational Enterprises Program is responsible for the promotion and follow-up on the Tripartite Declaration. It receives guidance from the decisions of the Multinational Division of the Policy Development Section of the ILO Governing Body.[44]

The WHO joined the regulation effort on the occasion of widespread unethical sales practices on the part the infant formula industry leading to malnutrition, disease, and increased infant mortality.[45] This followed massive civil society campaigns against the industry, particularly Nestlé. In 1981, the WHO issued its *International Code of Marketing of Breastmilk Substitutes*[46] and UNICEF has been keeping track of the global adoption of the code. As of April 2011, 84 countries have enacted legislation implementing the Code and subsequent WHO resolutions.[47] The WHO also became concerned about the pharmaceutical industry whose drive for profit was found to be in conflict with the promotion of health care. For example, it points out that companies currently spend one-third of all sales revenue on marketing their products, roughly twice what they spend on research and development; furthermore, the drugs chosen for development are those for use in the industrialized world, neglecting the diseases of the underdeveloped nations where patients cannot pay for the drugs. In 1988, the WHO adopted a set of *Ethical Criteria for Medicinal Drug Promotion.*[48] In 2001, the WHO turned its attention to the tobacco industry which, it pointed out, has been operating for years with the express intention of subverting the efforts of governments and of the WHO, to combat smoking. The WHO's Tobacco Free Initiative is intended to monitor the industry. It publishes monthly reports drawing global attention to the practices of the tobacco industry that have a negative effect on tobacco control endeavors.[49]

With the passing of time, developing nations began to change their outlook toward the multinationals. Some saw benefits in their services. In 1999, UN

Secretary-General Kofi Annan launched Global Compact, a voluntary partnership between the UN and multinational corporations that embraces ten principles of good international corporate practices covering human rights, labor standards, environment, and anticorruption.[50] By 2008, Global Compact had over 5,000 participants from 130 countries. This may be encouraging. But there are approximately 65,000 parent firms together with a total of 850,000 foreign affiliates.[51] Multinationals are powerful and increasing their profits remains their primary motive. Monitoring their activities will be critically important, and transparency should be an important objective for global governance. Multinationals are likely to remain on the global diplomatic agenda.

The global economy remains hard to manage. The disparity between states is enormous. But the international community has changed remarkably since the Second World War. Nations are more prepared to consult. They have created a variety of international institutions where none existed, for example, international banks. A surprising amount of global governance has been initiated. The WTO has become a reality with built-in methods of conflict settlement. The gap between rich and poor is still monumental and economic instability is still too much of a reality. This is no time for complacency. Our interdependent world is nevertheless better organized and diplomacy is generating more collective endeavors.

NOTES

1. F. P. Walters, *A History of the League of Nations* (Reprinted in one volume. New York: Oxford University Press, 1960), pp. 423–425, 427.

2. Daniel S. Cheever and H. Field Haviland, Jr. *Organizing for Peace: International Organization in World Affairs* (Boston: Houghton Mifflin, 1954), pp. 159–172.

3. Cheever and Haviland, pp. 227–231.

4. See Nicholas Bayne and Stephen Woolcock, eds., *The New Economic Diplomacy: Decision-Making and Negotiation in International Economic Relations* (3rd ed. Burlington, VT: Ashgate, 2011).

5. The other states included were Argentina, Australia, Indonesia, Mexico, Saudi Arabia, South Africa, South Korea, and Turkey. Gordon Smith, *G-7 to G-8 to G-20: Evolution in Global Governance.* Center for International Governance Innovation (CIGI) G-20 Papers, No. 6 (May 2011). www.cigionline.org/sites/default/files/G20No6 (Accessed September 23, 2012).

6. Peter I. Hajnal, *The G-8 System and the G-20: Evolution, Role, and Documentation* (Burlington, Vermont: Ashgate, 2007).

7. www.g20.org/about_what_is_g20 (Accessed August 24, 2011).

8. See Deborah Bronnert, "Making Government Policy: The G-8 and G-20 in 2010," in *The New Economic Diplomacy: Decision-making and Negotiation in*

International Economic Relations, edited by Nicholas Bayne and Stephen Woolcock (3rd ed. Burlington, VT: Ashgate, 2011).

9. www.g20.org/images/stories/canalfinan/docs/uk/07finalcomu   (Accessed September 27, 2012).

10. www.pecc.org/about-us/about-us (Accessed August 26, 2011).

11. www.pecc.org (Accessed September 27, 2012).

12. See Duncan Green and Phil Bloomer, "NGOs in Economic Diplomacy," in *The New Economic Diplomacy* (2011).

13. Cheever and Haviland, p. 247.

14. Campbell R. McConnell, *Economics: Principles, Problems, and Policies* (7th ed. New York: McGraw-Hill, 1978), p. 878.

15. Cheever and Haviland, p. 572.

16. Bennett, 6th ed., p. 289.

17. Lori Fister Damrosch, Louis Henkin, Richard Crawford Pugh, Oscar Schachter, and Hans Smit, *International Law, Cases and Materials* (4th ed. St. Paul, MN: West Group, 2001), pp. 1577–1593.

18. As of December 2013, http://mc9.wto.org (Accessed June 1, 2014). China was admitted to membership in December 2001.

19. www.unsystemceb.org (Accessed September 28, 2009).

20. Damrosch and others, pp. 1593–1596.

21. www.globalissues.org/article/46/who-protests-in-seattle-1999   (Accessed September 30, 2009). See Joseph E. Stiglitz, *Globalization and its Dissidents* (New York: Norton, 2002). Richard Peet, *Unholy Trinity: The IMF, World Bank, and WTO* (2nd ed. New York: Palgrave Macmillan , 2009).

22. http://mc9.wto.org (Accessed June 1, 2014).

23. Ibid.

24. See Susan Brown-Shafi, *Promoting Good Governance and Accountability: Implementation and the WTO* (New York: Palgrave Macmillan, 2011).

25. http://hdr.undp.org/en (Accessed October 15, 2009).

26. www.undp.org/poverty/about_us (Accessed January 21, 2010).

27. See Thierry Soret, *Governance Arrangements for Global Economic Challenges: Where Do We Stand? A Political Science Perspective* (New York: Office of Development Studies, UN Development Program, November 2009).

28. www.unido.org (Accessed June 2, 2014).

29. www.undg.org (Accessed September 2012). See also http://gpia.info/node/4718 (Accessed September 14, 2012).

30. www.rcgg.ufrgs.br/msd_ing (Accessed January 21, 2010).

31. www.un.org/esa/ffd/ffdconf (Accessed September 14, 2009).

32. www.bread.org/learn/global-hunger-issues/millenniun-challenge-account (Accessed September14, 2009).

33. www.un.org/esa/policy/mdggap (Accessed January 28, 2010).

34. www,globalpolicy.org/un-reform/un-reform-initiatives/millennium-summit-and-its-followup (Accessed February 2, 2010).

35. www.un/org/millenniumgoals/pdf/report-2013/mdg-report--2013-english (Accessed June 3, 2014).

36. www.un.org/en/ecosoc/about/mdg-shtm (Accessed June 30, 2014).

37. www.beyond2015.org (Accessed June 5, 2014).

38. See also international trade section of this chapter.

39. undp.org/content/ssc (Accessed June 6, 2014).

40. Ssc.undp.org/content/ssc and www. Sela.org/attach/258 (Accessed June 6 2014).

41. See Charles W. Kegley, Jr., and Eugene R. Wittkopf, *World Politics: Trend and Transformation* (9th ed. Belmont, CA: Wadsworth / Thomson, 2004), pp. 173–177, 216.

42. Seymour J. Rubin, "Transnational Corporations and International Codes of Conduct: A Study of the Relationship Between International Legal Cooperation and Economic Development," *American University International Law Review* Vol. 10, No. 4 (1995), pp. 1275–1289.

43. www.ilo.org/wcmsp5/groups/public/---ed_emp/---emp_ent/documents/publication/wcms_101234 (Accessed September 20, 2012).

44. www.ilo.org/empent/units/multinational-enterprises/lang--en/index (Accessed September 20, 2012).

45. See detailed account by Edward Baer, "Babies Mean Business," *New Internationalist Magazine* Issue 110 (April 1982). www.newint.org/features/1982/04/01/babies. "The World Health Organization Indicts the Infant Formula Industry" (Accessed September 17, 2012).

46. www.who.int/nutrition/publications/code_english (Accessed September 19, 2012).

47. "State of the Code by Country, April 2011" (New York: UNICEF, Nutrition Section, 2011). www.unicef.org/nutrition/files/State_of_the_Code_by_Country_April2011 (Accessed September 17, 2012).

48. www.who.int/trade/glossary/story073/en/index (Accessed September 19, 2012).

49. www.who.int/tobacco/surveillance/ti_monitoring/en/index (Accessed September 19, 2012). The 2003 WHO Framework Convention on Tobacco Control has the support of 176 states.

50. Tagi Sagafi-nejad, with John Dunning, *The UN and Transnational Corporations: From Code of Conduct to Global Compact* (Bloomington, IN: Indiana University Press, 2008).

51. Charles Kegley, Jr. *World Politics: Trend and Transformation* (11th ed. Boston: Thomson / Wadsworth, 2008), p. 205.

Chapter 7

Addressing Social Issues

Social issues were not traditionally on the diplomatic agenda. They were essentially domestic. But interdependence and changing cultural values broadened the boundaries of diplomacy and the nineteenth century engaged in some pioneering ventures, for example, in the field of public health.

HEALTH CARE

Disease, of course, does not respect international boundaries. Throughout history, epidemics of all kinds have devastated a multiplicity of societies. In the nineteenth century, with the advance of scientific knowledge and technology, states began to work together to stop infectious diseases. In 1851, in Paris, the French government convened the first international health conference.[1] The eleventh international health conference (Paris, 1903) produced an international convention establishing mechanisms for the international control of infectious diseases.[2] The convention led to the establishment of the International Office of Public Hygiene in Paris (1907).[3] Meanwhile, in 1902, the Second Conference of American States resolved to convene a conference of American Republics' Health Departments. It created the Pan American Sanitary Bureau, the predecessor of the current Pan American Health Organization.

At the end of the First World War, the League of Nations Covenant merely said that the members of the League "will endeavor to take steps in matters of international concern for the prevention and control of disease." Nevertheless, in early 1920, the League Council created a committee to draft plans for a League Health Organization. This diplomatic initiative proposed to absorb the Paris Office of Public Hygiene, a step that had the support of the Paris

Executive Committee. The draft proposal was approved by the League Council and the Assembly, but the United States, a member of the Paris organization, refused to accept the merger. The two organizations, however, found a creative way to work together: they decided to have a common policymaking body.[4]

The architects of post–Second World War institutions approached matters differently. Before the UN was created, the Allies launched independent Specialized Agencies eventually to be linked to the UN. This approach continued even after the UN was established. The Charter of the World Health Organization (WHO) was drafted in 1946 and became operational in 1948. The Pan American Sanitary Bureau was integrated into the WHO and serves as the regional WHO office for the Americas; in addition, it continues serving as the Secretariat of the Pan American Health Organization. The WHO also absorbed the International Office of Public Hygiene established in Paris. The WHO, headquartered in Geneva, has 194 member states including a few non-UN members. Like other Specialized Agencies of the UN, it is financed by annual assessments of its members, amounting to $929 million for the biennium 2014–2015, and, most importantly, by voluntary contributions of $3.536 billion for a total of $4.465 billion.[5] The main decision-making organ is the World Health Assembly, meeting annually in Geneva and engaging in critical policy negotiations. This is where much of the diplomacy of global health governance is conducted, new programs launched, and budget issues negotiated. The Assembly is composed of all member states and appoints a director-general every five years. A 34-member Executive Board is elected by the Assembly for three-year terms and meets twice a year. Because of the medical nature of many of the issues on the agenda of the World Health Assembly, member states include in their diplomatic delegations members of the medical profession and public health specialists—health professionals serving in diplomatic capacities—in addition to regular foreign service personnel. Many WHO member states, in fact, have in their national delegations more medical or health personnel than foreign service professionals. Almost all national delegations to the annual Assembly are headed by their health ministers. The heads of the permanent state missions in Geneva (usually foreign service, with the rank of ambassador) are also major participants. In addition, a number of UN bodies, for example, UNICEF and some NGOs, participate in the annual Assembly as well as non-UN international organizations such as the Arab League.[6] Few assemblies bring together so many constituencies and it can be said that world health issues are now discussed on a truly global scale.

The breadth of the WHO's mission is impressive. Fighting crippling diseases is of course a major endeavor. There is no comparison with what was being done even as late as the 1930s. In 1948, as the WHO opened its doors, some 50 million people were infected with yaws, a crippling and disfiguring disease proliferating as a result of poor hygiene (often caused by poverty and dismal living conditions). It affects children and leaves them with severe disabilities eventually keeping them from earning a living. The WHO set about persuading doctors that a mass campaign had to be conducted using strategies going beyond individual treatment. To modify the traditional clinical outlook of medical practitioners, it organized symposia, published manuals, trained doctors and nurses, and sent them where they could see how the disease was approached locally. By 1960, 49 countries had benefited from this help. The disease was not eradicated, but its consequences were vastly reduced. In Haiti alone, mass treatment returned 100,000 persons to productive work.[7]

The WHO is working on the eradication of a number of diseases—for example, polio, tuberculosis, and leprosy—a daunting endeavor. Smallpox was removed from the face of the earth by 1977, a historic first.[8] More tropical diseases have been attacked, with the help of a number of UN organizations such as UNICEF, and some private-sector organizations, such as the Carter Center. In the current campaign to address the 2014 Ebola crisis, the World Food Program (WFP) is extending its logistical capacity to support rapid response operations. Its helicopters are used to get medical personnel to remote rural areas and its engineers help the construction of treatment facilities. The World Bank Group has already raised about one billion dollars in financing for the countries hardest hit by the epidemic,[9] and the UN secretary-general established a UN Mission for Ebola Emergency Response. The WHO has launched a project to permit faster countermeasures in future outbreaks, especially when affected states are reluctant or unable to face the problem.

The WHO promotes research, and collects, analyzes, and disseminates data through several hundred reference centers. It publishes extensive numbers of medical studies and enlists the support of individual researchers and scientists. Maintaining the momentum is helped by its substantial Secretariat staffed by some 8,000 health and other support personnel, working at its headquarters in Geneva and at other posts.[10] The WHO works in association with organizations and collaborating institutes and universities, which are designated by the director-general to carry out activities in support of its programs. Currently, there are over 800 WHO Collaborating Centers in over 80 countries working in areas such as communicable diseases, mental health, and health technologies.[11] It maintains an extensive network of offices around the world. Six regional offices review the needs of their parts of the world.[12] Each is assisted by a Regional Committee consisting of all the health department heads in the countries of the region. Regional Committees set guidelines for the implementation in the region of WHO policies. They also serve as program review boards for WHO work in their regions.

Another form of local input is provided by the WHO representatives and liaison personnel. Its representatives are important in maintaining an effective working relationship with the governments of its member states. They are the equivalent of WHO diplomatic agents. In fact, each WHO representative has diplomatic status and enjoys diplomatic privileges and immunities. Significantly, the WHO representative is a trained physician and does not have the nationality of the host country, literally a new kind of health diplomat. The WHO resident representative is a member of the UN System Country Team supported by a UN Resident Coordinator. The WHO representative is assisted by a Country Office consisting of several health and other experts, both foreign and local, and a support staff. The Country Office is usually located in the capital and may be supplemented by satellite offices elsewhere depending upon local conditions and the size of the country. The WHO's Liaison Offices are similar to the preceding Country Office posts but on a smaller scale. They are established in countries desiring to work with the WHO but enjoying a high level of development and no major health problems. Liaison officers are citizens of the country in which they serve and are not entitled to any form of diplomatic immunity. WHO also maintains offices at the seat of important international organizations, for example, at the United Nations, in New York, the World Bank and IMF, in Washington, DC, the EU, in Brussels, Belgium, and the AU, in Addis Ababa, Ethiopia. These enable the WHO to interact with major centers of international activity affecting its health concerns.

HIV/AIDS

As reported in mid-2008, an estimated 33 million people worldwide were living with HIV, about 2.7 million were newly infected, and 2 million died of AIDS-related illnesses in 2007. Approximately 22 million living with HIV, or 67 percent of the global total, were in sub-Saharan Africa where the epidemic is most severe. Almost one-third of all new HIV infections and AIDS-related deaths worldwide occurred in this region. For every two individuals who started antiretroviral therapy, five were newly infected and only 40 percent of young people between the ages of 15 and 20 demonstrated accurate knowledge of HIV.[13] Given the magnitude of this devastating pandemic, the ECOSOC established UNAIDS in 1994, a coalition of ten, eventually eleven, UN institutions, identified as "co-sponsors." They are as follows: the UNHCR, UNICEF, the WFP, the UNDP, the UN Fund for Population Activities, UN Women, the UNODC, the ILO, UNESCO, the WHO, and the World Bank.[14]

Launching UNAIDS was tantamount to the establishment of a new agency with an unconventional structure. Its effectiveness is dependent upon these eleven institutions working together, hence, the importance of their diplomatic process. Some of them are independent, with their own, separate membership (the Specialized Agencies). A Program Coordinating Board (PCB) negotiates policy decisions and sets priorities for the eleven cosponsors.

It reviews the implementation of joint activities. The PCB is composed of the diplomatic representatives of twenty-two governments representing all regions in the world, the representatives of all eleven UNAIDS cosponsors, plus—and this is where the new institution becomes even more innovative—representatives of NGOs for the five regions of the world, participating as *equal members*, not just as observers, including associations of people living with HIV, another sign that participation in the diplomatic dialogue has expanded.[15] UNAIDS was the first UN program to have civil society formally represented on its governing body.

In an effort to enhance the participation of civil society in PCB decisions, in 2008, the civil society delegation created the Communication Facility, an independent mechanism to strengthen the capacity of the delegation to bring forward a consolidated message from the field to PCB meetings. With UNAIDS funding, the Facility recruited a consortium including the World AIDS Campaign as well as health and development networks. The Communication Facility works in two ways: it ensures that the diverse civil society voices are heard and influence the development of international policies that meet their needs; and, second, it is in a position to inform civil society about the decisions reached at the global level by the PCB. So it produces and distributes a variety of information materials.[16]

The PCB has its own Secretariat in Geneva, headed by an executive director with rank of UN under-secretary-general. The Secretariat has personnel in more than eighty countries.[17] A Committee of Cosponsoring Organizations enables the eleven UN-system organizations to meet on a regular basis as a standing committee of the PCB, to consider matters of major importance to UNAIDS, and to provide input from the eleven cosponsoring organizations into the policies and strategies of UNAIDS. This is how the eleven institutions interact on HIV/AIDS issues, that is, conduct their UNAIDS diplomacy. They review the UNAIDS proposed budget for each fiscal period and review the activities of each cosponsoring organization for consistency and to ensure coordination in the joint program. Each one of the eleven organizations also deals with the HIV/AIDS problem individually in connection with its own program—for example ILO addresses HIV/AIDS as a labor and workplace issue since more than 26 million workers in their productive prime are infected with HIV.[18]

In addition to this UNAIDS activity, there are currently four Special Envoys of the UN secretary-general for HIV/AIDS who are to advance the HIV/AIDS agenda and ensure that the disease is given high political priority around the world. They work with a wide range of partners including governments and civil society, championing the greater involvement of people living with HIV in national responses and promoting support from the private sector.[19] Partnership is critical in the global struggle against HIV/AIDS because so many governments—so many *people* at the grassroots level—refuse to face reality. As a consequence, they contribute to the spread of HIV infection. Stigmatization has been another difficulty to overcome. UNAIDS is now mobilizing the international business community to join the fight. In 2008, the World Economic Forum Global Health Initiative (supported by UNAIDS) released its first report at the annual meeting in Davos, Switzerland, reviewing how the business community is responding to the HIV/AIDS crisis.[20]

HUNGER

Globally, 1.02 billion people are undernourished today. One in nearly six people does not get enough food to be healthy and lead an active life. Hunger is the leading health problem worldwide, greater than HIV/AIDS, malaria, and tuberculosis combined. The causes, however, are wide ranging: poverty, underdevelopment, overpopulation, poor agricultural infrastructure, environmental destruction, armed conflict, and natural disasters are among the main culprits. The idea of bringing the problem to an end in our own lifetime is an illusion. But, given the diversity of the main causes, making progress in any one of them, or a combination of them, is feasible under some circumstances. And some of this is happening now.[21]

We saw earlier how, in the middle of the Second World War, the United States took the initiative to convene a conference of Allied and Associated Powers to make plans for ensuring food security after the war, and how the FAO was created for this purpose and eventually became one of the Specialized Agencies of the UN. It has 194 member states and is designed to promote the development of agriculture and a long-term increase in food supply rather than meeting food emergencies. It guides its members toward more effective food output, provides technical assistance, monitors agricultural production, and publishes statistical information. FAO sponsors programs (e.g., in land use and irrigation), works with other institutions such as the WHO on joint projects (e.g., nutrition), and has developed a set of international quality standards for food products (the *Codex Alimentarius*).[22]

Increased food demand generated by population growth, as well as problems caused by desertification and other environmental destruction, point to the continuing importance of FAO's mission. However, food emergencies led the UN General Assembly to create, in 1961, a three-year World Food Program (WFP) which began in January 1963 with a proposed budget of $100 million raised by voluntary contributions. In 1965, the WFP was made permanent and diplomatic efforts led to increased financial support reaching $1.7 billion by 1993 and $4 billion by 2009.[23] The WFP is run by a 36 UN-member board, the main organ in its diplomatic process, appointed jointly by the UN secretary-general and FAO's director-general. An executive director serves a five-year term.[24] The WFP is the world's largest humanitarian agency fighting hunger.[25] It proposes to reach more than 90 million people with food assistance in more than 70 countries in the early 2010s. Around 10,000 people work for the WFP, most of them in remote areas, directly serving the hungry poor.[26] It is designed to relieve emergency food needs and to contribute to agricultural development. A special feature is the use of food as a partial substitute for cash wages for persons engaged in development projects.

The global food emergency of 1972–1973 caused by massive crop failures and food depletion on the world markets, led the UN General Assembly to convene a World Food Conference in Rome in November 1974 to meet the crisis. The Conference issued a Declaration in which governments accepted responsibility to cooperate for higher food production and more equitable distribution. They agreed on the need to reduce barriers to food trade. The Conference mandated FAO to set up a Global Information and Early Warning System on Food and Agriculture and it created a 36-nation World Food Council at the ministerial level—a kind of global executive—to coordinate UN food policies and programs. The United States strongly advocated the creation of a world food reserve; but the participants could not agree on how this reserve would be administered to avoid disrupting world markets. Reserves remain a matter of national choice for the food-producing nations to create and use as they see fit.[27] The Council was terminated in 1993 when its functions were absorbed by the FAO and the WFP.

As a result of the Rome Conference, the International Fund for Agricultural Development (IFAD) was created. It began functioning in late 1977 as a new UN Specialized Agency. The members of the OPEC were to contribute at least 40 percent of its $1 billion initial capital—industrialized nations were trying to get oil-rich nations to increase their contribution to third-world development. However, with subsequent oil price fluctuations, OPEC contributions never reached this level. The purpose of this new fund is to provide grants and reduced-interest loans to help increase food production in developing countries. By 1993, IFAD was able to channel $12.8 billion to 337 projects in 96 countries. Most projects were concentrated in 68 low-income, food-deficit countries. This was accomplished by generating supplemental funds amounting to two and a half times its own resources from cofinancing agencies and recipient governments, a process taking place in a number of other UN assistance programs. Currently, IFAD supports about 200 ongoing projects with a total IFAD investment of $3.2 billion.[28]

Food emergencies, particularly in Ethiopia, Angola, Mozambique, Lesotho, Somalia, and Sudan, have been met by short-term exceptional programs. For example, in 1983, the UN General Assembly created the UN Office for Emergency Operations in Africa running from January 1984 to October 1986.

In 1986, a Special Program for sub-Saharan African Countries was established with separate funding by IFAD. The World Bank, by means of its basic needs policy, channeled funds directly to assist poor farmers and their families. The IMF, since 1981, has made loans to countries experiencing special problems through its Special Food Financing Facility.[29] The UN Conference on the Environment and Development (UNCED, Rio, 1992, "Earth Summit") stressed the issue of sustainable agricultural development and the improvement of the welfare of rural women to spur agricultural development in poverty-stricken countries. Better terms of agricultural trade ought to help farming in these countries; but world trade negotiations, which began in 2001 (the Doha Development Agenda) remained stalled because of conflict between developing nations, the United States, and the EU over protectionist agricultural policies and farm subsidies.[30]

In addition to the activities of the organizations involved in food diplomacy and the conferences addressing hunger issues, International Grains Agreements have been negotiated by grain-exporting and grain-importing nations. Their primary objective has been to bring stability to the grain market and bring the boom and bust cycles under control. These agreements go back at least to 1934 and the International Wheat Agreement negotiated in response to problems of oversupply, low prices, and spreading agricultural protectionism. New agreements were negotiated and brought into effect in 1949, 1953, 1956, 1959, and 1962 and an International Wheat Council was established in London to oversee the implementation of the conventions. The 1967 Wheat Trade Convention was negotiated in the context of the GATT Kennedy Round[31] and was supplemented by a companion Food Aid Convention involving pledges to provide annual aid to developing countries amounting to 4.5 million tons of grain. From the outset, this food aid has been an important resource for the WFP in support of its various projects.[32] The Food Aid Convention was renegotiated, considerably broadening the list of eligible products, and led to the Food Assistance Convention (2012).[33] In the 1980s and 1990s the International Grain Conventions were revised to include other grains and increase the amounts that donor nations pledge to distribute to less-developed countries. Global aid shipments exceeded 10 million tons in most years. The current International Grains Convention was revised in 1995 to take into account the changes brought about by the launching of the WTO. The parties to the Convention include nine exporting entities and sixteen importing states plus Vatican City.

The private sector has contributed to the diplomatic process aimed at increasing the availability of food. An example is provided by the Consultative Group on International Agricultural Research (CGIAR), an organization created in 1971 at the initiative of the Rockefeller Foundation with the World Bank, the FAO, the IFAD, and the UNDP as cosponsors. The purpose of the Consultative Group is to achieve sustainable food security in developing countries by means of scientific research in the fields of agriculture, forestry, fisheries, and the environment, as well as public policy in these areas. The organization is served by a permanent Secretariat of its own.

CGIAR is in a partnership founded by 64 governmental and nongovernmental members made up of 25 developing and 22 industrialized countries, 4 private foundations, and 13 international and regional organizations. The organization supports 15 International Centers working in cooperation with many private-sector institutions, among which are national and regional research institutes, farmers organizations, NGOs, and private businesses around the world. More than 8,000 CGIAR scientists and staff are working in over 100 countries on projects aimed at producing more and better food by means of genetic improvement and agricultural diversification. It is also concerned with water scarcity which already affects one-third of the world's population, sustainable management of land and forests, and climate change which poses a serious threat to rural livelihoods across the developing world. CGIAR donors contributed $531 million in 2008 to address these issues.[34]

The world food problem, however, is becoming more acute. The combination of population growth, underdevelopment, environmental destruction, and the economic crisis has contributed to a worsening of the situation. The World Bank points out that 60 percent of the world's hungry are women. In response to this crisis (aggravated by a food price spike in mid-2008) a G8-related meeting in L'Aquila, Italy, in July 2009, pledged more than $20 billion for food aid. Leaders at the G20 summit in Pittsburgh in September 2009 then called on the World Bank Group to develop a new trust fund for agricultural assistance to destitute countries. Diplomatic negotiations, with broad input from potential recipient representatives (e.g., from the African Union Commission), UN agencies, civil society organizations, multilateral development banks, and potential donors, led to the creation of the Global Agriculture and Food Security Program (GAFSP), a new Trust Fund administered by the World Bank. The Board of Executive Directors of the Bank approved the GAFSP in January 2010.[35]

Five initial contributors have made commitments amounting to close to $900 million (the United States, $475 million; Canada, $230 million; Spain, $95 million; South Korea, $50 million; and, a sign of the new global structure, the Gates Foundation, $30 million). Other countries are expected to make contributions. The Fund is to finance agricultural development in poor countries to raise agricultural productivity, for example, by investing in irrigation projects, or linking farmers to markets by improving rural roads. In order to make financial assistance more predictable, GAFSP makes multiyear funding commitments (subject to performance). Also included in the assistance program are projects aimed at improving the nutrition of mothers and young children.

Interestingly, assistance may be provided not only by means of public-sector funding but also in the form of *private-sector* assistance (funds held in trust by the International Finance Corporation [IFC], a member of the World Bank Group); for example, assistance to poorly financed small and medium-sized agribusinesses that are more likely to work with small farmers.[36]

Investment decisions are made by consensus (often requiring a good deal of negotiations) in a Steering Committee composed of an equal number of donor and recipient countries. Civil society organizations have a voice in the governance of the Fund. Upon allocating resources to selected proposals, the Steering Committee identifies supervising entities (e.g., the IFAD and the WFP) to assist recipient countries to implement selected proposals. A Technical Advisory Committee including agriculture and food security experts is responsible for evaluating investment proposals and making recommendations to the Steering Committee. The Fund's impact will be measured by means of a series of indicators such as changes in household income and improvement in agricultural productivity.[37] The participants in this new effort know that the Fund will not put an end to hunger. But it is another source of assistance, and another way to look for worthy projects. The task remains monumental, but each of the institutions involved is making a difference. More diplomatic efforts are needed to bring more hands to the vineyard.

POPULATION

Population growth is a critical element in any effort to achieve economic and social well-being in global society. And the challenge of its global expansion is daunting:[38] 1900, 1.55 billion; 1950, 2.55 billion; and 2012, 7.00 billion. Population growth is even more critical for the developing world in its state of woeful destitution.[39] The sheer number of people in need of assistance makes whatever resources devoted to social development seem totally inadequate. To make the matter more difficult, population issues tend to be controversial. Culture and traditions in given societies often hamper dialogue; so can religious dogma. National sensitivity may be another factor. Rich nations, with their limited rates of population growth, often show too much eagerness in urging developing nations to do something about their population explosion (some 80 percent of the world's population live in underdeveloped countries, and it is estimated that 97 percent of the population growth during 2000–2050 will be in those countries[40]). Diplomacy is therefore essential in approaching this problem and trying to foster international cooperation in addressing it.

A Population Commission was established by the ECOSOC as early as October 1946. In December 1994, the General Assembly renamed it the Commission on Population and Development. It is composed of 47 member-state representatives elected by the ECOSOC for four-year (staggered) terms from the five UN geographical categories, with a majority of developing nations. Initially, the UN limited its population work to meetings of experts, fact finding, and statistical analysis. In 1967, the UNFPA was created (renamed the UN Population Fund in 1987 while retaining the original acronym) to support population programs fostering international development and human rights.[41] Its initial budget amounted to some $5 million. Over the years, however, nations became more concerned about the global population issue. In 2008, voluntary contributions from 176 countries, from private donors and other sources, amounted to some $785 million.[42] But the population program remained controversial. In 1986, the United States, until then the largest contributor, discontinued all UNFPA financial support on the ground that organization funds financed some of China's harsh population policies (an allegation that the UNFPA denied). The United States continued giving considerable amounts in annual bilateral support for foreign population programs ($250 million at the time). Increased UNFPA contributions by other nations made up for the loss of US support.

UNFPA is conscious that attitudes toward reproductive health, gender relations, and sundry population questions vary widely among different cultures (and national diplomatic delegations) and seeks to be guided in its work by the pronouncements of the global conferences convened by the UN. The main areas of its current Program of Action are sustainable development, reproductive health, and gender equality (all affirmed by the landmark UN 1994 Cairo Conference on Population and Development).[43] With the 1974 Bucharest Conference, an attempt was made to give population conferences a greater role in shaping population policy by bringing together government representatives, thus giving greater attention to political considerations. Twenty years later, development became a major focus in the 1994 Cairo Conference, a major undertaking, with five regional conferences taking place in 1992 and 1993 (involving Africa, Arab states, Asia and the Pacific, Europe and North America, and Latin America and the Caribbean). These were of key importance in developing the Cairo Program of Action.[44] The 179 countries represented at the Conference agreed on a road map for progress with the following goals:

- Universal access to reproductive health care.
- Universal primary education and closing the gender gap in education.
- Reducing maternal mortality.
- Reducing infant mortality.
- Increasing life expectancy.
- Reducing HIV infection rates.

The Conference thus took a broader view of the population question. The fact that 179 governments agreed to support these goals is an achievement in this controversial field. And even if agreement on a Program of Action does not necessarily lead to member-state implementation, global conferences have a normative and educational function. Changing attitudes is often critical (particularly in the matter of population growth). Getting states to explore difficult issues and try to find solutions remains useful. In addition, the UN General Assembly and UNFPA took steps to review what UN member states were accomplishing in implementation of the 1994 Conference Program of Action, what difficulties they were encountering, and what additional efforts were needed for further implementation. In December 1997, the General Assembly decided to convene a high-level Special Session in New York (June 30–July 2, 1999) to review accomplishments over the preceding five years (ICPD + 5).[45]

The UN Population Fund, for its part, organized a series of activities in preparation for this Special Session. With the UN Regional Commissions, it conducted five-year regional reviews on population and development.[46] It also organized a number of round tables, technical meetings, and forums involving many of its partners—donor countries, international programs, UN system agencies, NGOs, and other representatives of civil society. For example, it organized a round table on Adolescent Sexual and Reproductive Health and Rights in New York (April 1998) and a technical symposium on International Migration and Development at the Hague (June–July 1998).[47] The outcome of all these meetings and round tables were discussed at a large International Forum at the Hague, The Netherlands (February 1999).[48]

The Hague Forum was attended by government ministers and senior officials from 177 countries and territories, representatives from some 16 UN bodies—such as UNICEF—and the five UN Regional Commissions, six UN Specialized Agencies—for example, the WHO—14 other intergovernmental organizations—such as the League of Arab States—four committees created by treaties—for example, the Committee on the Rights of the Child—six regional parliamentary groups—among them the Asian Forum of Parliamentarians on Population and Development—14 foundations—such as the Ford Foundation and the William H. Gates Foundation—in addition to civil society organizations—such as the International Union for the Scientific Study of Population—and numerous NGOs that had attended the Associated NGO and Youth Forums prior to the convening of the Hague Forum.[49] It is significant that representatives of civil society organizations and NGOs were invited to participate in this five-year review Hague Forum along with high government and international organization officials. The global arena is indeed changing. The UN member states attending the June 1999 General Assembly five-year review Special Session decided what needed to be done for the further implementation of the Cairo Program of Action. They identified new benchmark indicators of progress in four areas: (1) education and literacy; (2) reproductive health care and the unmet need for contraception; (3) maternal mortality reduction; and (4) HIV/AIDS.[50] The General Assembly also encouraged governments to facilitate the involvement of civil society in policy discussions and in the formulation and implementation of strategies to achieve the 1994 objectives.

The global approach to the population problem remained broad-based and tied to the larger issue of development. About one year later, the Millennium Summit produced the Eight MDGs incorporating some of the key elements of the Cairo Program of Action and generating an even larger global campaign for economic and social change, probably the best strategy to address the global population issue. Many organizations include in their agendas elements of the 1994 Cairo Action Plan which means that their own independent efforts are contributing to the implementation of the Plan. For example, the UN Commission on the Status of Women, in the course of its March 2010 meeting discussed the close links between reproductive health, the empowerment of women, gender equality, and their contribution to poverty reduction. This multiplicity of efforts and broader acceptance of the need to address the population problem have been helpful. It is more difficult for governments to hide their inaction and lack of concern. Credible data is available to action groups and international actors participating in the global population policy debate. For example, the UN publishes *World Population Policies* providing "Country Profiles": population policies and dynamics for each of the UN member states for given years and for each of the decades between the 1970s and the 1990s, showing for each nation, among other data, population level, trend, rate of change, and assessment in relation to other social and economic indicators, as well as the evolution of government views and policies on population growth, age, structure, health, spatial distribution, and international migration.[51]

Concerted international action has yielded some positive results. The annual rate of growth of the global population reached its highest level in 1962 and 1963 at 2.2 percent. In 2014 it was estimated at 1.07 percent and continuously declining. The absolute annual growth of the world population peaked in 1989 with 88 million. In 2014, 77.2 million were added to the world's total[52]—a staggering amount, nevertheless progress, even if unevenly experienced around the world. We must consider, however, that 97 percent of global population growth in the next 40 years will happen in Africa, Asia, Latin America, and the Caribbean. Africa had just passed one billion and is expected to grow by 100 percent by 2050. Niger has a fertility rate of 7.4 children per woman; Uganda, 6.7. In other words, international society is still facing a monumental crisis. And other issues are involved.

THE WELL-BEING OF CHILDREN

Very close to the concerns of the WHO, the welfare of children world-wide, particularly their health and the health of their mothers, came to be entrusted to a different UN organization as a result of circumstances. This effort started with the pioneering attempt by the Second World War Allies to provide assistance in war-torn areas with the creation of the UNRRA. When the US Congress put a premature end to this humanitarian mission—when so much remained to be done—the UN, in 1946, created UNICEF to permit this part of the UNRRA's mission to continue. This was a stop-gap effort to run for three years. It was a resounding success, except that saving children could not be done once and for all (and in three years). And the emergency program was extended for another three years. But new needs developed even as the wounds of the world conflict healed. Children were still at risk in many parts of the world; and UNICEF was made a permanent UN program in 1953, dropping the word "emergency" from its title. However, as UNICEF had become so well known around the world, the acronym was retained.

UNICEF is one of the best-run programs of the UN system. It is under the authority of the General Assembly (i.e., it is not an independent organization like the WHO) and it is included in the UN budget. However, it is authorized to raise funds for its own projects and to appeal to UN members for voluntary contributions including private-sector collections. In 2013, UNICEF's total financial resources amounted to $6.5 billion.[53] UNICEF has its own staff and executive director. It has a 36-member Executive Board, composed of the diplomatic representatives of UN member states. They represent the five regional groups at the UN. They are elected for three-year terms (staggered) by the UN ECOSOC, a number of representatives being elected every year. The executive director is appointed by the UN secretary-general in consultation with the Executive Board. The duties of the Executive Board are to authorize UNICEF policies, approve programs, and oversee administrative and financial operations.[54] Interaction between the states' representatives of the Executive Board requires diplomatic skill on the part of UNICEF's executive director to ensure their support for his/her activity program and budgetary decisions.

UNICEF has a strong presence in 155 countries, and it works with a large network of civil society people. The health of children and their mothers represents a huge part of its work. For this reason its partnership with the WHO is strong, and it works with many other UN Programs and Specialized Agencies, such as the World Bank and UNESCO. UNICEF is aiming at universal vaccination against all childhood diseases and it is involved in the fight against malaria, tuberculosis, and pneumonia. Equally important is the battle against diarrhea which causes three million deaths a year, many of which could be prevented by rehydration therapy, a simple and inexpensive remedy.[55] HIV/AIDS is also part of UNICEF's concerns. In 2008, 730,000 children under 15 were estimated to be living with HIV and in need of treatment. In 1965, UNICEF was awarded the Nobel Peace Prize.

Other UN programs and agencies have projects pertaining to children in their own areas of specialization. Member-state practices lead to such separate initiatives which, eventually, became objects of cooperation among other institutions such as the ILO with regard to child labor issues. The ECOSOC facilitates interagency cooperation in problem solving pertaining to economic and social issues.[56] In the UN Secretariat, the OCHA is responsible for bringing together humanitarian actors (representatives of agencies and humanitarian programs) to ensure coherent response to emergencies. This office provides a framework within which the various organizations responding to a crisis can be aware of what others are contributing and thus avoid duplication and waste of resources. The head of OCHA (a UN under-secretary-general) leads the Inter-Agency Standing Committee (IASC), a forum for coordination, policy development, and decision making involving key UN and non-UN humanitarian actors. What is done here is another form of diplomatic work between humanitarian agents, often of different cultures and professional backgrounds (physicians, refugee work specialists, government administrators from different political systems or NGO activists).[57]

YOUTH

It took longer for global society to recognize the special needs of those between the ages 15 and 24 estimated to number about 1 billion or 18 percent of the world population.[58] Two hundred million youth live on less than $1 a day, 130 million are illiterate, 10 million live with HIV, and 88 million are unemployed. It took the UN and its diplomatic process to bring those special needs to the attention of global society. The UN General Assembly declared 1985 International Youth Year. Ten years later, UN member states adopted the World Program of Action for Youth to the Year 2000 and Beyond,[59] which provided a policy framework identifying ten priority areas. In 2005, the UN General Assembly added five new priority areas of concern.[60] As nations and UN agencies recognize the difficulty of measuring the effect of their efforts, the General Assembly requested the UN Secretariat to establish a set of youth development indicators. This led to a meeting of experts bringing together representatives of youth organizations, UN agencies, other intergovernmental organizations, and academia to produce an instrument that could measure youth development over time.[61]

The UN General Assembly decided to make 2010 another International Year of Youth. A variety of international conferences were organized. For example in January 2010, an International Symposium on Youth and the Future in Tunis, Tunisia, organized by the Islamic Educational, Scientific and Cultural Organization jointly with the General Secretariat of the Arab Maghreb Union and the Arab League Educational, Cultural and Scientific Organization. In August, showing the diversity of the observance, the first-ever Youth Olympic Games in Singapore brought together some 5,000 athletes between the ages 14 and 18, and officials from the 204 National Olympic Committees along with 20,000 local and international volunteers, 370,000 spectators, and 1,200 media representatives.[62] Many UN bodies and other international organizations now include youth issues in their programs. Altogether, eight UN Specialized Agencies, six divisions of the UN Department of Economic and Social Affairs (UNDESA), all five of the UN Regional Commissions and fifteen of the UN programs and interagency projects (for a total of thirty-four) include youth issues in their own fieldwork or specialized projects, taking responsibility for the necessary fundraising and implementation.[63]

AGING

Another urgent concern is now on the global population agenda: people are living longer. Better health care, economic development, and improved living conditions are all factors in this phenomenon. The number of older persons has tripled over the last 50 years; it will more than triple again over the next fifty. In 1950 there were 205 million persons aged 60 or over throughout the world. 50 years later, in 2000, this number increased about three times to 606 million. The older population is growing faster than the total population in practically all regions of the world[64] although in Africa the proportion of older persons will only grow from 5 to 6 percent between 2000 and 2025. In sub-Saharan Africa, because of the HIV/AIDS pandemic and continuing economic and social hardship, the percentage will reach half that level. In Europe, it will increase from 20 to 28 percent.[65]

The international community responded somewhat more slowly to this demographic situation. In 1978, the ECOSOC's Commission for Social Development exercised leadership and prompted the General Assembly to convene a World Assembly on Aging, which met in Vienna in July 1982. In preparation for this global conference, a Forum on Aging was held in Vienna in March, and was attended by 336 delegates representing 159 NGOs.[66] Forums explore and exchange ideas rather than negotiating. The 1982 World Assembly produced the Vienna International Plan of Action on Aging endorsed by the General Assembly in December. This document focused on the contribution to society made by older persons and such concerns as health care, housing, family, social welfare, employment, income security, and retirement. Governments were expected to play a larger role in implementing the Plan of Action on Aging. UN agencies, such as the UN Population Fund, were expected to provide technical expertise. A UN Trust Fund for Aging was created as a means of supporting developing countries in meeting the needs of their aging populations.[67]

In 1987, the ECOSOC recommended the establishment in Malta of an International Institute on Aging which began functioning in 1988 as an autonomous body under the auspices of the UN, sponsoring seminars and cooperating with other research institutions, seeking to foster greater international understanding of aging as a social issue.[68] The UN General Assembly itself, in December 1991, adopted *The United Nations Principles of Older Persons* focusing on dignity, independence, participation in society, care, and self-fulfillment of older persons, inviting governments to incorporate these principles into their national programs.[69] Individual states could thus refer to the authority of the global body in launching their own programs. Ten years after the 1982 World Assembly on Aging, the General Assembly selected 1999 as the International Year of Older Persons. Furthermore, in preparation for the 1999 Special Session of the General Assembly on Population (Cairo + 5), the UN Population Fund organized a Technical Meeting on Population Aging in Brussels (October 1998).[70] Aging was getting into the global social agenda. It was also discussed in other meetings called in preparation for the 1999 Special Session. Adding to this expanding international attention, in May 2000, the UN General Assembly decided to convene a second World Assembly on Aging to take place in Madrid in April 2002, the twentieth anniversary of the first World Assembly.

The Madrid World Assembly was large: 159 diplomatic delegations from UN member states and representatives from 5 UN bodies and programs, 4 of the 5 UN Regional Commissions (the African Commission did not send any representatives), 7 Specialized Agencies, 12 other intergovernmental organizations, and numerous NGOs. Outside the official proceedings of the Madrid World Assembly, a number of related events took place: an NGO Forum on Aging was held on April 5–9 (The Assembly occurred on April 8–12), with more than 3,000 participants attending 170 workshops and panels. At the end of the Forum, one of the cochairs was invited to address the Assembly and read a summary of the conclusions reached by the NGO representatives. UN bodies and Specialized Agencies organized 8 events and panels. Moreover, a number of NGOs, alone and in association with member states, hosted 18 panels, workshops, and round tables in parallel with the Assembly.[71] The outcome of this massive deliberation was a new international plan of action adopted unanimously by the World Assembly. It recommended considerably more than two hundred items of policy to improve the quality of life of older persons, the presentation of which took *twenty-nine* pages. It was acknowledged that governments had the primary responsibility for implementing the plan. However, it must be remembered that a good two-thirds of the countries of the world are destitute. If they cannot even meet their most essential needs, how can they give their older citizens what the plan calls for? Large conferences have a consciousness-raising effect, and concern for older persons needs to have a place in international development programs.

The UN Commission for Social Development undertook to consecrate its 46th session (February 2008) on five-year reviews of the Madrid International Plan of Action on Aging. It mandated the five UN Regional Commissions to organize regional conferences for a review and appraisal of the implementation of the Plan. HelpAge International (an NGO working in more than 75 countries) noted, however, that these regional reports reflected a disappointingly low effort to monitor the implementation of the 2002 Plan of Action and no efforts to implement its proposed policies.[72] Other UN agencies have done better. The World Bank, for example, addressed the issue of income protection and poverty alleviation for the aged. It worked on pension reform. Between 1984 and 2004, the Bank gave over 200 loans and credits to 68 countries for the reform of pensions and provided $5.4 billion in pension-specific lending. It also worked on issues of health services for older persons.[73] It must also be noted that global conferences often have a catalytic effect, in the sense that a variety of organizations, agreeing with the objectives of a given conference, decide on their own to undertake projects in the same area. The WHO Executive Board, for example, discussed the issue of implementing the International Plan of Action on Aging.[74]

EDUCATION, SCIENCE, AND CULTURE

If sustainable development is to be achieved and the gap between rich and poor reduced, education, science, and culture need to be addressed globally. Ironically, this has remained a controversial task. The League of Nations Assembly created the Committee on Intellectual Cooperation in September 1921. It did not meet until August 1922 and its staff was inadequate. However, the French government created the International Institute of Intellectual Cooperation, which began working in 1926, and used its own staff to run League Committee projects to the point that it was called the "executing agency" of the League Committee.[75] Education became a major endeavor, training teachers, striving to eliminate national bias in textbooks, helping the exchange of ideas among instructors and school administrators, working with some forty national pedagogical centers, and, at the request of ILO, in 1931, helping the development of adult education. The League Committee undertook to facilitate cooperation among libraries and among museums. It sponsored dialogues among outstanding authorities on such topics as the future of European culture and helped cooperation and communication among scientific associations.[76] Although its accomplishments remained modest, this institution was the first effort to address the development of an international intellectual and cultural community, even if perhaps more European than global in its thrust.

In the process of creating the UN, the San Francisco Conference adopted a resolution advocating the establishment of a permanent UN cultural organization, and a UN Conference was convened in November 1945 for this purpose. It produced the constitution of UN Educational, Scientific, and Cultural Organization (UNESCO), signed on November 16, 1945. The first meeting of the new institution was held in Paris in December 1946. It is an independent organization, a Specialized Agency, linked to the UN, by an international agreement. It has currently 195 member states and eight associate members.[77]

UNESCO is governed by its General Conference, which consists of the diplomatic representatives of all member states. It meets every two years and is also attended by representatives of associate members, observers from nonmember states, international organizations, and NGOs. The General Conference negotiates UNESCO's policies and programs. Issues of education and culture are often controversial, member states being frequently oversensitive on matters perceived as touching national identity. Other differences are the result of conflict in the relations between rich and poor nations and issues of ideology. Diplomacy is therefore a critical element in the operation of this institution even though its agenda does not compare with that of the more politically involved institutions. Controversy in fact has led a number of member states to withdraw, most significant among them the United States, in 1984, followed by the United Kingdom in 1985. The United Kingdom rejoined in 1997, and the United States in 2003 after almost twenty years.[78] In 2011, once again, the United States withdrew, this time in protest over the admission of Palestine as a member state. The Executive Board, composed of fifty-eight member states, is elected by the General Conference and meets twice a year. It takes care of the overall management of the organization. The UNESCO Secretariat, with its headquarters in Paris, is headed by a director-general. It employs about 2,000 civil servants (as of mid-2009). More than 700 staff members work in UNESCO's 65 field offices around the world. In 1994, UNESCO introduced a *Program for Parliamentarians*, to maintain contact with elected representatives and generate greater understanding of UNESCO's objectives. In 2009, it organized a conference for parliamentary organizations.[79]

UNESCO's current global program is primarily focused on education. The task is monumental. At the turn of the century, adult illiteracy was estimated to have reached 880 million.[80] In 1990, UNESCO, the UNDP, the UN Population Fund, UNICEF, and the World Bank held a World Conference in Jomtien, Thailand, and launched the Education for All (EFA) movement. Ten years later, many countries remained far from having universalized primary education. Nevertheless, 34 million more children attend school and the number of children out of school has been halved since the year 2000.[81] UNESCO and its associates convened the World Education Forum in Dakar, Senegal, bringing together 1100 participants from 164 countries, international organizations, and NGOs. They identified six education goals (early childhood education, primary education, lifelong learning, adult literacy, gender parity, and quality education[82]) to meet the needs of all children, youth, and adults by 2015. This Framework for Action was supplemented by Regional Frameworks for Action arrived at in the course of six regional meetings. UNESCO was mandated to coordinate the international campaign.

To achieve the EFA goals, extensive partnerships are required involving governments, international organizations, bilateral and multilateral donors, NGOs, and other elements of civil society. To help them work together, a High-Level Group was created bringing together representatives from all these participating entities. Regular monitoring of the state of education in the world is of critical importance in the EFA campaign. This is done through the independent EFA Global Monitoring Report and the UNESCO Institute for Statistics. The annual report provides the latest data and analysis, and includes an EFA Development Index that measures the extent to which countries are meeting EFA goals.[83] UNESCO is also making use of its network of field offices to promote regional and subregional EFA forums, and it works with regional intergovernmental organizations such as the AU, to promote education and foster EFA networks. Another initiative is the creation of a Task Force on Teachers for EFA, an international alliance to address the global teacher gap. It is currently estimated that 18 million new primary teachers are needed to achieve Universal Primary Education.[84] Reaching EFA goals will be difficult. But progress is being made. In 2008, the rate of global adult literacy (i.e., beyond age 15) had risen from 76 percent to 86.6 percent over the previous two decades.[85]

Beyond this major focus on education, UNESCO has important programs in four areas, namely, natural sciences, social and human sciences, culture, and finally, communication and information. UNESCO is using its publications as an important means in the implementation of its vast mission. The very size of its endeavor, however, has frequently been attacked for a lack of focus. One of UNESCO's problems in carrying out its mission is that its pursuits are rarely at the top of national governments' agendas—even education for all. Politicians talk about them, but when it comes to state spending, or implementing their commitments, tasks that seem to be more urgent frequently take precedence. UNESCO keeps reminding global society of what it is neglecting. And by involving NGOs and other elements of civil society in its forums, round tables, and conferences it may compensate for political apathy.

The United Nations University

In 1969, UN secretary-general U Thant, in his annual report to the General Assembly, proposed the creation of an international university. The ECOSOC invited the General Conference of UNESCO to submit its opinion on this proposal. UNESCO produced a feasibility study and adopted a resolution (December 1972) recommending to the General Assembly the creation of the UN University (UNU). A UN Panel of Experts contributed a report and the government of Japan offered $100 million to establish University headquarters in Tokyo. The Assembly accepted the offer and approved the University's Charter in December 1973.[86] The University rector is the chief academic and administrative officer and is appointed by the secretary-general of the UN. University policies are determined by the University Council composed of twenty-four members appointed jointly by the UN secretary-general and the director-general of UNESCO. Council members serve six-year terms in their individual capacities rather than as representatives of their countries. Serving as ex officio members are the UN secretary-general, the director-general of UNESCO, the executive director of the UN Institute for Training and Research, and the University rector. The UNU maintains liaison offices at the UN headquarters in New York and UNESCO in Paris.

The UNU is funded by voluntary contributions from governments, bilateral and multilateral development assistance agencies, foundations, and other public and private sources. It is different from other universities. It does not have a campus of its own. It is a worldwide network composed of the UNU Center in Tokyo (the University's headquarters), and institutes located in thirteen countries, for example the UNU Institute for Natural Resources in Africa (in Accra, Ghana), the UNU World Institute for Development Economics Research (in Helsinki, Finland), or the UNU Institute of Advanced Studies in Sustainable Development (in Yokohama, Japan). The main focus of the University is to meet the needs of the developing world, with, for example, course offerings that do not conform to the curricula and schedules of regular institutions of higher learning.[87]

INTERNATIONAL MIGRATIONS AND
THE PLIGHT OF REFUGEES

A growing global crisis is that of massive migrations across international borders involving refugees or people seeking a better life. Dire economic conditions are making migration a matter of survival for increasing numbers of people, and so are armed conflicts and various forms of oppression. Many countries are affected by these extensive flows of people, whether as countries of origin, host countries, or transit states. There is much international disagreement as to how to respond to this phenomenon. It is estimated that almost 200 million people now live outside their birthplaces and the current annual rate of migration growth is about 2.9 percent and rising.[88] *Refugees* were the first to receive international attention. The League of Nations, however, did not get involved in the costly issue of relief and resettlement leaving the matter to private organizations. The League Council, though, in response to an appeal by the ICRC, created, in September 1921, the office of High Commissioner to provide limited assistance to Russian refugees fleeing the revolution (without any funds for this purpose). High Commissioner Nansen created a League of Nations passport to enable refugees to relocate. In 1930, the League Assembly created the "autonomous" International Refugee Office to raise funds for humanitarian purposes, but in 1931, decided that its mission would end in 1938, as if the issue could be disposed of that easily. The League, however, was instrumental in the negotiation of two refugee conventions (1933 and 1938) laying down a number of principles for their protection, such as an obligation not to refuse them admission or expel them except for reasons of national security and public order.[89]

With Hitler taking over in Germany, new waves of refugees flocked to near-by countries, and, in October 1933, the League created the High Commissioner for Refugees Coming from Germany. In 1938, the League brought together previously established refugee bodies under a new high commissioner to deal with all refugees. League diplomacy thus addressed the issue of refugees, but ever so hesitantly. President Roosevelt took the initiative to call an international conference in 1938 to explore better ways of dealing with the growing refugee problem, and an intergovernmental committee was created for this purpose; but little was accomplished and soon the Second World War created its own monumental refugee problem. The UNRRA was an imaginative institution established at a gathering of the 44 United and Associated Nations at the White House in November 1943—remarkably early compared with what was done in the First World War showing the critical importance of leadership. Large resources were made available for the relief effort, something that League diplomacy never managed to do. But, in 1946, the UNRRA became controversial and was abruptly and thoughtlessly terminated by the US Congress. By that time, the large majority of the Second World War refugees had been repatriated but 1.6 million remained in camps, and the UN General Assembly approved the creation of the International Refugee Organization (IRO), a UN Specialized Agency, in December 1946.[90]

Cold War tensions, however, hampered the functioning of the new organization. When the Middle East exploded in 1948–1949, the UN was ill-equipped to handle the new flood of refugees. In 1950, it created the UN Relief and Works Agency for Palestine Refugees in the Near East (UNRWA) to respond to the dire needs of about 750,000 people. Local tensions made it difficult to meet their needs and find permanent accommodations for them, and their numbers grew. There are today 4.7 million officially registered Palestine refugees. One-third of them, nearly 1.4 million, live in refugee camps in Jordan, Lebanon, Syria, the Gaza Strip, and the West Bank. The other two-thirds live in and around the cities of the host countries.[91]

Because of the Cold War the IRO could hardly do its job. It was allowed to work only in areas controlled by Western armies of occupation, leaving many refugees without any assistance. Eighteen countries became members (none from the Soviet camp). IRO faltered and finally came to an end in 1952. Another source of refugee protection was needed and the UN General Assembly established the UN High Commissioner for Refugees (UNHCR) in December 1950—with a three-year mandate (and not applicable to the Middle East). The illusion persisted that refugees were a temporary phenomenon. UNHCR's mandate was extended to the end of the decade; then, it became a permanent organization. The UNHCR won the Nobel Peace Prize in 1951 for helping the refugees of Europe and a second time in 1981 for its permanent functions. UN concerns for refugees also led to diplomatic negotiations for the 1951 Convention Relating to the Status of Refugees (modified in 1967 by means of a protocol), and the 1954 Convention Relating to the Status of Stateless Persons.[92] The global refugee problem, however, has become worse. The number of refugees, internally displaced persons and people seeking asylum, was close to a record 60 million by the end of 2014 and growing. UNHCR's financial requirements for 2015 amount to more than $6 billion.[93]

Monumental as the global refugee problem is today, *cross-border migration* is even more significant and potentially destabilizing.[94] The protection of migrant workers has received the attention of the ILO ever since its creation in 1919. The UN itself negotiated the 1990 Convention on the Protection of the Rights of All Migrant Workers and Members of Their Families. But the issue remains controversial. As of December 2009, 42 states had become parties, with industrialized nations still opposed to ratification. The protection of human rights probably seems less relevant to decision makers when it comes to migrant workers. The Convention aims at guaranteeing the same working

conditions for migrants and nationals and seeks to foster international cooperation to prevent clandestine movements and to act against traffickers and
employers of undocumented migrants. But states sharply restrict who is
allowed to enter.

National policies on migration are primarily formulated on the basis of
national concerns (and public emotions), but it has human dimensions, which
cannot be ignored. The General Assembly decided in 2004 to hold its first-
ever plenary session on migration issues in September 2006. In addition,
the UN decided to bring government ministers and high-ranking diplomats
together for informal round table discussions on related issues, such as remit-
tances, smuggling of migrants, trafficking in persons, and the creation of
diplomatic partnerships at the bilateral and regional levels. Over 140 member
states participated.[95] It is interesting how often workshops and seminars for
high-ranking officials are now organized in the margin of formal proceedings
to examine the complex ramifications of problems under consideration.

As a result of these discussions, a large number of UN members expressed
an interest in continuing the dialogue by means of state-led global forums.
It is of course easier to continue the dialogue than to agree to take effective
measures in this controversial issue. Belgium took the lead to organize the
first Global Forum on Migration and Development in Brussels from July 9
to 11, 2007. The program had two interrelated parts: a program of discussion
for government officials and diplomatic representatives (July 10–11), for
the purpose of dialogue rather than decision making, as well as a meeting
of civil society actors preceding the governmental meeting (July 9) organized by a Belgian foundation. Many civil society organizations are strong
advocates of addressing the problem of migrants and want to be heard.[96] The
Global Forum was attended by 156 UN member states. It facilitated dialogue
between countries of origin and host destinations and has become an annual
event held in various parts of the world.[97] The related civil society conference
now meets for two days just before the gathering of diplomatic delegations
and its recommendations are then presented to the government participants.[98]
Some civil society groups, such as Migrant Rights International, have organized events of their own leading up to and during the Forum. The Global
Forum on Migration and Development is not sponsored by the UN but is open
to all UN member-states. The UN, however, plays a role in its work. The
secretary-general participates in Forum meetings and has appointed a Special
Representative for Migration and Development. In early 2006, the secretary-
general created an interagency "Global Migration Group" to permit dialogue
and cooperation among agencies involved in migration-related activities.[99] It
also provides expert support in the preparation of Global Forum meetings and
for the implementation of their outcomes. The Global Migration Group meets
several times a year.

An earlier independent initiative has contributed to the international dialogue on the migration issue. The International Organization for Migration (IOM) was established in 1951, based in Switzerland, and unrelated to the UN. It has 127 member states, including the United States, and the major industrialized states. 40 NGOs enjoy observer status and IOM convenes annual consultations for a wider NGO audience as it strives for increased NGO participation in migration policy dialogue. It maintains a staff of 7,000 serving in over 450 field offices in more than 100 countries. Its program budget exceeds $1 billion, funding over 2,000 projects and programs. IOM works with other international organizations, states, and civil society groups to uphold the human dignity and well-being of migrants, including refugees and displaced persons, and encourages social and economic development through migration, while addressing the growing problems involved in this massive phenomenon.[100]

The IOM was created as the Provisional Intergovernmental Committee for the Movement of Migrants from Europe to help European governments identify resettlement countries for the estimated 11 million people uprooted by the Second World War (at the time they were mainly identified as refugees). Eventually the organization expanded and became involved in migrations following the crises of the twentieth and early twenty-first centuries, including, for example, Hungary (1956), Czechoslovakia (1968),[101] and now the spreading turmoil in the Middle East and Africa. The IOM signed a cooperation agreement with the UN in 1996 and is a member of the interagency Global Migration Group. It has a Permanent Observer Office at the UN headquarters in New York. This office is in regular contact with the UN Secretariat, notably the OCHA and fosters the exchange of information with New York-based UN bodies such as the UN Population Agency, all of which involves a good deal of diplomacy to maintain effective working relationships. More diplomacy is involved in the IOM's extensive fieldwork. IOM Chiefs of Mission (the organization is involved in more than one hundred countries) are frequently invited by UN Resident Coordinators to work with UN Country Teams, sometimes as full partners. The IOM works extensively with UN agencies in the field for joint execution of programs (e.g., with the UNHCR).[102]

The IOM is dependent upon the interaction of government diplomatic representatives for its governance and policy process. The highest authority is the Council. Each member state has one representative and one vote and negotiates IOM policies. The Council meets twice a year but the diplomatic interaction of member states also takes place in the margin of official meetings, particularly now, as migration is reaching crisis proportions. The Executive Committee is made up of the representatives of 33 member states serving two-year terms. This body meets annually. The Standing Committee on Programs and Finance, open to the entire membership, meets twice a year and reviews policies, programs, and other activities of the organization. The Secretariat ("The Administration") is headed by a director-general and a deputy director-general. It is responsible for administering and managing the organization. Both of these offices are independently elected by the Council for a period of five years and play important diplomatic roles aside from (and in connection with) the administration of the organization.[103]

It must be noted that much more work is now anticipated in the migration area on the part of specialized international organizations in their own fields of work. For example, the WHO is now cooperating with the OECD on a Health Workforce and Migration Project, stressing the importance of improved international cooperation to address the growing demand for health personnel in light of the international migration of doctors and nurses both among developed societies and between these and some underdeveloped nations.[104]

DISASTER RELIEF

As the Second World War wound down, the UNRRA had the monumental task of providing relief assistance to the victims of war as territories were liberated by the Allied Forces. It was an unprecedented humanitarian venture unfortunately cut short before the task could be completed. Other institutions were called upon to fill the void, such as refugee organizations, or the WHO. But, as many expected, the need for disaster relief did not disappear with reconstruction. Between June 2008 and June 2009, 343 disasters linked to natural hazards (e.g., earthquakes) affected more than 42 million people, taking more than 14,000 lives and causing economic damage totaling $57.4 billion. Asia had the highest occurrence rate (36 percent), Africa the highest mortality (60 percent), and the Americas the highest economic losses (88 percent).[105]

In 1964, the ECOSOC requested the UN secretary-general to study arrangements for coordinating international disaster relief. Spontaneous bilateral assistance was often chaotic; but it was the disasters of 1970 that prompted the General Assembly to create the United Nations Disaster Relief Office in Geneva. Its two main functions were: (1) relief coordination (mobilizing and coordinating aid to stricken nations); and (2) prevention and preparedness in disaster-prone areas.[106] In December 1991, the General Assembly decided to strengthen the UN response to both complex emergencies (the result of a number of human factors including political conflicts) and natural disasters while improving the overall effectiveness of humanitarian operations in the fields. The same General Assembly resolution also created the new high-level position of Emergency Relief Coordinator combining the functions carried out by representatives of the secretary-general for major complex emergencies as well as the functions of the previous UN Disaster Relief Coordinator.[107]

Soon thereafter, the secretary-general established the Department of Humanitarian Affairs (in the UN Secretariat) providing the necessary staff to implement the expanded program (i.e., institutional support). The Emergency Relief Coordinator was given the rank of under-secretary-general for Humanitarian Affairs with offices in New York and Geneva. The same General Assembly resolution revising the UN disaster relief system also created three instruments to enhance the effectiveness of the Emergency Relief Coordinator:

1. The IASC, an institution for coordination, policy development, and decision making involving key UN and non-UN intergovernmental organizations and civil society humanitarian partners for a total membership of twenty.
2. The Consolidated Appeals Process (CAP), a tool used by aid organizations to work together and appeal for money. Since 1992, more than one hundred donor countries have provided in excess of $42 billion for 330 appeals to meet urgent needs in more than fifty countries and regions.[108]
3. The Central Emergency Revolving Fund (CERF), later changed to Central Emergency Response Fund, to act immediately when disaster strikes by making funds available for life-saving activities to UN programs, Specialized Agencies and the IOM. CERF is funded by voluntary contributions from UN members, private businesses, foundations, and individuals. Its program was expanded in 2005. In 2011, 73 member states pledged $450.4 million to the Fund.[109]

In 1998, the Secretariat Department of Humanitarian Affairs was reorganized into the OCHA and given more responsibilities. OCHA performs its coordination functions primarily through the IASC. Partnership remains a critical element in its effectiveness, which means that, more than ever, the diplomatic process involves the private sector. OCHA now maintains a larger number of field offices than its predecessor (more than 20), plus the offices of three regional disaster-response advisors, and three regional coordinators. The integration of international facilities for humanitarian relief in complex disaster situations (particularly of the political type, in peacekeeping/peace-building operations) can create tension because of the partiality involved in dealing with certain political actors in the process of restoring peace (some actors remain a threat) and the impartiality needed in humanitarian work.

OCHA assesses situations and humanitarian needs. As emergencies evolve, needs change. OCHA works with humanitarian agencies both within and outside the UN system to develop realistic Action Plans and avoid duplication of efforts by arriving at a workable division of responsibility, hence the need for negotiations. It monitors progress, adjusting programs if necessary, and leads the CAP to mobilize resources. OCHA has an important responsibility involving humanitarian diplomacy in efforts to prevent further emergencies and in negotiations with parties in conflict to ensure access to people in need (e.g., whose homes have been destroyed), or to those working with UN security officials in complex peacekeeping operations, facilitating relations between humanitarian and military components. A Civil-Military Coordination Section (UN-CMCoord) based in Geneva is the essential dialogue instrument.[110] OCHA serves as the Secretariat for all these interagency bodies.

An important tool in OCHA's disaster relief work is ReliefWeb, updated around the clock by means of more than 3,700 information providers (NGOs, academic and research institutions, UN and non-UN international organizations, and governments, among others) offering coordination and support services, as well as information on the full range of humanitarian issues, such as food, health, shelter, human rights protection, water, and sanitation covering 193 natural disasters and 33 complex emergencies in 2009. The website received some 10 million visits in 2009 from 237 countries and territories. In addition, ReliefWeb services over 152,000 subscribers providing resources specifically targeted to relief professionals.[111] In 2015, ReliefWeb reported that in 2014 it had over 4.97 million users accessing the website more than 12 million times.[112]

The Virtual OSOCC is another important tool in disaster relief serviced by OCHA. Its purpose is to assist local authorities with the management of a particular disaster including the coordination of relief work. This website is restricted (password protected) for disaster managers in governments and response organizations. It is to facilitate decision making for a widespread response to major disasters by means of real-time information exchange among all actors involved in such operations including governments, international organizations, and NGOs. OSOCC enables relief actors to coordinate their efforts, and discuss the evolving crisis continuously and simultaneously from anywhere in the world.

OSOCC is used by the International Search and Rescue Advisory Group (INSARAG), a global network of more than 80 countries and disaster-response organizations specializing in earthquake rescue. It is serviced by OCHA. OSOCC is also of great importance to the UN Disaster Assessment and Coordination service (UNDAC), a standby team of disaster management professionals who are nominated and funded by member governments, OCHA, the UNDP, and humanitarian UN agencies such as UNICEF, the WFP and the WHO. Upon request of a disaster-stricken country, the UNDAC team can be deployed within hours to carry out assessment of priority needs and assist local authorities to coordinate international relief on site. Members of the UNDAC team are permanently on standby to deploy following disasters.

The team is responsible for providing first-hand information on the disaster and priority needs of the victims through OCHA.[113] OSOCC is also available to the Global Disaster Alert and Coordination System (GDACS), also serviced by OCHA in Geneva. This organization seeks to strengthen the network of providers and users of disaster information worldwide, to provide accurate alerts and impact estimates immediately upon the onset of disasters, and to improve international cooperation in relief work. It has more than 9,000 subscribers and users of Virtual OSOCC worldwide. The EU has been funding GDACS since its creation in 2004 and providing the benefits of the European Commission Joint Research Center in Ispra, Italy.[114]

DISASTER REDUCTION

With the increasing incidence and magnitude of disasters, the UN General Assembly decided to launch the International Decade for Natural Disaster Reduction, 1990–1999, and issued a Framework for Action. In 1994, the UN convened the World Conference on Natural Disaster Reduction in Yokohama, Japan, which produced an International Strategy for Disaster Reduction (ISDR) to enable communities to become resilient to the effects of natural crises, technological hazards (e.g., a nuclear reactor meltdown) and environmental problems, and to proceed to the management of risk.[115] In 2005, the UN convened the Second World Conference on Disaster Reduction (Kobe, Hyogo, Japan). It was a landmark gathering that adopted the *Hyogo Framework for Action 2005–2015*: "Building the Resilience of Nations and Communities to Disasters," which was endorsed the same year by the UN General Assembly.[116] This Framework for Action is intended to promote disaster reduction as an integral component of sustainable development and the fulfillment of the MDGs, which explains the target date. This enabled the Hyogo Project to share some of the excitement generated by the MDG campaign (see chapter 6).

But nature is difficult to control when it comes to what generates natural disasters. The Hyogo strategy has to do with preparedness, conscious human action to reduce vulnerability, and mitigation of consequences. It seeks the development of institutions and mechanisms at all levels to address the issue and build resilience to hazards, as well as the inclusion of risk reduction in programs of emergency preparedness. It shows concern for early warning.[117] The strategy involves, essentially, a system of partnership and global cooperation among many types of actors—states, international organizations (including many units of the UN system), NGOs, their networks, and other elements of civil society, such as scientific and technical bodies—hence the multiplicity of diplomatic efforts. For that reason, the UN organized a biennial forum, the Global Platform for Disaster Risk Reduction bringing together all concerned groups, including more than 160 states and as many institutions, involving them in a large number of workshops and plenary sessions on implementing the Hyogo Framework, and reviewing the progress made. All of these add to the visibility of the project. The UN secretary-general gives the General Assembly a regular overview of the situation; for example, how approximately one billion people live in vulnerable makeshift shanty towns around cities, mostly in the developing world, with this number actually growing by about 25 million per year.[118]

The ISDR has its own Secretariat in Geneva, a part of the UN Secretariat, to coordinate and guide all the ISDR partners, with the help of five regional offices. The ISDR Secretariat maintains PreventionWeb serving the information needs of the disaster risk reduction community and facilitating collaboration.[119] Regional Platforms for Disaster Risk Reduction, including ministerial meetings, are led by regional intergovernmental organizations, for example, the Second Africa Ministerial Conference on the implementation of the Africa Regional Strategy, in April 2010, in Nairobi, Kenya, involving more than 250 participants from 42 African countries.[120] Thematic programs are led by UN Specialized Agencies or technical institutions, for example, on early warning.[121] Several stakeholder groups and networks are associated with ISDR, among them, the Global NGO Network and the Parliamentarian Network.

As the Hyogo Framework for Action was to come to an end in 2015, the UN convened a third World Conference to create a successor program. The Conference met in Sendai, Japan, in March 2015, after extensive negotiations that began in July 2014, with three meetings of a Preparatory Committee, a number of ministerial round tables and partnership dialogue . It was a massive, remarkable event with 6,500 delegates including 187 states, the UN secretary-general Special Representative for Disaster Risk Reduction, UN institutions, non-UN international organizations, and private-sector representatives. 40,000 people took part in a wide range of conference-related events and, most importantly, the World Conference issued the *Sendai Framework for Disaster Risk Reduction, 2015–2030.*[122] It remains a difficult undertaking, but there is agreement on its importance as indicated by the international response. The keen interest generated by the previous phase of the project permits expectations of a lively campaign in the years to come.

ROAD TRAFFIC ACCIDENTS

While road traffic accidents may not qualify as a "global disaster," they are a major public hazard and a leading cause of death and injury around the world.

It has been estimated that each year nearly 1.2 million people die and millions more (perhaps 20 to 50 million) are injured or disabled as a result of road traffic accidents. These figures are expected to increase by 65 percent by 2020. Traffic accidents are now the largest cause of preventable death in the age group between 10 and 24.[123] The UN has acknowledged the need to address the problem for almost 60 years, and extensive road safety work has been carried out by global and regional organizations, including the WHO, the World Bank, and the UN Regional Commissions. The UN Economic Commission for Europe pioneered road safety work with the establishment of an Ad Hoc Working Group on the Prevention of Road Accidents in March 1950, followed by the creation of a Group of Experts on Road Traffic Safety and, since 1988, with the establishment of the Working Party on Road Traffic Safety, an intergovernmental body in which other related international organizations as well as NGOs play an active role. This Working Party is the only permanent international body in the UN system focusing on improved road safety. The UN Economic Commission for Europe became responsible for the development of road safety conventions and traffic regulations. In its global function, the Working Party is assisted by the World Forum for the Harmonization of Vehicle Regulations, composed of all UN member states, other UN bodies, regional organizations (e.g., the EU), related NGOs, and technical bodies. In 1998, the UN decided that the World Forum would be the single recognized institution to negotiate and approve technical rules for wheeled vehicles and their equipment, in particular to provide global performance requirements.

This UN machinery has created a number of international conventions, for example, the 1968 Convention on Road Traffic, the 1968 Convention on Road Signs and Signals, and the 1997 Agreement on Periodic Technical Inspection of Vehicles. Many of these treaties have been periodically revised or supplemented by a number of protocols.[124] The WHO has long been concerned about traffic accidents. It issued its first call to improve road safety in 1960. With the help of more than 100 experts from 40 countries, and jointly with the World Bank, it produced the World Report on Road Traffic Injury Prevention in 2004. In April of the same year the UN General Assembly debated this issue and adopted a historic resolution calling for greater attention and resources to be directed toward road safety efforts. This resolution invited the WHO to act as a coordinator on road safety issues. Working with the five UN Regional Commissions, in 2004, the WHO launched the UN Road Safety Collaboration, a new partnership involving a number of UN agencies, other international organizations (such as the EU), national governments, foundations, research institutions, a large number of NGOs, and private-sector institutions. The Collaboration is an informal mechanism that has created a global web-based database on road safety legislation and coordinated activities aimed at implementing the WHO World Report.

In 2009, the Russian Federation hosted the First Global Conference on Road Safety. 1500 persons attended this historic event in Moscow, including state ministers, representatives of UN agencies, civil society organizations, and private companies. The meeting concluded with the adoption of the Moscow Declaration, which invited the General Assembly to declare a Decade of Action for Road Safety, 2011–2020.[125] The General Assembly endorsed the idea of a Decade of Action in March 2010 and called upon member states to address road safety issues, particularly in the areas of road management, road infrastructure, vehicle safety, road user behavior, and post-crash care. It also encouraged member states to become contracting parties to the UN road safety–related conventions developed by the UN Economic Commission for Europe. With the explosive growth of traffic on the roads of industrializing nations, particularly India and China, a challenge of monumental proportions is now facing the members of global society.

NARCOTIC DRUG TRAFFIC

International society took a long time to address the problems of drugs. In the nineteenth century, a number of great powers were involved in the lucrative drug trade. The growing drug abuse problem led to the first drug treaty, the International Opium Convention (1912).[126] But it was ratified by only eight countries. In 1919 the Convention was made a part of the peace treaty at Versailles. In 1925, a new International Opium Convention was signed and ratified by 56 countries.[127] It established the Permanent Central Opium Board intended to be an impartial body made up of experts (appointed by the League Council). In 1931, the Board was empowered to institute embargoes against countries that exceeded their import or export quotas,[128] but the European colonial powers continued to tolerate and profit from opium smoking.[129] A conference negotiated the Convention for Limiting the Manufacture, and Regulating the Distribution, of Narcotic Drugs (1931), which was eventually endorsed by 67 states. And in 1936, a Convention for the Suppression of the Illicit Traffic in Dangerous Drugs was the first agreement characterizing this traffic as criminal action. But it never gained widespread acceptance.

With the creation of the UN, diplomatic relations changed dramatically. In 1946, the ECOSOC established the 40-member Commission on Narcotic Drugs, enlarged in 1991 to 53. Commission members are elected by the ECOSOC from states to achieve adequate representation of countries that are important drug producers and of countries in which drug addiction is a serious problem. Right away, the Commission produced an agreement to bring under control the new synthetic narcotic drugs.[130] Next, the Commission turned its attention to making existing conventions more effective.

Negotiations started to consolidate these documents leading to the 1961 Single Convention superseding all previous international agreements.[131] In 1968 the International Narcotics Control Board (INCB) was created to facilitate implementation. It is independent and identifies weaknesses in national and international practices. The Board maintains a permanent dialogue with governments to assist them in complying with their treaty obligations. It may also recommend sanctions in case of noncompliance.[132] The INCB is composed of thirteen members elected by the ECOSOC for five-year terms. To ensure their independence, they serve in their personal capacity. Three members with medical, pharmaceutical or pharmacological experience are elected from a list of persons nominated by the WHO, and ten members are elected from a list of persons nominated by governments.[133]

In the 1960s, however, drug use increased dramatically most notably with new drugs such as amphetamines, and the Single Convention proved insufficient. The Commission on Narcotic Drugs and the WHO debated the issue. A diplomatic conference convened in Vienna negotiated the 1971 Convention on Psychotropic Substances.[134] The United States proposed creating a government-funded, UN-administered antidrug fund, and the UN established the Fund for Drug Abuse Control (UNFDAC) in 1971, with a $2 million US contribution. This fund, however, did not receive widespread support. INTERPOL became a sponsor of local, regional, and global drug enforcement meetings. The UN General Assembly requested the ECOSOC in 1984 to instruct the Commission on Narcotic Drugs to prepare a draft convention against illicit drug trafficking. In 1988, the UN convened a diplomatic conference in Vienna during the course of which 106 states produced the final text of the Convention against Illicit Traffic in Narcotic Drugs and Psychotropic Substances (the Trafficking Convention).[135] This treaty is essentially an instrument of criminal law intended to harmonize national drug-related criminal laws and enforcement action around the world.[136] The Convention, remarkably, came into force in record time—just under two years. The measures taken to implement the Convention were successful in dismantling some of the world's largest criminal networks in the first half of the 1990s, and extraditions for drug-related offenses increased.

In 1989, the G7 summit established the Financial Action Task Force on Money Laundering (FATF) a policymaking body composed of 34 member states. In addition, 27 international organizations and regional banks are associate members or observers and participate in its work. In 1990 FATF drew up a set of international standards (later expanded) to combat money laundering.[137] In 1991 the UN drug-control machinery was reorganized.[138] The UN General Assembly merged existing drug bodies into a single International Drug Control Program (UNDCP) based in Vienna.[139] Six years later, the UNDCP was merged with the UN Center for International Crime Prevention to form the UNODC.[140]

Despite all these efforts, drug abuse kept expanding. By the mid-1990s, the international community felt that more global action was urgently needed, and the UN held a Special Session of the General Assembly on the World Drug Problem in June 1998. It produced an Action Plan including measures to promote judicial cooperation.[141] Other UN bodies, particularly the Specialized Agencies, are themselves working on aspects of the drug problem related to their own missions. For example, the WHO's Global Program on Drug Dependence involves interaction with member states for the prevention, treatment, and management of drug addiction. It also carries out activities assigned to it by international drug-control treaties. The UNESCO focuses on the prevention of drug abuse through public education and awareness.

INTERNATIONAL CRIME CONTROL

Aside from drug traffic, the international community is facing other forms of criminal activity requiring international cooperation and extensive diplomacy. In the nineteenth century, concern developed about the proliferation of crime. The first International Congress on the Prevention and Repression of Crime was held in London in 1872,[142] leading to the First International Criminal Police Congress in 1914. Police officers, lawyers, and magistrates from 14 countries discussed arrest procedures and centralized international criminal records and extradition matters. The year 1923 marked the birth of INTERPOL, then officially called the International Criminal Police Commission, headquartered in Vienna, intended to facilitate police cooperation across international borders. A new constitution was adopted in 1956. It is an independent organization currently with 188 member states, governed by a General Assembly. A 13-member Executive Committee is elected by the General Assembly. A General Secretariat, now located in Lyon, France, operates 24 hours a day, 365 days a year, under the direction of a secretary-general. It has seven regional offices around the world, and maintains Special Representatives at the United Nations in New York and at the EU in Brussels. Each member state has a National Central Bureau staffed by national law-enforcement officers serving as a link to the INTREPOL Secretariat, to regional offices and to other member states. A web-based communication system, launched in 2002, has significantly increased the effectiveness of the organization.[143]

In 1948, the UN set up its first office for the purpose of fighting international crime. The General Assembly decided to resume the practice, established at the 1872 conference, to hold an International Conference on Crime Control (Crime Congress) every five years.[144] Accordingly, such gatherings have been held since 1955 in different parts of the world, attended by heads of state, government policymakers, parliamentarians, representatives of UN bodies, non-UN international organizations, NGOs, practitioners in the areas of crime prevention, and academics. Regional preparatory meetings are organized for the purpose of making action-oriented recommendations. As a part of the Congress, the UN organizes workshops, for example, on "Practical Approaches to Preventing Urban Crime."[145] In 1971, in response to the Fourth UN Crime Congress held in Kyoto in 1970, the UN created the UN Committee on Crime Prevention and Control, a body of 27 members nominated by their governments, elected by the ECOSOC, and reporting to it. It was charged with the coordination of the growing responsibilities of UN bodies in this area and preparation for the international crime congresses.[146]

With the global increase of crime, a November 1991 meeting at the ministerial level attended by 114 state ministers was held in Versailles, France. This meeting called for a new UN crime prevention program. The General Assembly responded by requesting the ECOSOC to take action in the matter, which led to the creation of the UN Commission on Crime Prevention and Criminal Justice in 1992. The 40-state Commission is the principal UN policymaking and coordination body on criminal justice and meets annually in Vienna. Many of its decisions are forwarded to the ECOSOC or, occasionally, to the UN General Assembly, for endorsement.[147] Shortly after its creation, the Commission became concerned about the loose networks of criminal groups exploiting new market opportunities. It therefore recommended the negotiation of a new international convention against transnational crime. The General Assembly gave its approval. Diplomatic negotiations continued through six sessions in 1999, and five more in 2000. The General Assembly endorsed the new Convention against Transnational Organized Crime (the Palermo Convention) and two of its supplementary protocols in November 2000.[148] A third protocol was endorsed in May 2001.[149] They constitute a significant advance in international criminal justice.

The first protocol is to *Prevent, Suppress and Punish Trafficking in Persons, Especially Women and Children.* It applies not only to cases of sexual exploitation but also forced labor, and practices similar to slavery. Such practices affect an estimated 21 million people with global profits put at $150 billion annually.[150] It also makes provision for the protection of the victims and addresses issues of repatriation or permanent settlement.[151] It is the first global legally binding instrument with an agreed definition on trafficking in persons. The second protocol pertains to the *Smuggling of Migrants by Land, Air and Sea.* It makes provision for the criminal prosecution of the people engaging in this kind of trade, specifying, however, that the migrants will not be liable to criminal action. Provision is made for the humane treatment of the victims.[152] The third protocol is *Against the Illicit Manufacturing of, and Trafficking in, Firearms, Their Parts and Components and Ammunition.* It requires unique marking and special procedures for firearms export and import.[153] It is the first binding instrument on small arms adopted at the global level.

The negotiators of the Palermo Convention and its three protocols debated whether corruption should be covered by these instruments, but they decided that the matter was too complex. The UN had debated the issue for more than two decades and the Commission on Crime Prevention and Criminal Justice was concerned about it from the time of its creation. Several regional organizations such as the EU negotiated legal instruments of their own to combat corruption. In other words, there was widespread interest in combating this criminal activity.[154] In December 2000, the General Assembly established an Ad Hoc Committee for the negotiation of a Convention against Corruption. More than 130 national delegations participated and produced a new convention adopted by the General Assembly in October 2003.[155] It was the first legally binding global instrument against corruption. Countries are required to criminalize a wide range of acts of corruption. In fact, the Convention goes beyond usual forms of corruption and includes trading in influence. Obstruction of justice as well as private-sector corruption are also dealt with. In a major breakthrough, countries agreed on asset recovery, particularly important where high-level corruption leads to the plundering of national wealth and where resources are needed for reconstruction under new governments. Countries are required to give mutual assistance in gathering and providing evidence to extradite offenders.[156] Implementation of the Convention is facilitated by the UNODC.

The UNODC (see preceding section) is currently the major organ dealing with criminal justice. Headquartered in Vienna, it maintains 21 field offices around the world and liaison offices at the EU in Brussels and at the UN in New York. Its work involves extensive collaboration with governments, international and regional organizations, and civil society.[157] It is also involved in counterterrorism technical assistance (see chapter 5) supporting states requesting help in achieving a universal legal regime against terrorism, not only helping criminal justice officials, but also guiding policymakers toward the implementation of global conventions against terrorism. There are 16 UN antiterrorism conventions and protocols providing a framework for international cooperation (see Textbox 5.4). In 2002, the UN General Assembly decided to strengthen the program of the UNODC's Terrorism Prevention Branch.[158] It is now a member of the UN Counter-Terrorism Implementation Task Force established by the secretary-general in July 2005 to ensure coordination and coherence in the UN counterterrorism efforts. The UNODC works closely with the Security Council's Counter-Terrorism Committee and its Executive Directorate.[159]

Also related to the UNODC's extensive mission, research and analysis must be mentioned. The UNICRI in Turin, Italy,[160] was created in 1968 to assist intergovernmental, governmental, and nongovernmental organizations in formulating and implementing criminal justice policies. It studies emerging forms of crime and helps the integration of national and international efforts to identify effective crime prevention and criminal justice practices. It adapts them to different national situations. The purpose of its programs is to promote national self-reliance and foster institutional capabilities. It provides high-level expertise and contributes to the training of specialized personnel.

The Turin Institute cooperates with fifteen institutes and centers around the world. These are private, national, or intergovernmental bodies and constitute the UN Crime Prevention and Criminal Justice Program Network, which entails a substantial amount of interaction among professionals of different cultures and political systems. It illustrates a new form of international interaction requiring interpersonal skills for effective international and transnational cooperation. It is fostered by growing interdependence and integration of services around the world.[161] Global crime prevention and criminal justice work are now facilitated by modern communication technology, as can be witnessed by the UN Crime and Justice Information Network (UNCJIN), a global electronic clearinghouse mandated by the ECOSOC and established in 1989, where information on crime prevention and criminal justice is exchanged on an unprecedented scale. It permits communication between criminal justice documentation centers and libraries around the world—a new dimension in law enforcement.[162]

Considering the global social arena, a remarkable amount of diplomatic work has taken place—a genuine contribution to the global common good. It is an amazing evolution over what states and other international actors were willing to do barely fifty years ago. Granted, much less gets done than laid out in the Action Plans created by international conferences. But a remarkable amount of collective work is now taking place around the world and a great many institutions are striving to build on it.

NOTES

1. Valeska Huber, "The Unification of the Globe by Disease? The International Sanitary Conferences on Cholera, 1851–1894," *The Historical Journal* Vol. 49, No. 2 (2006), pp. 453–476.

2. David P. Fidler, "From International Sanitary Conventions to Global Health Security: The New International Health Regulations," http://chinesejil.oxfordjournals. org/cgi/content/full/4/2/325 (Accessed February 5, 2010).

3. http://jama.ama-assn.org/cgi/content/ (Accessed February 9, 2010).

4. Daniel S. Cheever and H. Field Haviland, Jr. *Organizing for Peace: International Organization in World Affairs* (Boston: Houghton Mifflin, 1954), pp. 178–179.

5   WHO, "Overview of Funding. Approved Programme Budget, 2014–2015." http://extranet.who.int/programmebudget/Financing (Accessed April 17, 2015).

6. World Health Assembly, *List of Delegates and Other Participants.* A62/DIV/1 Rev.1 May 21, 2009. http://apps.who.int/gb/ebwha/pdf_files/A62/A62_DIV1Rev1 (Accessed February 13, 2010).

7. See *Four Decades of Achievement, 1948–1988: Highlights of the Work of WHO* (Geneva: WHO, 1988).

8. See for example David A. Koplow, *Smallpox: The Fight to Eradicate a Global Scourge* (Berkeley, CA: University of California Press, 2003).

9. *Ebola: World Bank Group Mobilize Emergency Funding.* www.world-bank.org/en./topic/health/brief/world-bank-group-ebola-fact-sheet (Accessed April 2, 2015).

10. www.who.int/governance/en/index (Accessed February 11, 2010).

11. www.who.int/collaboratingcenters/en (Accessed September 9, 2011).

12. See for example Regional Office for Europe, www.euro.who.int/.

13. UNAIDS Annual Report (Geneva: UNAIDS, 2009), p. 7.

14. See a sample of what these organizations contribute to the campaign against HIV/AIDS, "Cosponsor Highlights," 2008 UNAIDS Annual Report (Geneva: UNAIDS, 2009), pp. 45–60.

15. www.unaids.org/en/AboutUNAIDS/Governance (Accessed April 15, 2010).

16. 2008 UNAIDS Annual Report, p. 39.

17. www.unaids.org/en/AboutUNAIDS/Secretariat (Accessed April 15, 2010).

18. See for example www.unaids.org/en/Cosponsors/ILO/default (Accessed April 6, 2010).

19. www.unaids.org/en/AboutUNAIDS/Leadership/SpecialEnvoy (Accessed April 15, 2010).

20. *2008 UNAIDS Annual Report*, p. 40.

21. Jennifer Clapp, *Hunger in the Balance: The New Politics of International Food Aid* (Ithaca, NY: Cornell University Press, 2012).

22. See www.fao.org (Accessed October 14, 2009). See also chapter 5, Rule of Law section.

23. www.wfp.org/about/donors/wfp-donors/2009 (Accessed June 4, 2010).

24. www.wfp.org/about/corporate-information (Accessed October 14, 2009).

25. Sandy Ross, *The World Food Program and Global Politics* (Boulder, CO: First Forum Press, 2011).

26. See *Annual Report.* www.wfp.org/about (Accessed June 4, 2010).

27. Edwin McC. Martin, *Conference Diplomacy. A Case Study: The World Food Conference, Rome, 1974* (Washington, DC: Institute for the Study of Diplomacy, Edmund A. Walsh School of Foreign Service, Georgetown University, no date).

28. www.ifad.org/governance/index (Accessed October 14, 2009).

29. Bennett (6th ed.), pp. 322–326.

30. www.wto.org/english/tratop_e/dda_e/dda_e (Accessed September 13, 2011).

31. See International Trade section in preceding chapter.

32. International Grains Council, *Grains Trade and Food Security Cooperation.* www.igc.int/en/aboutus/default (Accessed June 6, 2010).

33. www.foodassistanceconvention.org/en/about_fac/about (Accessed June 9, 2014).

34. CGIAR: www.cgiar.org/who/index (Accessed October 14, 2009).

35. World Bank, http://siteresources.worldbank.org/NEWS/Resources/GAFSP-QuestionsAnswers_ext042210 (Accessed June 7, 2010).

36. U.S. Treasury Department announcement of April 22, 2010. www.america.gov/st/trexttrans-english/2010/April/20100422174942eaifas0.422146 (Accessed June 7, 2010).

37. http://siteresources.worldbank.org/NEWS/Resources/GAFSPQuestionsAnswers_ext042210 and www.america.gov/st/texttrans-english/20100422174942eaifas0.422146 (Both accessed June 7, 2010).

38. US Census Bureau, International Data Base. www.census.gov/main/www/popclock (as of September 2012) (Accessed September 3, 2012).

39. See World Development Indicators, World Bank. www.worldbank.org/data (Accessed March 5, 2010).

40. Bennett and Oliver, p. 337.

41. www.unfpa.org/public/about (Accessed September 14, 2011).

42. www.unfpa.org/public/about (Accessed March 1, 2010).

43. www.unfpa.org/public/cache/offonce/about (Accessed February 25, 2010).

44. www.un.org/ecosocdev/geninfo/population/icdp (Accessed February 27, 2010).

45. General Assembly Resolution of December 18, 1997. www.un.org/en/development/devagenda/population (Accessed march 3, 2010).

46. www.un.org/popin/icpd5reg (Accessed March 8, 2010).

47. www.unfpa.org/icpd/icpd5/meetings/hague_forum/reports/forumrept-ch2 (Accessed March 8, 2010).

48. www.unfpa.org/icpd/icpd5-keyactions (Accessed March 4, 2010).

49. www.unfpa.org/icpd/icpd5/meetings/hague_forum/reports/forumrept-ch2 (Accessed March 8, 2010).

50. www.unfpa.org/icpd/icpf5-keyactions (Accessed March 4, 2010).

51. United Nations, *World Population Policies, 2009* (New York: United Nations Publications, 2009). 2007 volume is accessible online at www.un.org/esa/population/publications/wpp2007/wpp2007 (Accessed March 4, 2010).

52. www.census.gov/population/international/data/worldpop/table_population (Accessed July 4, 2015).

53. www.unicef.org/about/execboard/files/financial_managementt_orientation_session-15Jan2015 (Accessed May 20, 2015).

54. Ibid.

55. Ibid.

56. See www.un.org/en/ecosoc (Accessed February 24, 2010).

57. http://ochaonline.un.org (Accessed February 24, 2010).

58. www.un.org/events/youth98/backinfo/ywpa2000 (Accessed March 9, 2010).

59. www.un.org/events/youth98/backinfo/ywpa2000 (Accessed March 9, 2010).

60. www.un.org/esa/socdev/unyin/youthindicatiors1 (Accessed March 10, 2010).

61. www.un.org/esa/socdev/unyin/youthindicators1 (Accessed March 10, 2010). To assess what the UN system accomplishes with regard to youth, see *World Youth Report* published every other year by the UN Department of Economic and Social Affairs, also online, for example, for 2007, www.un.org/esa/socdev/unyin/wyr07 (Accessed March 10, 2010).

62. http://assets.olympics.org/YOG/en/index and www.singapore2010.org/public (Accessed September 15, 2011).

63. www.un.org/esa/socdev/unyin/agenda (Accessed March 10, 2010).

64. United Nations Department of Economic and Social Affairs, Population Division, *World Population Ageing: 1950–2050* www.un.org/esa/population/publications/worldageing19502050 (Accessed March 11, 2010).

65. www.un.org/esa/socdev/ageing/madrid_intlplanaction (Accessed March 12, 2010).

66. Bennett and Oliver, 2002, pp. 366–367.

67. *Ageing International* Vol. 13, No. 2 (June 1986), pp. 17–19.

68. www.inia.org.mt/activities (Accessed March 12, 2010).

69. www.un.org/NewLinks/older/99/principles (Accessed March 12, 2010).

70. www.unfpa.org/icpd/icpd5-keyactions (Accessed March 4, 2010).

71. http://daccess-dds-ny.un.org/doc.UNDOC/GEN/N02/397/51 (Accessed March 14, 2010).

72. www.helpage.org/Researchandpolicy/MadridInternationalPlanofActionon-Ageing/MIPAA5review (Accessed March 14, 2010).

73. *The World Bank and Ageing*, www.brettonwoodsproject.org/art (Accessed March 16, 2010). See also *Pension Reform: An Evaluation of World Bank Assistance.* Report (June 2006), same online source.

74. http://apps.who.int/gb/ebwha/ (Accessed March 14, 2010).

75. www.unesco.org/new/en/unesco/about--us/who-we-are/history (Accessed April 8, 2010).

76. See Cheever and Haviland, pp. 619–623.

77. en.unesco.org/about/about-us (Accessed June 10, 2014).

78. Other departures were Portugal (1972), returning in 1974, South Africa (1956), returning in 1994, and Singapore, following Britain in 1985, returning in 2007. http://erc.unesco.org/portal/UNESCOMemberStates.asp?language=en (Accessed April 10, 2010).

79. http://portal.unesco.org/en (Accessed April 10, 2010).

80. Bennett and Oliver, p. 373.

81. United Nations, April 15, 2015. www.ipsnews.net/2015/04 (Accessed April 18, 2015).

82. www.unesco.org/en/efa/the-efa-movement/efa/goals (Accessed April 11, 2010).

83. www.unesco.org/en/efa/monitoring (Accessed April 12, 2010).

84. www.uneco.org/en/efa/international-cooperation/task-force-on-teachers (Accessed April 11, 2010).

85. Mark Richmond, Clinton Robinson, and Margarete Sachs-Israel, eds. *The Global Literacy Challenge: A Profile of Youth and Adult Literacy at the Mid-Point of the United Nations Literacy Decade, 2003–2012* (Paris: UNESCO, 2008), p. 7.

86. "UN University Chronology" (Tokyo: UN University, 1980), p. 1.

87. www.unu.edu/about (Accessed April 13, 2010).

88. www.iom.int/jahia/Jahia/about-migration/lan/en (Accessed March 18, 2010).

89. Cheever and Haviland, pp. 615–619.

90. See IRO Constitution at http://avalon.law.yale.edu/20th_century/decad053. asp (Accessed March 29, 2010).

91. Scott B. Lasensky, "Arab-Israeli Conflict," in *The Middle East*, edited by Robin Surratt (11th ed. Washington, DC: CQ Press, 2007), pp. 49–96.

92. www.unhcr.org/ (Accessed March 19, 2010).

93. Office of the UN High Commissioner for Refugees, reported by the *New York Times*, on June 18, 2015, pp. A1 and A4. And www.un.org/apps/news (Accessed on July 4, 2015).

94. Emory Elliott, Jasmine Payne, and Patricia Ploesch, *Global Migration, Social Change, and Cultural Transformation* (New York: Palgrave Macmillan, 2007).

95. www.un.org/migration (Accessed March 20, 2010).

96. See Kristof Tamas and Joakim Palme. *Globalizing Migration Regimes: New Challenges to Transnational Cooperation* (Burlington, VT: Ashgate Publishing, 2006).

97. www.gfmd.org/en/gfmd-process (Accessed June 10, 2014).

98. www.gfmd.org/en/gfmd-process (Accessed March 22, 2010).

99. www.globalmigrationgroup.org/gmg_members (Accessed March 22, 2010).

100. See Erica Usher, *The Millennium Development Goals and Migration* (Geneva: International Organization for Migration, 2005). www.iom.int/jahia/web-day/site/myjahiasite/shared/shared/mainsite/ (Accessed March 20, 2010).

101. www.iom.int/jahia/Jahia/about-iom/history/lang/en (Accessed March 24, 2010).

102. Ibid.

103. www.iom.int/jahia/Jahia/about-iom/governing-bodies (Accessed March 24, 2010).

104. *Policy Brief on the International Migration of Health Workforce (OECD/ WHO)*, Health Workforce and Migration Project, www.oecd.org/health/workforce (Accessed March 20, 2010).

105. Report of the Secretary-General, UN General Assembly A/64/280 (August 10, 2009). www.unisdr.org/eng/about_isdr/basic_docs/SG-report/SG-Report-64-280-eng (Accessed April 19, 2010).

106. www.nationsencyclopedia.com/United-Nations/Social-and-Humanitarian-Assistance (Accessed April 18, 2010).

107. http://ochaonline.un.org/OCHAHome/AboutUs?Historyof OCHA (Accessed April 19, 2010).

108. http://ochaonline.un.org/humanitarianappeal/webpage (Accessed April 19, 2010).

109. http://ochaonline.un.org/cerf/CERFFigures (Accessed October 13, 2011).

110. http://ochaonline.un.org//OCHAHome/AboutUs/Coordination/CivilMilitary-Coordination (Accessed April 22, 2010).

111. ReliefWeb, *Annual Statistics, 2009.* www.reliefweb.int/rw/hlp.nsf/db900by-key/stats2009?OpenDocument (Accessed April 21, 2010).

112. Report published on February 24, 2015. See www.reliefweb.int/report/world/reliefweb-highlights-2014 (Accessed July 6, 2015).

113. http://ochaonline.un.org/OCHAHome/AboutUs/Coordination/UNDACSystem (Accessed April 21, 2010).

114. Tom De Groeve, Thomas Peter, Alessandro Annunziato, and Luca Vernaccini, *Global Disaster Alert and Coordination System* (Joint Research Center of the European Commission and OCHA, 2009). www.gdacs.org/documents/2009_GDACS_overview (Accessed April, 2010).

115. www.unisdr.org/who-we-are/history (Accessed July 9, 2015).

116. www.unisdr.org/2005/wcdr/wcdr-index (Accessed July 9, 2015).

117. www.preventionweb.net/english/hyogo/isdr/history (Accessed April 19, 2010). See also Damon P. Coppola, *Introduction to International Disaster Management* (Burlington, MA: Elsevier, 2007).

118. www.unisdr/org/eng/about_isdr/basic_docs/SG-report/SG-Report-64–280-eng (Accessed April 19, 2010).

119. www.preventionweb.net/english/about (Accessed April 24, 2010).

120. www.unisdr.org/?pid:50&pih:2 (Accessed April 27, 2020).

121. See Reid Basher, *Global Early Warning Systems for Natural Hazards: Systematic and People-Centered* (London: Philosophical Transactions of the Royal Society, 2006).

122. www.preventionweb.net/english/professional/news (Accessed July 9, 2015).

123. www.who.int/violence_injury_preventon/publications/road_traffic/world_report/en/index (Accessed June 9, 2010).

124. Michael A. R. Bernhard, *Global Road Safety and Accident Prevention: How the United Nations, the European Union and the World Health Organization Interrelate in the Legal, Technical and Promotional Sectors* (June 2004). www.fiva.org/CommonDownloads/GLOBALROADSAFETY (Accessed June 9, 2010).

125. www.who.int/roadsafety/ministerial_conference/en/index (Accessed June 5, 2010).

126. United Nations Office on Drugs and Crime, *A Century of International Drug Control* (New York: UN Publications, 2008), pp. 7–32.

127. Ibid., pp. 52–53.

128. Cheever and Haviland, p. 180.

129. William B. McAllister, *Drug Diplomacy in the Twentieth Century* (New York: Routledge, 2000), p. 86.

130. UN Office on Drugs and Crime, p. 59.

131. As of 2008, the Convention had 183 parties. UN Office on Drugs and Crime, p. 60.

132. www.incb.org/incb/en/mandate (Accessed May 12, 2010).

133. www.incb.org/incb/en/membership_actual (Accessed May 12, 2010).

134. Vladimir Kuševic, "Drug Abuse Control and International Treaties," *Journal of Drug Issues* Vol. 7, No. 1 (Winter 1977), pp. 35–53.

135. UN Office on Drugs and Crime, pp. 68–70.

136. David P. Stewart, "Internationalizing the War on Drugs: The UN Convention against Illicit Traffic in Narcotic Drugs and Psychotropic Substances," *Denver Journal of International Law and Policy* Vol. 18, No. 3 (Spring 1990), pp. 387–404.

137. www.fatf-gafi.org/pages and www.fatf-gafi.org/document (Accessed May 16, 2010).

138. Mendy Bentham, *The Politics of Drug Control* (London: Macmillan, 1998), pp. 106–110.

139. www.un.org/documents/ga/res/46/a46r104 (Accessed May 16, 2010).

140. www.unodc.org/unodc/en/about-unodc/index (Accessed May 2, 2010). See also, *infra*, this chapter, under crime control.

141. www.ungassondruds.org/index (Accessed May 15, 2010).

142. International Penal and Prison Congress (Ithaca, NY: Cornell University Library, Digital Collection).

143. www.interpol.int/Public/ICPO/default (Accessed May 19, 2010).

144. www/un.org/ar/conf/crimecongress2010/pdf/55years_ebook (Accessed May 21, 2010).

145. www.unodc.org/unodc/en/crime-congress (Accessed October 18, 2012).

146. www.unac.org/en/link_learn/monitoring/susdev_bodies_crime (Accessed May 21, 2010).

147. www.unodc.org/unodc/en/commissions/CCPCJ/index (Accessed May 17, 2010).

148. www.unodc.org/unodc/en/treaties/CTOC/index (Accessed May 23, 2010).

149. Ibid.

150. UN Foundation. *UN Wire* on line (May 29, 2014). http://mail.google.com/mail (Accessed June 9, 2014).

151. www.uncjin.org/Documents/Conventions/ (Accessed May 26, 2010).

152. Ibid.

153. www.unodc.org/pdf/crime/a_res_55/255e (Accessed May 26, 2010).

154. www.uncjin.org/Documents/corrupt (Accessed May 27, 2010).

155. www.unafei.or.jp/english/pdf/PDF (Accessed May 27, 2010).

156. www.unodc.org/unodc/en/treaties/CAC/index (Accessed May 26, 2010).

157. www.unodc.org/unodc/en/money-laundering/partnerships (Accessed May 15, 2010).

158. www.unodc.org/unodc/en/terrorism/index (Accessed September 4, 2012).

159. Ibid.

160. www.unicri.it/wwa/contacts/location (Accessed June 2, 2010).

161. www.unodc.org/unodc/en/commissions/CCPCJ/institutes (Accessed May 23, 2010).

162. www.ifs.univie.ac.at/uncjim2/mosaic/handbook (Accessed June 3, 2010).

Chapter 8

Human Rights and the Diplomatic Process

For the longest time, literally until the Second World War, human rights were a matter of domestic jurisdiction, that is, practically left to the sovereign authority of the national state. Nations or international organizations were expected not to meddle with foreign human rights issues. Human rights were not on the diplomatic agenda. There were exceptions. Nineteenth-century agreements protected religious groups in the Ottoman Empire and the 1919 Peace Conference led to treaties protecting minorities created by the redrawing of international boundaries. But the international community was not attuned to the larger issue of the international protection of human rights.

Earlier efforts to reduce the barbarity of war had led to the development of rules of international law applicable in international armed conflicts as found in Hugo Grotius's 1625 treatise.[1] The nineteenth century, with the creation of the International Committee of the Red Cross (ICRC), saw the development of more international rules—for example, for the protection of the wounded in the field. More rules of war were written at the Hague Conferences in 1899 and 1907. However, these rules were not perceived as protecting *individual* human rights. *States* were undertaking the obligation to follow the law of war—for example, to care for the wounded and sick. This was eventually characterized as humanitarian law. At the time, individuals were seen as objects (not subjects) of law in the international legal system (in the sense that states had rights and obligations under international law, the object of which was the protection of individuals. These individuals did not have an international right to protection). This legal practice was not limited to the field of humanitarian law. It pertained to the place of the private individual in international law. Eventually this conceptualization began to change as global society evolved.[2]

THE INTERNATIONAL LABOUR ORGANIZATION

International concern for the well-being of workers and their human rights goes back to the nineteenth century. Widespread exploitation and abusive conditions in the workplace led to reform movements, unrest, and calls to revolt. The International Socialist Congress (Paris, 1889) created the new Socialist International ("The Second International"). Then came the Bolshevik Revolution of November 1917 in Russia, and the Communist International or Comintern ("The Third International"), founded in Moscow in March 1919.[3] These momentous developments were among the factors leading the nations assembled at the Paris Peace Conference to create an unprecedented institution, the International Labour Organization (ILO), to address the protection of workers, worldwide.[4] It was incorporated into the Versailles Treaty, but independently from the League of Nations.[5] It was the first large-scale effort to protect human rights, although it was not yet presented as a matter of human rights.

ILO is now a UN Specialized Agency with a current membership of 185 states. Its structure is unusual. Each member state is represented by two government delegates, as well as one labor and one management representative chosen by each government in consultation "with the industrial organizations, if such organizations exist, which are most representative of employers or workpeople, as the case may be, in their respective countries" (ILO Constitution, Art. 3). Labor and management representatives participate and vote independently. They do not have to support the policies of their home states so that labor delegates, for example, can coalesce to defend labor interests across national lines, an unprecedented arrangement in international organization and a pioneering venture to hear the voice of civil society in global diplomacy.

Labor issues are thus effectively debated at the ILO annual meeting (the "International Labour Conference")[6] which creates international labor standards (the "International Labor Code") by enacting conventions which are binding upon ratification. It can also issue nonbinding recommendations. To date, the ILO has adopted almost 200 conventions and more than 180 recommendations.[7] An executive organ, "the Governing Body," is made up of twenty-eight government delegates and fourteen labor and fourteen management representatives. Ten of the government delegates must be from the states of "chief industrial importance." The labor and management representatives are "elected respectively by the Employers' and the Workers' delegates to the Conference."[8] The ILO Secretariat (the International Labour Office, in Geneva) is headed by a director-general, elected by the Governing Body. From the very beginning he has been a labor activist, a leader in the ILO's diplomatic process.

The ILO has taken steps to foster the implementation of the labor conventions. Member states must report regularly on the extent to which their laws and practices conform to ILO standards, and what steps they have taken to secure the ratification of the conventions. Governments are required to submit copies of their reports to employers' and workers' organizations. These organizations may comment on the governments' reports and send observations on the application of the conventions directly to the ILO.[9] A Committee of Experts on the Application of Conventions and Recommendations examines the government reports and submits an annual report on issues of implementation identifying the governments concerned. The experts' report is sent to the International Labour Conference where it is examined by the Conference Committee on the Application of Standards (made up of government, employer, and worker delegates).

The governments identified by the experts as involved in implementation problems are invited to respond before the Conference Committee and provide information on the situations discussed in the experts' report. The Conference Committee, in many cases, recommends that these governments take specific steps to remedy identified problems or invite ILO missions to provide assistance, or seek technical help. The Conference Committee's discussion and recommendations are published in its report (available online) thus contributing to international accountability. Situations of special significance are highlighted in these reports.[10] The ILO has also devised complaint procedures that can be initiated against states that fail to comply with the conventions they have ratified, and a Committee on Freedom of Association reviews complaints concerning violations of workers' rights whether or not a member state has ratified the relevant conventions.[11]

The ILO is concerned about the condition of labor in the developing world and is involved in Decent Work Country Programs, and poverty reduction. It administers programs in education, skills development, and employability,[12] and maintains, in cooperation with the Italian government, the ILO Training Center in Turin (established in 1964) using ILO's expertise on human-resources development and capacity building. The ILO's global Gender Network organizes an annual Inter-Regional Learning Forum in which the ILO's work on gender equality is discussed.[13] The ILO works with other UN agencies on joint projects, for example, with UNESCO on migration and the human rights of migrant workers, and with UNAIDS on the protection of workers with HIV. The ILO also remains in contact with the ECOSOC, which coordinates the UN's Specialized Agencies' network and helps in a variety of activities of vital importance for the well-being of working people worldwide.

Research and information are important parts of ILO's mission. Economic and labor market analysis is used in the ILO's large employment program.[14]

The International Institute for Labour Studies was established by the ILO in Geneva in 1960. It publishes the annual *World of Work Report* and the *International Labour Review*, a global, multidisciplinary journal of labor and social policy, and it also publishes books and reports. The Institute is a center for policy dialogue among ILO members, staff, the academic community, and policymakers by means of policy forums, seminars, panel discussions, online conferences, and study visits. The Institute offers an annual Internship Course on Labour and Social Policies for the Promotion of Decent Work. The course is intended for middle-level officials in ministries of labor and in employers' and workers' organizations who are expected to rise to positions of greater responsibility. About 20 fellowships are offered including travel and living expenses in Geneva. The three component groups of the ILO Governing Body nominate the countries and organizations to be invited. The final selection is the responsibility of the director of the International Institute.[15]

THE LEAGUE OF NATIONS

The League Covenant itself contained no mention of human rights, although the League had occasion to show its interest in some international aspects of human rights. In 1924, the League Council appointed a Temporary Slavery Commission whose report led to the 1926 Convention to Suppress the Slave Trade and Slavery.[16] The League was also concerned about the rights of the child, as a result of the endeavors of the International Save the Children Union (Geneva), an NGO that adopted the first children's rights proclamation in 1923. The League of Nations endorsed this proclamation in September 1926 as the Geneva Declaration on the Rights of the Child.[17] But it took the monstrous Nazi abuses of the late 1930s and war years to change international attitudes. Allied pronouncements, particularly President Roosevelt's, stressed the international protection of human rights as an important objective of the war effort. This concern for global human rights remained strong during the negotiations to create the UN, particularly in San Francisco, and the UN Charter reflects this new outlook.

THE UNITED NATIONS

The Preamble of the UN Charter proclaims:

> "We the Peoples of the United Nations, determined . . . to reaffirm faith in fundamental human rights, in the dignity and worth of the human person, in the equal rights of men and women and of nations large and small . . . have resolved to combine our efforts to accomplish these aims."

Article 1 specifies that the purposes of the UN are:

> to achieve international cooperation in solving international problems of an economic, social, cultural, or humanitarian character, and in promoting and encouraging respect for human rights and for fundamental freedoms for all without distinction as to race, sex, language, or religion

In Article 56, UN members "pledge themselves to take joint and separate action in co-operation with the Organization for the achievement of the purposes set forth in Article 55," namely, "universal respect for, and observance of, human rights and fundamental freedoms for all without distinction as to race, sex, language, or religion." UN member states thus undertook a formal obligation to respect and observe human rights. The powers conferred upon the UN, however, remain limited. The General Assembly is authorized to "initiate studies and make recommendations for the purpose of . . . assisting in the realization of human rights and fundamental freedoms" (Article 13), and the ECOSOC is likewise given the power to make recommendations for the same purpose (Article 62)—in other words, much less than might have been expected from the wartime pronouncements. Nevertheless, the ECOSOC is given the mandate to "set up commissions . . . for the promotion of human rights," and this is how it proceeded. In the course of its first meeting, the ECOSOC created its first Functional Commission, the Commission on Human Rights (December 10, 1946), composed of eighteen countries chosen by the ECOSOC itself with due regard for geographical distribution.[18] At its first meeting the new Commission made the crucial decision of unanimously electing Eleanor Roosevelt as chair.[19] Her stature, skill, and dedication would soon be critical elements in its work. Another momentous early decision was to embark upon the ambitious task of drafting an International Bill of Human Rights.

It was a challenging task. There was no enunciation anywhere of the human rights to be universally protected. Each nation state has its own political system and its own culture. Even Western democracies, despite their long-standing interest in the protection of human rights, had different views as to what those rights were. For example, in the United States, segregation was still the law of the land in 1946. Some countries, for example, the United Kingdom, wanted those rights identified in a binding treaty, which would have made agreement even more difficult. In late 1947, the Commission agreed to start with a nonbinding declaration, to be followed later by a binding instrument and still later, by measures of implementation.

But the task remained a difficult one. The negotiations took enormous patience and diplomatic skill. Remarkably, it was accomplished in about one year, a feat matched only by the historic approval of the Universal

Declaration of Human Rights by the General Assembly on December 10, 1948, *without a dissenting vote.*[20] Eight countries abstained (the Soviet Bloc, Saudi Arabia, and South Africa). For all their opposition to some of the rights included in the Universal Declaration, they did not vote against it. Given its Marxist-Leninist ideology, one can imagine how the Soviet Bloc reacted to, say, Article 18: "Everyone has the right to freedom of thought, conscience and religion; this right includes freedom to change his religion or belief, and freedom, either alone or in community with others and in public or private, to manifest his religion or belief in teaching, practice, worship and observance." For Saudi Arabia "freedom to change his religion or belief" is equally jolting. It is significant, however, that the communist states of Europe formally accepted the Universal Declaration of Human Rights in 1975 in the Final Act of the Helsinki Conference on Security and Cooperation in Europe, which specifies: "In the field of human rights and fundamental freedoms, the participating states will act in conformity with the purposes and principles of the Charter of the United Nations and with the Universal Declaration of Human Rights. They will also fulfill their obligations as set forth in the international declarations and agreements in this field" (Final Act).

The Universal Declaration is very comprehensive and straightforward in its presentation of universal human rights. It includes *civil and political rights*, for example, freedom of expression, the right of assembly, and the right to take part in government (Articles 19–21); *legal rights* such as equality before the law, freedom from arbitrary arrest, and the right of due process of law (Articles 7–11); *personal rights*, including freedom of movement, the right to found a family with the free and full consent of the intending spouses, and the right to own property (Articles 12–18); *economic rights*, among them, the right to work (free from any discrimination), the right to rest, and the right to join labor unions (Articles 22–25); and finally, *social and cultural rights*, including the right to education and to participate in cultural life (Articles 26–28). The Universal Declaration also clarifies that "everyone has duties to the community in which alone the free and full development of his personality is possible" (Article 29).

This Declaration was not a treaty, but it quickly acquired enormous respect and authority in global society. It was invoked to condemn national violations of human rights, and given the effect of international law. The US Court of Appeals, in the case of *Filartiga v. Pena-Irala* (1980), illustrated this transformation when it reasoned:

> This Declaration [in this case, the UN General Assembly Declaration on the Protection of all Persons from Torture], like the Declaration of Human Rights before it, was adopted without dissent by the General Assembly.

These UN declarations are significant because they specify with great precision the obligations of member nations under the Charter. Since their adoption, "members can no longer contend that they do not know what human rights they promised in the Charter to promote." Moreover, a UN declaration is, according to one authoritative definition, "a formal and solemn instrument, suitable for rare occasions when principles of great and lasting importance are being enunciated" (34 UN ESCOR, Supp. [No.8] 15, U.N. Doc. E/cn. 4/1/610 [1982] [memorandum of Office of Legal Affairs, UN Secretariat]). Accordingly, it has been observed that the Universal Declaration of Human Rights "no longer fits into the dichotomy of 'binding treaty' against 'non-binding pronouncement,' but is rather an authoritative statement of the international community." E. Schwelb, Human Rights and the International Community 70 (1964).[21]

The UN Commission on Human Rights, having achieved its first objective, set out to convert the Universal Declaration into legally binding treaty rights. But, as anticipated in 1947, producing a human rights treaty proved to be a much more difficult task. To facilitate the negotiations, it was decided to draft two documents: an International Covenant on Civil and Political Rights and an International Covenant on Economic, Social and Cultural Rights. But deciding how the terms of the Universal Declaration could be made into rules of law remained extremely controversial. It took eighteen years before the two Covenants could be approved by the General Assembly and opened for signature in December 1966. It took another ten years before they entered into force in 1976 upon ratification by thirty-five states.[22] The Civil and Political Rights Covenant now has 168 parties[23] and the Economic, Social and Cultural Rights Covenant 164.[24]

Aside from these important Covenants, the UN was given to address other, more specialized, human rights issues, some of them taking a different diplomatic path. The Commission on the Status of Women, established by the ECOSOC in June 1946, formulated a considerable number of international conventions adopted by the General Assembly—for example, for the protection of the political rights of women, which was particularly important as in 1945, only 25 of the original 51 UN member states allowed equal voting rights for women. The new convention was the first international law instrument to recognize the right of women anywhere to vote, run for office, and exercise any public function.[25] More conventions for women were adopted over the years, including the 1979 Convention on the Elimination of All Forms of Discrimination against Women.[26] Some of these treaties were subsequently supplemented by international protocols.

The development of UN human rights conventions has been a continuing process as a variety of UN bodies faced human rights issues in their own areas of specialization, for example, UNESCO with regard to education, or the ILO with regard to the Convention on Equal Remuneration for Men and Women for Work of Equal Value. All of this has led to a large body of UN human rights conventions that will continue to grow in the future (see Textbox 8.1).

Textbox 8.1   Post-1945 Global Human Rights Conventions

1. Convention on the Prevention and the Punishment of the Crime of Genocide, 1948.
2. Convention for the Suppression of the Traffic in Persons and of the Exploitation of the Prostitution of Others, 1949.
3. Convention Relating to the Status of Refugees, 1951.
4. Convention on the International Right of Correction, 1952.
5. Convention on the Political Rights of Women, 1952
6. Protocol Amending the 1926 Slavery Convention, 1953.
7. Convention Relating to the Status of Stateless Persons, 1954.
8. Supplementary Convention on the Abolition of Slavery, the Slave Trade, and Institutions and Practices Similar to Slavery, 1956.
9. Convention on the Nationality of Married Women, 1957.
10. Convention against Discrimination in Education, 1960.
11. Convention on the Reduction of Statelessness, 1961.
12. Convention on Consent to Marriage, Minimum Age for Marriage and Registration of Marriages, 1962.
13. Protocol Instituting a Conciliation and Good Offices Commission to be Responsible for Seeking the Settlement of Any Disputes which May Arise between States Parties to the Convention against Discrimination in Education, 1962.
14. International Convention on the Elimination of All Forms of Racial Discrimination, 1965.
15. Protocol Relating to the Status of Refugees, 1966.
16. International Covenant on Civil and Political Rights, 1966.
17. Optional Protocol to the International Covenant on Civil and Political Rights, 1966.
18. International Covenant on Economic, Social and Cultural Rights, 1966.
19. Convention on the Non-Applicability of Statutory Limitations to War Crimes and Crimes against Humanity, 1968.
20. International Convention on the Suppression and Punishment of the Crime of Apartheid, 1973.
21. Convention on the Elimination of All Forms of Discrimination against Women, 1979.
22. Convention against Torture and Other Cruel, Inhuman or Degrading Treatment or Punishment, 1984.
23. International Convention against Apartheid in Sports, 1985.
24. Convention on the Rights of the Child, 1989.
25. Second Optional Protocol to the International Covenant on Civil and Political Rights, Aiming at the Abolition of the Death Penalty, 1989.
26. International Convention on the Protection of the Rights of All Migrant Workers and Members of Their Families, 1990.

27. Agreement Establishing the Fund for the Development of the Indigenous Peoples of Latin America and the Caribbean, 1992.
28. Amendments to Articles 17 (7), and 18 (5) of the Convention against Torture and Other Cruel, Inhuman or Degrading Treatment or Punishment, 1992.
29. Amendment to Article 20 (1) of the Convention on the Elimination of All Forms of Discrimination against Women, 1995.
30. Amendment to Article 43 (2) of the Convention on the Right of the Child, 1995.
31. Optional Protocol to the Convention on the Elimination of All Forms of Discrimination against Women, 1999.
32. Optional Protocol to the Convention on the Rights of the Child on the Involvement of Children in Armed Conflict, 2000.
33. Optional Protocol to the Convention on the Rights of the Child on the Sale of Children, Child Prostitution and Child Pornography, 2000.
34. Optional Protocol to the Convention against Torture and Other Cruel, Inhuman or Degrading Treatment or Punishment, 2002.
35. Convention on the Rights of Persons with Disabilities, 2006.
36. Optional Protocol to the Convention on the Rights of Persons with Disabilities, 2006.
37. International Convention for the Protection of All Persons from Enforced Disappearance, 2006.
38. Optional Protocol to the International Covenant on Economic, Social and Cultural Rights, 2008.

Note: This listing does not include the conventions adopted by the International Labour Organization (ILO), which as of June 2010, numbers 188, counted from its inception in 1919. A large number of these labor conventions (constituting the International Labor Code) implement human rights acknowledged in the Universal Declaration of Human Rights, for example, the Convention on the Right to Organize and Collective Bargaining (1949) or the Convention on the Abolition of Forced Labor (1957). See a full list of these conventions at www.ilo.org/ilolex/english/convdisp1 (Accessed June 15, 2010).
Sources: United Nations, *Human Rights: A Compilation of International Instruments of the United Nations* (New York: United Nations, 1968), and United Nations, *Status of Treaties*. IV. Human Rights, http://treaties.un.org/Pages/Treaties (Accessed June 17, 2010).

The UN General Assembly has also adopted nonbinding declarations which are easier to negotiate and often serve as a foundation for subsequent negotiations for international conventions (see Textbox 8.2).

It must be noted also that authoritative declarations help the creation of international regimes—informal acceptance by states and other international actors of modes of international behavior. International norms can also lead to the development of unwritten rules of law.[27] Legal practice has tended to settle on two criteria for the use of such declarations as law: they must be in the form of a rule (or rules) of general application, and they must have

Textbox 8.2 Human Rights Declarations Contained in General Assembly Resolutions

1. Universal Declaration of Human Rights, December 10, 1948. (*)
2. Declaration of the Rights of the Child, November 20, 1959. (*)
3. Declaration on the Granting of Independence to Colonial Countries and Peoples, December 14, 1960.
4. Declaration on the Elimination of All Forms of Racial Discrimination, November 20, 1963. (*)
5. Declaration on the Elimination of Discrimination against Women, November 7, 1967. (*)
6. Declaration on Territorial Asylum, December 14, 1967.
7. Declaration on Social Progress and Development, December 11, 1969.
8. Declaration on the Rights of Mentally Retarded Persons, December 20, 1971.
9. Charter of Economic Rights and Duties of States, December 12, 1974.
10. Declaration on the Protection of Women and Children in Emergency and Armed Conflict, December 14, 1974.
11. Declaration on the Rights of Disabled Persons, December 9, 1975.
12. Declaration on the Protection of All Persons from Being Subjected to Torture and Other Cruel, Inhuman or Degrading Treatment or Punishment, December 9, 1975. (*)
13. International Declaration against Apartheid in Sports, December 14, 1977. (*)
14. Declaration on Namibia and Program of Action in Support of Self-Determination and National Independence for Namibia, May 3, 1978.
15. Charter of Rights for Migrant Workers in Southern Africa, December 20, 1978.
16. Declaration on the Elimination of All Forms of Intolerance and of Discrimination Based on Religion or Belief, November 25, 1981.
17. Principles of Medical Ethics Relevant to the Role of Health Personnel, Particularly Physicians, in the Protection of Prisoners and Detainees against Torture and Other Cruel, Inhuman or Degrading Treatment or Punishment, December 18, 1982. (*)
18. Declaration on the Participation of Women in Promoting International Peace and Cooperation, December 3, 1982.
19. Declaration on the Rights of Peoples to Peace, November 12, 1984.
20. Declaration of Basic Principles of Justice for Victims of Crime and Abuse of Power, November 29, 1985.
21. Declaration on the Human Rights of Individuals Who Are Not Nationals of the Country in Which They Live, December 13, 1985.
22. Declaration on Social and Legal Principles Relating to the Protection and Welfare of Children, with Special Reference to Foster Placement and Adoption Nationally and Internationally, December 3, 1986.
23. Declaration on the Right to Development, December 4, 1986.
24. Body of Principles for the Protection of All Persons under Any Form of Detention or Imprisonment, December 9, 1988.
25. Declaration on Apartheid and Its Destructive Consequences in Southern Africa, December 14, 1989.
26. Basic Principles for the Treatment of Prisoners, December 14, 1990.
27. United Nations Principles for Older Persons, December 16, 1991.
28. Principles for the Protection of Persons with Mental Illness and for the Improvement of Mental Health Care, December 17, 1991.

29. Declaration of the Rights of Persons Belonging to National or Ethnic, Religious and Linguistic Minorities, December 18, 1992.
30. Declaration on the Protection of All Persons from Enforced Disappearance, December 18, 1992. (*)
31. Standard Rules on the Equalization of Opportunities for Persons with Disabilities, December 20, 1993. (*)
32. Principles Relating to the Status of National Institutions for the Promotion and Protection of Human Rights (Paris Principles), December 20, 1993.
33. Declaration on the Elimination of Violence against Women, December 20, 1993
34. Declaration on the Right and Responsibility of Individuals, Groups and Organs of Society to Promote and Protect Universally Recognized Human Rights and Fundamental Freedoms, December 9, 1998.
35. Declaration Reaffirming Commitment to the Goals and Objectives of the Beijing Declaration and Platform for Action and the Nairobi Forward-Looking Strategies for the Advancement of Women, June 10, 2000.
36. United Nations Millennium Declaration, September 8, 2000.
37. World Summit Declaration Reaffirming the United Nations Millennium Declaration, September 25, 2005.
38. Basic Principles and Guidelines on the Right to a Remedy and Reparation for Victims of Gross Violations of International Human Rights Law and Serious Violations of International Humanitarian Law, December 16, 2005.
39. United Nations Declaration on the Rights of Indigenous Peoples, September 13, 2007.
40. Declaration Reaffirming Commitment to the Implementation of the Declaration and Plan of Action of the Special Session of the General Assembly on Children, December 13, 2007.
41. Declaration on the Sixtieth Anniversary of the Universal Declaration of Human Rights, December 10, 2008.

Source: www.un.org/documents/instruments/docs_subj_en (Accessed June 25, 2010). Declarations identified with (*) were subsequently written into international conventions.

general support—consensus or support from states across the global political spectrum.[28]

Aside from the development of international conventions and declarations, the protection of human rights has taken other forms. The Commission on the Status of Women recommended to the General Assembly that 1975 be designated as International Women's Year in observance of the Commission's 25th anniversary. The Commission also called for the organization of an international conference to coincide with International Women's Year. The conference was held in Mexico City and was attended by 133 governments while 6,000 representatives of NGOs convened in a parallel forum. The women's movement worldwide is probably the best hope for the elimination of discrimination. More global women's conferences were held in Copenhagen (1980), Nairobi (1985), and Beijing (1995), the latter being the largest ever.[29]

In addition to the Commission on the Status of Women, a number of UN bodies were created to foster women's rights: the International Research and Training Institute for the Advancement of Women (INSTRAW), established in 1976; the UN Development Fund for Women (UNIFEM), created later in the same year; and the Office of the Special Adviser on Gender Issues and Advancement of Women (OSAGI), which was established in 1997. Then, in 2010, after years of negotiations between UN member states, and civil society women's groups, the UN General Assembly created a new agency called UN Women, merging the UN Secretariat's Division for the Advancement of Women and the three institutions just mentioned. This consolidated body is intended to help UN member states to implement women's rights and hold the UN system accountable for its application of these rights.[30]

Implementing human rights, particularly the UN Conventions, has been a difficult and frustrating issue. The UN's initial efforts to protect human rights created great expectations and began to generate large numbers of petitions from individuals and NGOs. From 1947 to 1957, some 65,000 such communications were received by the UN, even reaching 20,000 annually in later years.[31] But the UN Commission on Human Rights decided that it had no power to take any action in regard to any complaints concerning human rights, and that decision was confirmed by the ECOSOC, its parent organization,[32] which of course meant that the member states serving on these bodies were against facing the implementation problems surfacing in the petitions. A large number of states have remained opposed to the creation of implementation procedures. Many have a poor human rights record. They coalesce to preserve their lack of accountability and block efforts to investigate allegations of human rights violations. If enough member states refuse to act, nothing gets done.

In 1965, developing countries wanted action against apartheid in South Africa and racial discrimination elsewhere. The General Assembly requested action eventually leading the ECOSOC to empower the Human Right Commission to devise a variety of procedures to investigate and publicly discuss human rights violations. In the late sixties, the Human Rights Commission appointed working groups focused on events in only three areas: South Africa, Palestine, and Chile—the latter then under Pinochet. The international outcry was very selective. After 1979, however, many situations were discussed in the Commission, and the threat of formal condemnation led some governments to initiate corrective measures.[33] Nevertheless the Commission was attacked for failing to discuss some notorious violators such as Iran and China.

In 1989, the UN General Assembly called for a World Conference on Human Rights to assess progress made since the Universal Declaration. Much was done to make it a success. Four Preparatory Committee meetings took place in 1991 in the course of which governments, dozens of UN bodies, international organizations, and thousands of NGOs dialogued. Three regional meetings (in Africa, Latin America and the Caribbean, and Asia) as well as informal meetings elsewhere, provided their views of the progress made. The World Conference met in Vienna in 1993 and brought together 171 governments, 7,000 participants from the human rights community, international organizations, academics, experts, and representatives from more than 800 NGOs. They produced a plan of action which recommended the appointment of a UN High Commissioner for Human Rights to oversee efforts in the field. The General Assembly created the post the same year with the rank of under-secretary-general.[34] The document also called for the creation of a Special Rapporteur on Violence against Women (appointed in 1994).[35] The Conference made provision for a 5-year implementation review in 1998 by the Human Right Commission, the ECOSOC, and the General Assembly.[36]

The membership of the Human Rights Commission (as elected by the ECOSOC) undermined the Commission's legitimacy as a number of states became members despite their dismal human rights records. These states included Cuba, Saudi Arabia, and even Sudan, despite its role in Darfur.[37] Worse yet, Libya served as chair of the Commission in 2003 in total disregard of its own human rights abuses and past involvement in international terrorism. The politicization of the Commission's proceedings became a major issue. Member states focused on the misdeeds of their opponents while attempting to shield their own allies, not an unusual occurrence in international politics, but a serious liability in an institution supposed to monitor human rights performance.[38] In 2005 UN Secretary-General Kofi Annan declared, in a statement to the UN General Assembly, "the Commission's capacity to perform its tasks has been increasingly undermined by its declining credibility and professionalism,"[39] a remarkable acknowledgment on the part of the UN chief diplomat.

The 2005 UN World Summit meeting followed through on the secretary-general's statement and replaced the Human Rights Commission with a new Human Rights Council, raising expectations among some human rights advocates. But in the end, the main flaws remained. The new Council is still too large with 47 member states (instead of 53 for the Commission) elected by an absolute majority of the General Assembly, instead of the two-thirds majority sought by the secretary-general. Although it is an improvement over the election of the Commission by the 54 state members of the ECOSOC, there is no rule to prevent human rights violators from being elected to the new Council. The selection is supposed to be done in the diplomatic process leading up to the election. And some of it does take place: Iran lost its bid to become a member of the new Council in 2006. But, in the give and take of the negotiations, deals are made; networks support their own allies, particularly as nominations are done by the five regional groups (for the sake of balanced geographic distribution). In 2010, the number of candidates proposed by each region *equaled* the number of seats earmarked for the region! The General Assembly was not given a choice of candidates—although unwanted candidates could have been denied a majority. Libya received the lowest number of votes of any country in any region—but still won 155. Not promising.[40]

The Millennium Summit contributed to the protection of a number of human rights in its advocacy for the MDGs and the massive campaign it launched to reach them. Among them were far-reaching efforts to combat poverty, hunger, illiteracy, child mortality, disease, and to foster gender equality. Some UN agencies, in *their specialized humanitarian missions, are implementing human rights* "on the ground" by physically helping the victims of various conditions such as destitution. This is not enforcing human rights by punishing violators. But it works by feeding the hungry and providing the means for a more decent existence—a different kind of human rights work by such bodies as UNICEF and the WHO. The UN is deeply involved in humanitarian pursuits protecting human rights.

Civil society and NGOs deserve more attention than is given them in the field of human rights. They played an important role in San Francisco pressing negotiators to include human rights provisions into the UN Charter, and their efforts have continued. Their advocacy has contributed to keeping human rights on the diplomatic agenda. They expose abuses and seek to protect victims. Technology has given them better means of communication and more groups have joined the campaign. NGOs network and cooperate with groups having different specializations. It may be difficult to lobby governments in totalitarian societies or in corrupt political systems but pressure can be applied internationally. NGOs are heard in international conferences and in their representatives' endeavors to influence the diplomatic process. In fact, international organizations are now more conscious of their importance, and are helping them play a greater role. The Commission on the Status of Women involved them in their work from the outset. It is true that civil society actors and NGOs can be unwieldy. The alienated are more inclined to protest and disrupt. But many are anxious to contribute to social change and can be constructive partners in a variety of international ventures. A more systematic harnessing of their power is worth adding to the diplomacy of human rights.

REGIONAL LEVEL

In the promotion of human rights much has been done at the regional level. And it must be remembered that regional accomplishments are a direct result of what has been done at the global level starting in 1945, and more particularly with the 1948 approval of the Universal Declaration.

Europe

The European Convention on Human Rights was signed on November 4, 1950. It was created by the Council of Europe (COE) and deals mainly with civil and political rights. Ratification of the Convention is now a prerequisite to become a member of the COE, which means that 47 states are bound by this human rights Convention. Furthermore, these rights are enforceable in the European Court of Human Rights, a remarkable development. Not only can member states bring human rights violations before the court, but private individuals may also bring a case against a state—even against their own state, and this is unprecedented.[41] With the demise of the Soviet Union and satellite regimes, so many people have sought redress from abusive conditions under their former communist governments that the entire redress system had to be expanded and simplified in 1998 to face the spectacular increase of the Court's caseload. However, the number of cases received continued to grow, reaching 27,200 in 2003 when around 65,000 applications were already pending. In 2004, the Committee of Ministers of the COE adopted Protocol 14 to improve once again the Court's effectiveness. The Protocol was designed also to help the Committee of Ministers, which supervises the execution of judgments. But the number of cases continued to increase. In 2009, 57,200 applications were allocated to the Convention's judicial bodies. The backlog reached 119,300 applications. A ministerial conference on the future of the Court was held in 2010 and developed an Action Plan to address the issue with short- and middle-term measures. But another revision of the Court process will probably take place. In the meantime, the European human rights program and its judicial enforcement system are making an important contribution. It must be noted also that European Court of Human Rights decisions can be appealed to the Grand Chamber of the Court[42]—an option that is still rare enough in the international judicial process. Grand Chamber judgments are final. Once it has been decided that a violation of the European Convention occurred, the state concerned must prevent future recurrence. The payment of compensation may be ordered. Court judgments are monitored by the Committee of Ministers of the COE to assist victims and ensure that judgments are carried out.

It is important to remember that these developments would have been unthinkable prior to 1950. However, less was done with economic, social, and cultural rights. The European Social Charter was adopted in 1981 and protects rights pertaining, for instance, to housing, health, education, and employment. It was revised in 1996 but remains outside the enforcement procedures found in the European Convention on Human Rights. The application of the Charter is monitored by the European Committee of Social Rights composed of independent experts serving six-year terms. States must submit annual reports on how they have followed the Charter standards. These reports are reviewed by the Committee, which publishes its findings as "Conclusions." If a state ignores a finding of violation, the Committee of Ministers of the COE will request rectification—but this does not match the enforcement measures of the Human Rights Convention. An additional Protocol to the European Social Charter entered into force in 1998 permitting workers' groups and NGOs to file collective complaints. But the Protocol had been ratified by only 14 states by March 2010.[43]

The COE negotiated additional instruments for the protection of human rights in Europe. In 1987, it adopted the European Convention for the Prevention of Torture and Inhuman or Degrading Treatment or Punishment, later supplemented by two protocols. The convention has been ratified by all 47 members of the COE, and is now a precondition for joining the Council.[44] Interestingly, non-COE member states are now allowed to become parties to the Convention. It is monitored by the Committee for the Prevention of Torture, composed of independent impartial experts (one per signatory state). Committee members may pay unscheduled visits to places of detention, as well as mental health and elderly care institutions, and are allowed to interview privately people detained there as well as any other person who may provide relevant information, including NGOs concerned with human rights. The Committee writes reports on country visits, making recommendations to ensure prevention of ill treatment. Governments are required to respond to the Committee's recommendations and the Committee may issue public statements if these governments fail to address its recommendations.[45]

The COE also adopted a European Charter for Regional or Minority Languages in 1992 and a Framework Convention for the Protection of National Minorities in 1995,[46] the first post–Second World War treaty to offer protection to minorities (particularly significant in light of the radical political changes in Central and Eastern Europe following the collapse of the Soviet Union). The Convention is monitored by the Committee of Ministers of the COE, assisted by an Advisory Committee of Independent Experts. In addition, in 1993, the Council established a European Commission against Racism and Intolerance (one government-appointed member per member state, but serving independently). In 1999, the Council created a Commissioner for Human Rights[47] whose function is to promote respect for human rights in the 47 member states with country visits and dialogues with national authorities and civil society.

All members of the EU have ratified the European Convention on Human Rights and accepted the jurisdiction of the Human Rights Court. The EU, however, is a separate legal entity. It has its own Court of Justice. Problems have been avoided in that the Court of Justice of the EU declared, in a series of decisions, that respect for human rights was a part of the general principles of law the Court was required to apply, and that it looked to the European Convention on Human Rights in determining the nature of those rights.[48] It is to be noted also that the Maastricht Treaty (which transformed the European Community into the EU), declared, under Title I, Common Provisions, Article F(2): "The Union shall respect fundamental rights, as guaranteed by the European Convention for the Protection of Human Rights and Fundamental Freedoms signed in Rome on 4 November 1950 and as they result from the constitutional traditions common to the Member States, as general principles of Community law."[49]

The Organization for Security and Cooperation in Europe (OSCE), which found its origins in the Final Act of the 1975 Helsinki Conference, is also involved in the protection of human rights. This agreement was a significant effort to reduce Cold War tensions and contained an explicit commitment to act in conformity with the Universal Declaration of Human Rights (remarkable enough on the part of the Soviet Bloc given its Marxist-Leninist foundations and the role of ideology in the Cold War). This agreement remained significant after the end of the Cold War and, in 1995, led to the establishment of the OSCE currently composed of 56 member states, including all European states, Canada, the United States, and the former Soviet republics of Central Asia. In 1989, OSCE established a methodology known as the Vienna Mechanism to deal with allegations of human rights violations. This procedure involves a choice of fact finding, diplomatic negotiations or, if the problem is not resolved, bringing it to a conference of member states. In 1991, this was supplemented by the Moscow Mechanism, which allows the establishment of ad hoc missions of independent experts to assist in the resolution of human rights issues. In extreme situations, an investigation may be carried out without the consent of the state in question. The OSCE Office for Democratic Institutions and Human Rights is to provide support for the implementation of the Moscow Mechanism and it maintains a list of experts to carry out human rights investigations. The Moscow Mechanism was used, for example, in 1992 by the 12 states of the European Community and the United States in the issue of atrocities and attacks on unarmed civilians in Croatia and Bosnia-Herzegovina.[50]

With the end of the Cold War and potential minority issues in Eastern and Central Europe and in the former Soviet republics, the OSCE established in 1992 the post of High Commissioner on National Minorities to provide early warning in situations that may eventually lead to conflict. It may also endeavor to guide the governments concerned toward peaceful accommodation. It is a difficult mission requiring diplomatic skill and timely consultations. An example of success in this role is provided by Max van der Stoel, a former Dutch foreign minister, appointed to the post in 1993 for a three-year term. His stature and diplomatic ability enabled him to achieve success in leading a number of governments and national minorities away from dangerous confrontation. The task is often one of mediation. The situation in Eastern Ukraine is a monumental challenge for the current High Commissioner Astrid Thors as she addresses the crisis.[51]

Latin America

Other regional organizations devised their own ways to protect human rights. The Ninth International Conference of American States proclaimed the American Declaration of the Rights and Duties of Man on May 2, 1948, some seven months before the Universal Declaration was accepted. It has much in common with the Universal Declaration and includes civil and political as well as economic, social, and cultural rights. It also covers duties—toward society, the community, and the nation; toward children and parents; as well as the duty to vote, to obey the law, to pay taxes, and to work.[52] As the Universal Declaration, it was adopted as a declaration rather than a convention subject to ratification. It eventually came to be regarded as an authoritative statement of the "fundamental rights of the individual" mentioned in the constitution of the OAS. In November 1969, the Inter-American Specialized Conference on Human Rights produced the American Convention on Human Rights (also known as the "Pact of San José"), which created two institutions to ensure the protection of these rights: the Inter-American Commission on Human Rights at the OAS headquarters in Washington, DC, and the Inter-American Court of Human Rights in San José, Costa Rica.[53]

The Inter-American Commission on Human Rights functions somewhat as the European Commission on Human Rights did prior to the 1998 restructuring. It is empowered to receive petitions from private individuals against a state party to the Convention, but it can only receive complaints from one state against another if these states have accepted the interstate jurisdiction of the Commission. The Commission will investigate the facts and may hold hearings; it remains open to reaching a friendly settlement between the parties. If no friendly settlement is reached, the commission will draw up a report setting out the facts and the conclusions it has reached. It may also choose to bring the case to the Inter-American Court of Human Rights, or the state concerned may bring the case to the Court. Individuals have no standing before the Court but the Commission brings their cases to the Court. The Commission is not a party before the Court but will help it reach a decision. A state may bring to the Court a case against another state only if both have accepted the jurisdiction of the Court. The Convention did not establish any procedure to supervise the enforcement of the Court's judgments but it is to submit, to each regular session of the OAS General Assembly, a report on its work during the previous year specifying the cases in which states did not comply with its judgments. The Assembly may discuss the issue and take whatever measure it deems appropriate, but Assembly actions are not legally binding on member states.[54] The outcome will thus depend upon diplomacy, power, and political relations among the OAS member states. The work of the Inter-American Court of Human Rights has increased over the years (see Textbox 8.3). Furthermore, the Inter-American Commission on Human Rights has promoted the development of inter-American conventions supplementing legal instruments created by UN institutions (see Textbox 8.4). In addition, the OAS has a number of bodies and programs focused on human rights (see Textbox 8.5).

Textbox 8.3   Inter-American Court of Human Rights Caseload

Contentious Cases before the Court and in Stages of Monitoring Compliance with Judgment

Year	Number of Cases
1986	3
1990	5
1995	14
2000	28
2005	74

1979–2005 Practice

19	advisory opinions
139	judgments issued
68	cases solved
62	provisional measures

Source: Inter-American Court of Human Rights, *2005 Annual Report*. University of Minnesota, www1.umn.edu/humanrts/iachr/Annuals/annual-06 (Accessed July 5, 2010).

Textbox 8.4   Inter-American Instruments for the Protection of Human Rights

American Declaration of the Rights and Duties of Man

American Convention on Human Rights

Additional Protocol to the American Convention on Human Rights in the Area of Economic, Social and Cultural Rights (Protocol of San Salvador)

Protocol to the American Convention on Human Rights to Abolish the Death Penalty

Inter-American Convention to Prevent and Punish Torture

Inter-American Convention on Forced Disappearance of Persons

Inter-American Convention on the Prevention, Punishment and Eradication of Violence against Women (Convention of Belém do Pará)

Inter-American Convention on the Elimination of All Forms of Discrimination against Persons with Disabilities

Declaration of Principles on Freedom of Expression

Principles and Best Practices on the Protection of Persons Deprived of Liberty in the Americas

Inter-American Democratic Charter

Statute of the Inter-American Commission on Human Rights

Statute of the Inter-American Court of Human Rights.

Source: Inter-American Commission on Human Rights. *Basic Documents Pertaining to Human Rights in the Inter-American System.* www.cidh.oas.org/Basicos/English/ Basic.TOC (Accessed July 5, 2010).

Textbox 8.5   Other OAS Facilities Pertaining to the Protection of Human Rights

Inter-American Commission of Women

Inter-American Program on the Promotion of Women's Human Rights and Gender Equity and Equality

Rapporteur on the Rights of Women

Inter-American Program for the Promotion and Protection of the Human Rights of Migrants, Including Migrant Workers and Their Families

Rapporteur on the Rights of Migrant Workers and their Families

Office of the Special Rapporteur for Freedom of Expression

Rapporteur on the Rights of the Child

Unit for Human Rights Defenders

Rapporteur on the Rights of Persons Deprived of Liberty

Rapporteur on the Rights of Indigenous Peoples

Rapporteur on the Rights of Afro-Descendants and against Racial Discrimination

Source: OAS, Inter-American Commission on Human Rights. www.cidh.oas.org/rela- torias.eng (Accessed July 5, 2010).

Africa

Progress has been more difficult in Africa. In the 1960s and 1970s there was not much democracy in Africa and even less concern for the protection of human rights. But with mounting pressure from the UN and civil society for regional mechanisms to monitor the protection of human rights, in 1979, the Organization of African Unity (OAU) established a committee of experts to draft a human rights instrument for the African continent. The African Charter on Human and Peoples' Rights was unanimously approved by the OAU Assembly in 1981 and came into effect (as a binding instrument) in 1986.[55] It has now been ratified by 53 members of the AU (the OAU successor).

The Charter protects economic, social, and cultural rights along with civil and political rights but it imposes some restrictions on the rights it proclaims. For example, Article 9 (2) specifies: "Every individual shall have the right to express and disseminate his opinions *within the law*" (emphasis added). And in less than democratic societies, the law can be very restrictive. The Charter proclaims not only rights but also duties, and some of these are dangerously vague—for example, in Article 27 (2) "The rights and freedoms of each individual shall be exercised with due regard to . . . collective security, morality, and common interest." Beyond these, the Charter promulgates another category of rights, collective rights ("Peoples' rights"), such as the right of states parties to the Charter, individually and collectively, to the "free disposal of their wealth and natural resources" (Article 21.4), and the right of "all peoples" to "their economic, social and cultural development" (Article 22.1). These were rights that, at the time, African states strenuously claimed at the UN, in their quest for a New International Economic Order.

To implement these rights, the Charter created the eleven-member African Commission on Human and Peoples' Rights. It is elected by the Assembly of Heads of State and Government, to serve in their individual capacities rather than as government representatives. For years, however, the Commission included high-ranking government officials, which raised questions regarding their independence.[56] The Commission was given a function both promotional and quasi-judicial. In its first function (promotional), the Commission has resorted to educational programs and state visits to create greater awareness of the Charter and the rights protected, and it has used the services of Special Rapporteurs and working groups to promote human rights in Africa. The Commission grants observer status to NGOs to enable them to participate in its ordinary sessions. They contribute to the discussion and propose strategies to resolve issues of human rights. NGO forums enable civil society organizations to submit draft resolutions for the Commission's consideration. Some of these resolutions have condemned states' complicity in human rights violations such as in Darfur and Rwanda. More national human rights institutions, high-ranking state delegates, and other interested parties now participate in the sessions of the Commission.[57]

The second Commission function is quasi-judicial. It has extensive authority to interpret all the provisions of the Charter at the request of not only a state party, but also at the request of an institution of the AU or an African organization recognized by the it.[58] In addition, it has the power "to formulate and lay down, principles and rules aimed at solving legal problems relating to human and peoples' rights and fundamental freedoms upon which African governments may base their legislation" (Article 45). It is to be guided not only by the Charter on Human and Peoples' Rights, but also by the UN and AU Charters, the Universal Declaration on Human Rights and "other instruments adopted by the United Nations and by African countries in the field of human and peoples' rights," and "the provisions of various instruments adopted within the Specialized Agencies of the United Nations of which the parties to the present Charter are members" (Article 60). The Commission may also be guided by other human rights agreements to which AU members are parties and by African practices consistent with international norms on human and peoples' rights (Article 61). These are very constructive directions that could counter parochial notions of human rights.

The Commission is empowered to hear complaints and receive petitions from private individuals, NGOs and other nonstate entities having to do with grave human and peoples' rights violations. Thus anyone having an interest in the protection of human rights in Africa has access to the Commission even if not a victim. The Commission, however, is not authorized to deal with individual cases of victimization. If the Commission determines that the complaint is admissible it must refer it to the Assembly of Heads of State or Government which is not obligated to do anything about the case. But it may decide to request the Commission to undertake an in-depth study of the matter, produce a report, and present its recommendations. The Assembly is of course a political body. The report must remain confidential until the Assembly decides otherwise. Thus the Commission cannot even count on the sanction of publicity (Articles 58 and 59).

State party complaints may be filed with the Commission, at which point fact finding begins and the Commission is not limited to the information provided by the parties. It may draw upon any sources and may hold hearings in which states concerned may make presentations. If a friendly resolution is not achieved, the Commission must write a report presenting its findings and recommendations. It must send it to the states concerned and the Assembly— but the Charter does not require any action by the Assembly (Articles 47, 48, 52, and 53). Another problem is that cases before the Commission often take years to be processed. Numerous postponements of cases are the norm.

This is due in part to the short period of time that the Commission spends each year to consider cases. But the problem is also due to the fact that state parties work to delay the finalization of cases. Frequent requests of postponement are made by the states concerned on the pretext that they are not ready to proceed, despite constant reminders from the Commission.[59]

Beginning in 1994, efforts were made to improve the protection of human rights in Africa by creating an African Court on Human and Peoples' Rights. The General Secretariat, in cooperation with the Commission and the Geneva-based International Commission of Jurists, convened a group of legal experts in January 1994 in Geneva, Switzerland, to draft a protocol for the creation of the African Court. Interestingly, members of civil society took an active part in the drafting of the document, the International Commission of Jurists being instrumental in bringing together judges, practicing lawyers, human rights activists, and academics across Africa to participate in deliberations on the project. Some of these discussions were held alongside the regular sessions of the Commission in what has since become known as the NGO Forum. The draft was presented to a meeting of government experts in September 1995 in Cape Town, South Africa.

But African governments wanted to have greater control over the African Court and another meeting of experts was needed in April 1997 in the Mauritanian capital. The final text of the Protocol to the African Charter on Human and Peoples' Rights on the Establishment of an African Court was adopted by the OAU Assembly of Heads of State and Government in June 1998 after intense diplomatic negotiations and compromise. African governments remained hesitant.[60] The Protocol entered into force in January 2004 upon ratification by fifteen states. But by the end of 2007 only 24 ratifications had been received (out of 53 African states, now 54). In the meantime, the OAU had become the AU in 2002. In 2006 the AU Executive Council elected the first eleven judges but the Court delivered its first judgment only in December 2009—15 years after the first drafting talks had taken place.

In July 2004 the new AU decided that the African Court of Human and Peoples' Rights should be merged with the African Court of Justice (a new organ of the AU created by the Protocol of July 2003) but the merger process has stalled. The Protocols of the two Courts will have to be harmonized if the project is to come to fruition and one of the most contentious issues relating to the merger is the potential right of individual and NGO access to the Court. In the African Court on Human and Peoples' Rights, their direct access to the Court is limited to those states that have allowed individuals and NGOs to institute cases against them—and only Mali and Burkina-Faso have done so.[61] In the meantime the Commission and the African Court on Human and Peoples' Rights have failed to reach an agreement with regard to their relationship. It is going to take some time before it is possible to assess what an African Court will contribute to the protection of human rights on the African continent.

Despite all these difficulties, it must be noted that the diplomatic process among the 53 (now 54) countries, a good deal of it in the OAU and the AU, has led to the development of a number of human rights conventions, particularly in the last fifteen to twenty years (see Textbox 8.6). Granted, it is one thing to create legal rights and quite another to apply them. But progress away from authoritarianism and the development of a number of democratic systems in the region would seem to justify some hope for the future of human rights in this part of the world.

Asia-Pacific Region

Unfortunately, the same cannot be said of the Asia-Pacific region. None of the Asian regional organizations have a specific mandate to promote or protect human rights and a number of Asian countries are accused of serious human rights abuses by the international community and human rights organizations. NGOs, drawing upon a broad spectrum of civil society across the region, drew up an Asian human rights charter of their own, a "People's Charter,"

Textbox 8.6   African Instruments Related to the Protection of Human Rights

Charter of the Organization of African Unity, 1963.
Convention Governing the Specific Aspects of Refugee Problems in Africa, 1969.
OAU Convention for the Elimination of Mercenaries, 1972.
African Charter on Human and Peoples' Rights, 1981.
Dar es-Salaam Declaration on Academic Freedom and Social Responsibility of Academics, 1990
Kampala Declaration on Intellectual Freedom and Social Responsibility, 1990.
Khartoum Declaration on Africa's Refugee Crisis, 1990.
African Charter on the Rights and Welfare of the Child, 1990.
Addis Ababa Document on Refugees and Forced Population Displacements in Africa, 1994.
Protocol to the African Charter on Human and Peoples' Rights on the Establishment of an African Court on Human and Peoples' Rights, 1998.
OAU Convention on the Prevention and Combating of Terrorism, 1999.
Constitutive Act of the African Union, 2000.
Protocol to the African Charter on Human and Peoples' Rights on the Rights of Women in Africa, 2000.
Declaration on the Decade of a Culture of the Rights of the Child in West Africa, 2001.

Source: University of Minnesota Human Rights Library. www1.umn.edu/humanrts/instree/afrinst (Accessed July 9, 2010).

in 1998, in Kwangju, South Korea.[62] Amnesty International welcomed this expression of legitimate aspiration when confronted with their governments' lack of interest in the protection of human rights. The People's Charter calls for the adoption by governments of a regional convention on human rights. Such a regional objective, however, may not serve its intended purpose until a larger number of the governments in the region ratify and implement existing international conventions, particularly the two Covenants embodying the Universal Declaration.

The ten-member ASEAN in September 2009 created a consultative body, the ASEAN Intergovernmental Commission on Human Rights. This Commission is composed of one government representative per member state, responsible to the appointing government. And to reinforce the primacy of government policy, Article 5(6) of the terms of reference specifies that "Each appointing Government may decide, at its discretion, to replace its Representative." Among the member states are Vietnam, Laos, Myanmar, and Cambodia. Thus, the effective protection of human rights may not be just around the corner.

Middle East

This region presents a different problem. Many Arab states have ratified the major human rights treaties, but with extensive reservations restricting the application of a number of the essential rights protected in these treaties. For example, Saudi Arabia, probably the state having the most comprehensive system of institutionalized discrimination against women, ratified (along with 17 other Arab states) the Convention on the Elimination of All Forms of Discrimination against Women with reservations based on Islamic law. Using "Islamic law" for this purpose, however, is problematic because it is not formally codified and there are various methods of interpretation. Jurists and scholars often arrive at widely divergent conclusions as to what the law enjoins. As Denmark noted in its objection to Saudi Arabia's reservations, the references to the provisions of Islamic law are "of unlimited scope and undefined character."[63] The Gulf states of Oman, Qatar, Saudi Arabia, and the United Arab Emirates did not ratify the basic International Covenants on Civil and Political Rights and on Economic, Social and Cultural Rights. It must be noted, however, that a number of Arab states have been less restrictive in their endorsement of international human rights. Morocco, for example, whose king bears the title of Amir al Muminin, Commander of the Faithful, has been a supporter of women's rights. King Hassan II's sister was a women's rights activist.

A number of civil society human rights organizations are regularly urging Arab states to display greater attention to the serious human rights abuses taking place in the region. For example, Amnesty International, on the occasion of the Arab League summit of March 2010, urged Arab heads of state to make respect for human rights a cornerstone in their deliberations, particularly regarding conflicts in Sudan, Somalia, Yemen, and between Israel and the Palestinian territories.[64] Many human rights organizations monitor what is happening in the region and keep these issues in the news.

In 1994, the Arab League adopted an Arab Charter on Human Rights[65] which was widely criticized by human rights organizations in and out of the region for failing to correspond to accepted international standards. It remained unratified. In 2002, the Council of the League passed a resolution asking for a revision of the 1994 Charter and the secretary-general cautioned that it should mean a document supportive of international human rights standards. The project was accepted by a League summit meeting in May 2004. The League agreed to ask independent Arab human rights experts to produce a new draft. This group received submissions from international and regional NGOs. However, upon review by the Arab League Commission on Human Rights, substantial changes were made, intended to accommodate the views of a number of Arab states on such issues as women's rights, freedom of expression, and religion. The Charter came into force in March 2008. Although the document affirms the universality and indivisibility of human rights and recognizes many of the rights found in international conventions, a number of Middle East human rights organizations called on governments not to ratify the new Charter because it conflicts with international law in many fundamental areas.[66]

In the final analysis, the international protection of human rights is uneven around the world. Many governments violate human rights with impunity. Yet, it must be acknowledged that since the end of the Second World War progress has been made. The UN has greatly contributed to the development of a global interest in the protection of human rights with the Universal Declaration and numerous international conventions ratified by more than half of the states of the world. Many specialized UN bodies—such as UN Women—focus on human rights. And some regional organizations have done a remarkable job enforcing human rights in their own regional courts. In addition, the many UN humanitarian institutions and Specialized Agencies have given millions of destitute people the benefit of some very basic rights such as freedom from hunger and access to education.

Also significantly, the influence of civil society has escalated in the promotion and protection of human rights.[67] The communication revolution is an invaluable tool to mobilize public opinion and wield international pressure. And civil society's influence is felt in the diplomatic process. The UN and its agencies are helping them play a greater role. In fact, some of these bodies are mandated to seek civil society input. Moreover, NGOs are increasingly important in monitoring the performance of governments in implementing their human rights commitments.[68] The national reports that states must present on their human rights performance can be assessed against what NGOs have in fact observed—and it is hard to muzzle civil society. The application of human rights remains a challenge but global society is not giving up.

NOTES

1. Hugo Grotius, *De Jure Belli ac Pacis* (1625).

2. Lori F. Damrosch, Louis Henkin, Richard Crawford Pugh, Oscar Schachter, and Hans Smit, *International Law: Cases and Materials* (4th ed. St. Paul, MN: West Group, 2001), pp. 396–404.

3. www.marxists.org/history/international (Accessed April 2, 2010).

4. Robert W. Cox, "ILO: Limited Monarchy," in *The Anatomy of Influence: Decision Making in International Organization* edited by Robert W. Cox, Harold K. Jacobson, and others (New Haven, CT: Yale University Press, 1974), p. 102.

5. www.history.com/this-day-in-history/international-labor-organization-founded (Accessed May 25, 2015).

6. Antony Alcock, *History of the International Labor Organization* (New York: Octagon Books, 1971).

7. www.ilo.org/global/What_we_do/InternationalLaborStandards/lang-en/index (Accessed April 5, 2010).

8. ILO Constitution, Article 7.

9. www.ilo.org/global/standards/applying-and-promoting-international-labour-standards/committee-of-experts-on-the-application-of-conventions-and-recommendations/lang-en/index (Accessed September 20, 2011).

10. www.ilo.org/global/standards/applying-and-promoting-international-labor-standards/conference-committee-on-the-application-of-standards/general-survey/lang-en/index (Accessed September 20, 2011).

11. www.ilo.org/global/What_we_do/InterantionalLaborStandards/lang--en/index (Accessed April 5, 2010).

12. Ibid.

13. www.ilo.org/gender/Projects/lang--en/index (Accessed April 6, 2010).

14. www.ilo.org/empelm/lang--en/index (Accessed April 6, 2010).

15. www.ilo.org/public/english/bureau/inst (Accessed April 7, 2010).

16. www.unesco.org/new/en/...slave.../1-slavery-convention-1926 (Accessed January 11, 2013).

17. See background at www.crin.org/resources/infoDetail (Accessed June 21, 2010).

18. Over the years, membership was expanded as more states joined the UN.

19. www.nps.gov/archive/elro/glossary/human-rights-commission (Accessed June 12, 2010). See Mary Ann Glendon, *A World Made New: Eleanor Roosevelt and the Universal Declaration of Human Rights* (New York: Random House, 2001).

20. www.nps.gov/archive/elro/glossary/human-rights-commission (Accessed June 12, 2010).

21. *Filartiga v. Pena-Irala.* United States Court of Appeals, Second Circuit, 1980. Damrosch and others, *Cases and Materials,* pp. 143–145.

22. http://treaties.un.org/Pages/Treaties (Accessed June 15, 2010).

23. As of 2014. https://en/wikipedia.org/wiki/International_Covenant_on_Civil_and_Political_Rights (Accessed on July 13, 2015).

24. As of 2015. https://en/wikipedia.org/wiki/International _Covenant_on_Economic_Social_and_Cultural_Rights (Accessed July 13, 2015).

25. http://treaties.un.org/Pages/ViewDetails (Accessed June 23, 2010).

26. Ibid.

27. See the Filartiga case cited earlier in this chapter.

28. See Damrosch and others, pp. 142–154.

29. http://atdpweb.soe.berkeley.edu/quest/history/Beijing (Accessed June 24, 2010). See also Erin Leslie Coomer, *Women's Rights as Human Rights: The Role of NGOs in Integrating Women's Rights into Human Rights Theory and Advocacy* (London: Greenwood, 2000).

30. www.unwomen.org/about-us/about-un-women (Accessed October 22, 2012).

31. Buergenthal, p. 87.

32. Ibid.

33. See Philip Alston, "The Commission on Human Rights," in *Human Rights* by Louis Henkin, Gerald L. Neuman, Diane F. Orentlicher, and David W. Leebron (New York: Foundation Press, 1999), pp. 688–692.

34. Was eventually given a staff of 1,000 to monitor human rights issues around the world. www.ohchr.org/EN/Pages/WelcomePage (Accessed on October 9, 2014).

35. www.ohchr.org/EN/AboutUs/Pages/ViennaWC (Accessed July 14, 2015).

36. Clarence J. Dias, "The United Nations World Conference on Human Rights: Evaluation, Monitoring and Review," in *United Nations-Sponsored World Conferences on Human Rights: Focus on Impact and Follow-up.* Michael G. Schechter, ed. Tokyo: UN University Press, 2001, pp. 29–62.

37. Jacques Formerand, "Human Rights Council Elections, a Flawed Process at Heart." www.unausa.org/worldbulletin/100623/formerand (Accessed June 24, 2010).

38. www.ngo-monitor/article (Accessed June 27, 2010).

39. www.un.org/largerfreedom/sg-statement (Accessed June 27, 2010).

40. Guglielmo Verdirame, *The UN and Human Rights: Who Guards the Guardians?* (Cambridge: Cambridge University Press, 2011).

41. A condition is that they must have exhausted all domestic legal remedies available. *The European Human Rights System.* www.hrea.org/index (Accessed June 28, 2010).

42. www.echr.coe.int/NR/rdonlyres/57211BCC-C88A-43C6-B540-AFo642E8/D2C/O/CPProtocole14EN (Accessed October 22, 2012).

43. Although 43 states have ratified the Social Charter. www.coe.int/t/dghl/monitoring/socialcharter/Presentation/Overview_en (Accessed June 30.2010).

44. http://conventions.coe.int/Treaty/en/Treaties (Accessed June 30, 2010).

45. www.hrea.org/index (Accessed June 28, 2010).

46. http://conventions.coe.int/Treaty/EN/Treaties (Accessed July 1, 2010).

47. www.hrea.org/index (Accessed June 28, 2010). The Commissioner is elected by the Council of Europe's Parliamentary Assembly.

48. http://europa.eu/scadplus/glossary/eu_human_rights_convention_en (Accessed July 2, 2010).

49. www.eurotreaties.com/maastrichteu (Accessed July 2, 2010).

50. www.hrea.org/index (Accessed June 28, 2010), and www.osce.org/odihr/13483 (Accessed July 1, 2010).

51. www.osce.org/hcnm (June 12, 2014).

52. See full text: www.hrcr.org/docs/OAS_Declaration/oasrights5 (Accessed July2, 2010).

53. www.hrcr.org/docs/American_Convention/oashr (Accessed July 5, 2010).

54. www.cidh.oas.org/Basicos/English/Basic.TOC (Accessed July 5, 2010).

55. www1.umn.edu/humanrts/instree (Accessed June 12, 2014).

56. George Mukundi Wachira, *African Court on Human and Peoples' Rights: Ten Years on and Still No Justice.* Report (London: Minority Rights Group International, 2008), p. 10.

57. Ibid., pp. 9–10.

58. www1.umn.edu.humanrts/instree/z1afchar (Accessed July 7, 2010).

59. Wachira, pp. 11–12.

60. Ibid., pp. 13–14. See also The African Court on Human and Peoples' Rights, www.aict-ctia.org/courts_conti/achpr/achpr/home (Accessed July 6, 2010).

61. www.achpr.org/english/_info/court_en (Accessed July 6, 2010).

62 www.unhcr.org/refworld/publisherASIA (Accessed July 10, 2010).

63. www.al-bab.com/arab/human (Accessed July 10, 2010). See also Ann Elizabeth Mayer, *Islam and Human Rights: Tradition and Politics* (4th ed. Boulder, CO: Westview, 2007).

64. www1.voanews.com/englksh/news/Africa/decapua-arab-states-amnesty-26mar10-89268237 (Accessed July 10, 2010).

65. www1.umn.edu/humanrts/instree/arabhrcharter (Accessed July 12, 2010).

66. www.carnegieendowment.org/arb?fa=show&article=23951 (Accessed July 10, 2010).

67. See Henkin and others, "Implementation by Non-Governmental Organizations." pp. 737–769.

68. Hans Thoolen and Berth Verstappen, "Human Rights Missions: A Study of the Fact-Finding Practice of Non-Governmental Organizations," in Henkin and others, pp. 742–745, and Diane F. Orentlicher, "Bearing Witness: The Art and Science of Human Rights Fact-Finding," in the same volume, pp. 745–746, 753–754, and 758–760.

Chapter 9

Environmental Diplomacy

Global environmental issues are a recent addition to the diplomatic agenda, even more recent than universal human rights. Although a small number of international initiatives were taken in the nineteenth and early twentieth centuries, these were of limited scope.[1] After the Second World War, international society began to gain awareness on environmental degradation. Environmental protection became an international cause. New NGOs and activist groups were organized in this regard. In 1962, Rachel Carson, a biologist, published *Silent Spring* on the impact of pesticides on the natural environment, which triggered a massive questioning of the consequences of human activity on global ecology.[2] Others focused on population growth and the limits of global resources, for example, Paul Ehrlich and his widely read *Population Bomb* (1968).[3]

INITIAL ENVIRONMENT ACTION

It was the ECOSOC that took the first global diplomatic step, in 1968, to address environmental concerns by recommending to the General Assembly that it convene a global diplomatic conference on environmental issues. The states represented on the ECOSOC were thus taking the first global environmental initiative—an illustration of the diplomatic practicality of international institutions at a time when most countries remained essentially passive. The General Assembly endorsed the initiative and convened the Conference on the Human Environment to be held in 1972, in Stockholm, noting "the continuing and accelerating impairment of the quality of the human environment." The General Assembly created a Preparatory Committee of

27 member states, which met four times before the Conference and received more than one hundred national reports and proposals.

Unfortunately, Cold War politics marred the preparatory efforts: The Soviet Bloc withdrew from the preparatory process, and refused to participate in the Conference because West Germany, and not East Germany, was invited. Confrontations between developing and industrialized nations were another major problem.[4] Developing countries objected that environmental discussion was too oriented toward the interests of the industrialized states and feared that environmental concerns would lead to a reduction of antipoverty efforts. They implied they might thus boycott the conference. Maurice Strong, the Conference's secretary-general, embarked upon his own campaign to improve their disposition. He visited thirty developing countries explaining the importance of environmental integrity for the development process. He succeeded in obtaining a commitment from Prime Minister Indira Gandhi of India to become personally involved and attend the Conference. In addition, the Conference Secretariat organized a seminar of twenty-seven leading experts in development and the environment from around the world who met in Fournex, near Geneva, in June 1971 and their work did much to win the support of the bulk of the developing nations.[5]

THE 1972 STOCKHOLM CONFERENCE

The first global environmental conference (June 5–16, 1972) was attended by delegates from 114 countries. Representatives from about 500 NGOs came to Stockholm hoping to be heard by the diplomats. The Conference Secretariat organized an Environment Forum for accredited NGOs, which became a model for other world conferences. Some NGO delegates were invited to present formal statements at the Conference. Two additional forums did not have the endorsement of the UN Conference: the Peoples' Forum and Dai Dong, which took a more confrontational approach as the Vietnam War sparked much radical protest. These (larger) informal gatherings tended to be impatient with the slow response of governments.[6]

Following the pattern of other global conferences, the Stockholm gathering produced a Declaration, which amounted to a wish list, and an Action Plan, which was really a catalogue of concerns. It also recommended the creation of a new UN agency to address environmental issues, which the General Assembly did in December 1972 when it established the UN Environment Program (UNEP). This new body is headed by an executive director, under the control of a Governing Council composed of UN member states. Accredited NGOs may sit as observers at Council meetings and are allowed to make oral statements if invited by the chair. They may provide written statements related to agenda items.[7] The new agency has its headquarters in Nairobi, Kenya, undoubtedly to elicit greater support from the developing world but complicating relations with other UN bodies. This is somewhat offset by UNEP's Liaison Office at the UN headquarters in New York, which remains in contact with the entire UN membership and all UN bodies. UNEP also maintains six regional offices in various parts of the world focusing on their special environmental issues[8]—for example, the 2012 project of the Office for Africa to investigate the spectacular mammal migration corridor between Ethiopia and South Sudan, one of the largest in the world. It also participates in a variety of environmental events, such as the 4th African Rift Geothermal Conference "Geothermal Solution to Africa's Energy Need" (November 2012, Nairobi, Kenya).[9]

URBAN SETTLEMENTS AND THE ENVIRONMENT

In the course of the 1972 Stockholm Conference, it became clear that urgent action was needed to meet the growing environmental impact of urban centers around the world, but it was evident that urban problems were too complex to be addressed in Stockholm. The UN General Assembly therefore decided to call another global conference in 1976, the UN Conference on Human Settlements (Habitat), to be held in Vancouver. When the UN was created, just three decades earlier, two-thirds of humanity was still rural. But the world was now beginning to witness the fastest urban migration in history, especially in the developing countries. By the end of the twentieth century, half of the world population was living in urban settlements with one billion people living in urban slums and thousands joining them every day. In the next fifty years, two-thirds of humanity would live in cities.

Habitat marked the first time global society recognized the environmental consequences of rapid urbanization. In December 1978, the UN General Assembly created a new agency in Nairobi, Kenya, the Center for Human Settlements (UN-Habitat), to address urban environment issues on a con-tinuing basis.[10] Initially poorly funded, UN-Habitat was strengthened, as the urban crisis escalated. In 1996, the UN convened a second global conference on human settlements, Habitat II, focused on two themes, "Adequate shelter for all," and "Sustainable human settlements: Development in an urbanizing world."[11] Five years later (June 2001), the 25th Special Session of the UN General Assembly assessed the implementation of the 1996 Conference rec-ommendations and, in January 2002, UN-Habitat was promoted to the status of a full UN program.[12]

UN-Habitat now organizes a biennial World Urban Forum for the broadest discussion of urban issues, the first one taking place in 2002 in Nairobi, Kenya.[13]

Participation in the Forum is extremely open to allow dialogue between all actors working on urban issues (local and national), government officials, NGO representatives, other members of civil society, professionals, and academics. The popularity of these gatherings has increased. The dialogue does not follow the rules of procedure of formal UN meetings. Interaction is very free and informal. The first Forum in Nairobi attracted 1,200 participants; the third, in Vancouver, in 2006, brought together 11,400 people; and the one in 2014, in Medellin, Colombia, 24,000.[14] Now, this is not diplomatic work creating new international commitments. But these gatherings generate new ideas among people who have a stake in reducing slums and creating better living conditions in the expanding urban settlements of global society, another example of civil society and transnational actors being invited by intergovernmental organizations to participate in global problem-solving dialogues, an activity no longer restricted to officialdom.[15]

EXPANDING ENVIRONMENTAL EFFORTS

In the meantime, a number of agreements, some of them regional, were negotiated—for example, the Convention on the Protection of the Marine Environment of the Baltic Sea, Helsinki, 1974 was undoubtedly constructive, but incremental and piecemeal. In 1976, the World Meteorological Organization (WMO), a UN Specialized Agency, issued the first authoritative statement on climate change. In 1979, it convened the first World Climate Conference, and in 1988 cooperated with the UNEP to establish the Intergovernmental Panel on Climate Change (IPCC) involving over 1,000 scientific, legal, and policy experts from over sixty countries.[16] The IPCC received the 2007 Nobel Peace Prize jointly with Al Gore "for their efforts to build up and disseminate greater knowledge about man-made climate change, and to lay the foundations for measures that are needed to counteract such changes."[17]

Ozone depletion became a major concern, but it was simpler than climate change, involving fewer causes. Moreover, industrial substitutes permitted production changes without economically destabilizing consequences. In 1987, negotiations for the Vienna Convention for the Protection of the Ozone Layer were successfully completed to phase out the substances responsible for ozone depletion. The treaty was amended several times, leading to the 1997 Montreal Protocol, which was ratified by 196 states—a huge success.[18] In 1990, the WMO held the second World Climate Conference and the UN General Assembly created an intergovernmental negotiating committee for the creation of a Framework Convention on Climate Change, which was signed in 1992. The goal was to stabilize greenhouse gas emissions, but divergent economic and political interests prevented agreement on limitation targets, particularly due to US opposition.[19] Negotiations continued in successive conferences of the states that had become parties to the Framework Convention.

An agreement was reached for the Kyoto Protocol (1997) at the third conference of the parties. The Protocol supplements the Framework Convention. It entails some binding emission reductions of at least 5 percent below 1990 levels for all developed states that are parties to the agreement, that is, 37 industrialized states listed in Protocol Annex I.[20] Developing states are exempt as greenhouse gas emissions normally come overwhelmingly from industrialized states. The catch however is that India, China, and Brazil are *exempt* as not included in the industrialized category of Annex I. Yet, in 2008, China became the world's largest emitter of CO_2 gas. The United States refused to become a party to the Kyoto Protocol.[21] Negotiations have continued at subsequent conferences of the parties. Complex rules for the implementation of the Kyoto Protocol were adopted in 2001 at the seventh conference. G8 summits in 2007, 2008, and 2009 addressed the issue but no agreement on emission reductions was reached. The parties continued negotiating. The thirteenth conference (Bali, 2007) agreed to launch a new set of global negotiations and produced a road map for this purpose, with a target date of December 2009 for a binding emission reduction agreement.[22] But this failed, and so did the sixteenth conference (Cancún, 2010). At the seventeenth conference (Durban, December 2011), the parties to the Framework Convention started yet another round of negotiations. Not promising! However, they agreed to retain the Kyoto Protocol that was to expire in 2012.

The UNEP was long concerned with another problem: the worsening of species extinction caused by human activity. But nations wanted to retain sovereignty over the use of their domestic resources; moreover, rich and poor countries had conflicting interests in this area. In November 1988, the UNEP convened an Ad Hoc Working Group of Experts on Biological Diversity. Based on their work, the UNEP established, in May 1989, a Working Group of Technical and Legal Experts to prepare a convention for the conservation and use of genetic resources. This led to intergovernmental negotiations and the adoption of the Biodiversity Convention in Nairobi, Kenya, in May 1992. It was signed by more than 150 states, but not by the United States.[23] The Convention has three functions: the conservation of biological diversity, the sustainable use of genetic resources, and the fair and equitable sharing of benefits in the use of these resources.[24] As of 2015, the Convention had 196 parties. Conferences of the parties developed machinery for the implementation of the Convention and its harmonization with the WTO and the WIPO, as a great deal of the controversy over biological diversity pertains to property rights in the exploitation of biological resources.

A different issue was added to the diplomatic agenda: modern biotechnology modifying living organisms. Economic benefits need to be balanced with the requirements of public health in addition to protecting biodiversity. Negotiations were undertaken and, in 2000, the Cartagena Protocol on Biosafety was added to the Biodiversity Convention. The negotiations continued and a new agreement was reached in 2010—the Nagoya Protocol—to protect access to the genetic resources while sharing the benefits.[25] This was a significant achievement as the issue had pitted developed and developing countries against one another for decades.

TOWARD THE RIO SUMMIT CONFERENCE

In 1983, the UN General Assembly became concerned about environmental destruction and created a special independent commission to formulate a long-term agenda for action—the World Commission on Environment and Development (the Brundtland Commission. The Commission was headed by Gro Harlem Brundtland, prime minister of Norway and former environment minister). More than half of its twenty-two members, serving in their independent and expert capacities, were from developing countries. The Commission appointed a number of expert special advisers and three Advisory Panels. It held a series of public hearings around the world over a period of two years to hear from a wide variety of people from both the public and private sectors. The report, *Our Common Future*, was presented in 1987 and laid the groundwork for the convening of the 1992 Earth Summit. It launched the concept of sustainable development.[26]

The G7 itself for the first time, agreed in 1989 that decisive action was urgently needed to protect the earth's ecological balance. In December, the UN General Assembly adopted several resolutions on the need for environmental protection and initiated proceedings for the convening of the UNCED (the 1992 Rio Earth Summit).[27] The movement was gathering diplomatic momentum. In 1991, the World Bank, in cooperation with the UNDP and the UNEP, established the Global Environment Facility (GEF) as a $1 billion pilot program to assist in the protection of the environment and the promotion of environmentally sustainable development.[28]

The UN resolution calling for the Rio Conference expressed the General Assembly's deep concern about "the continuing deterioration of the state of the environment," and the risk of "ecological catastrophe" if allowed to continue, and specified in comprehensive terms a multiplicity of objectives for the conference, showing how perceptions had changed since 1968 when the first efforts to address the issue of the global environment began.[29] To plan the Conference, the General Assembly established a Preparatory

Committee composed of member states and chaired by Ambassador T. T. B. Koh of Singapore who had demonstrated his diplomatic skills when presiding over the complex proceedings of the Law of the Sea Conference. It must be remembered that a good deal of the negotiations of global conferences takes place in the meetings of preparatory committees. Equally skillful was the decision to appoint Maurice Strong as secretary-general of the Rio Summit. He held the same position at the Stockholm Conference and was the first executive director of the UNEP.

The UN General Assembly made provision for five meetings of the Preparatory Committee to take place between 1990 and 1992 and invited all UN member states to participate, as well as NGOs. UN funds were made available to assist the least-developed countries to participate in the negotiations of the Preparatory Committee and attend the conference. Three working groups were established.[30] They often broke into smaller negotiating bodies. Some accepted the participation of NGOs; others, in which delicate diplomatic compromise was sought, kept them out. Some of the negotiations, particularly toward the end of the Preparatory Committee sessions, continued until 4:00 or 5:00 a.m.

THE RIO EARTH SUMMIT

The UN Conference on Environment and Development was held from June 3–14, 1992, following two days of preliminary consultations—that is, more negotiations. The final two days of the Conference were set aside for the participation of heads of state or government. 172 state delegations attended the Conference including 108 chief executives. 2,400 persons represented accredited NGOs and 17,000 people attended the Parallel Forum some 25 miles away. 13 NGOs were invited to address the conference plenary meeting, and many government delegations included NGO representatives. Other NGOs participated in national and regional meetings held in preparation for the Rio conference. Each country was to submit a report outlining its concerns on development and the state of the environment. NGO input was specifically requested in the invitation sent to governments.

At the Global Assembly of Women and the Environment, a special presummit international conference organized under the auspices of the UNEP, some 500 participants from nearly 70 countries discussed grassroots-level cases of environmental management.[31] And there were some 10,000 journalists at the Earth Summit spreading news of the proceedings to the four corners of the world.[32] NGOs and civil society worldwide were invigorated, and there is political capital in this, even where governments are hostile to the cause.[33]

The Conference produced an Action Plan ("Agenda 21") and a Declaration of principles supporting the campaign for environment and development. Agenda 21 was overwhelming (700 pages divided into 40 chapters), but these documents, endorsed by such a prominent global gathering could be invoked by international actors in their environmental pursuits. Taking advantage of its summit character, the conference formally signed the two conventions negotiated earlier, that is, the Framework Convention on Climate Change and the Convention on Biological Diversity. The aura of the Rio Earth Summit gave additional importance to these documents although much more remained to be done in both areas.

The Conference wanted to take steps to protect forests. But competing economic interests made the subject extremely controversial and the negotiators at Rio decided to settle for a *Statement of Forest Principles*, the first global agreement on saving forests.[34] This opened the door to a good deal of diplomatic work in subsequent years, starting with an Intergovernmental Panel on Forests, from 1995–1997. It was replaced by an Intergovernmental Forum on Forests, established by the ECOSOC. These bodies were instrumental in negotiating the *Instrument on All Types of Forests* (nonlegally binding), a landmark document in this highly contentious area, adopted by the UN General Assembly in 2007.[35] The UN succeeded in launching a program for Reducing Emissions from Deforestation and Forest Degradation in Developing Countries (REDD) in 2008. This was the result of a collective initiative of the FAO, the UNDP, and the UNEP. Deforestation through agricultural expansion, pasture land additions, or destructive logging, accounts for nearly 20 percent of global greenhouse gas emissions, more than the entire global transportation emissions.[36] UN-REDD involves twenty-nine partner countries across Africa, Asia-Pacific, and Latin America. To date, the program has approved a total of $51.4 million for nine national pilot projects.[37]

Immediately following the Earth Summit, the General Assembly established the CSD in December 1992 for the purpose of monitoring the implementation of what was accomplished in Rio and providing assistance in follow-up activities. The CSD was composed of 53 member states elected by the ECOSOC with due regard to geographical representation. It met annually in New York. In the hope of generating more effective implementation, the Commission opened its sessions to multiple stakeholder dialogue and broad participation from representatives of UN system organizations, other intergovernmental organizations, and accredited nongovernmental actors. The Commission, however, acknowledged that the rate of implementation would remain slow.[38] It was replaced in 2013 by the High-Level Political Forum on Sustainable Development meeting every four years under the General Assembly and every other year under the ECOSOC.[39]

For the purpose of increasing international participation and generating more funding, the Rio Conference sought to expand the GEF and recommended its restructuring in Agenda 21. This was accomplished and put into effect in 1994. The GEF is now an independent financial organization of 182 member governments in partnership with 10 international agencies, and the private sector including NGOs. Since 1994, the World Bank has served as trustee of the GEF Trust Fund and has provided administrative services. The GEF is governed by a Council of 32 member states and an Assembly, meeting every three or four years. It is assisted by the Scientific and Technical Advisory Panel, which reviews every project and provides advice regarding GEF policies. The GEF Office of Monitoring and Evaluation (an independent entity within the GEF) reports on results and lessons from GEF projects directly to the GEF Council.[40] NGOs often play a key role in the process of project identification, formulation, and implementation.

The GEF provides grants to developing countries and countries with economies in transition, for projects related to its six main areas of specialization (climate change, biodiversity, water, land degradation, persistent organic pollutants, and the ozone layer).[41] It also serves as a financial mechanism for a number of international conventions. Today, the GEF is the largest provider of funds for projects to improve the global environment. It has allocated $8.8 billion, supplemented by more than $38.7 billion in cofinancing, for more than 2,400 projects in more than 165 developing countries and countries with economies in transition. Through its Small Grants Program, the GEF has also made in excess of 10,000 grants directly to NGOs and community organizations in 120 countries. In partnership with the Montreal Protocol of the Vienna Convention on Ozone Layer Depleting Substances, the GEF started funding projects that enable the Russian Federation and nations of Eastern Europe and Central Asia to phase out their use of ozone-destroying chemicals.[42]

FOUR SPECIAL ISSUES

The Rio Summit created momentum for other environment projects.[43] The Conference participants requested the UN to address four special issues: desertification, the development of small island states, conservation of fish stocks, and land-based sources of marine pollution, to which we must now turn.

1. Desertification

The international community had long recognized that desertification, the degradation of land in arid and semiarid areas, was a major economic, social, and environmental problem. Some 66 percent of Africa is desert or arid and 73 percent of its dry land agriculture is already degraded, adding to malnutrition and poverty.[44] In 1977, the UN held an international conference on desertification, which adopted a plan of action.[45] Despite efforts to achieve its objectives, the UNEP concluded in 1991 that desertification had intensified. In 1992, the Rio Summit therefore called upon the UN to establish an intergovernmental negotiating committee to prepare a Convention to Combat Desertification. The General Assembly acted on it in December. The UN Committee completed its negotiations in five sessions and the Convention was adopted in Paris in June 1994.[46] This international agreement uses national, regional, and subregional plans of action to address the problem. The desertification problem is monumental; climate change is aggravating it. This is not a problem that can be solved once, and for all and it highlights the importance of a continuing diplomatic process to devise strategies as the situation evolves.[47]

2. Small Island Developing States

The vulnerability of small island developing countries was brought to the attention of global society during the 1992 Rio Summit in which 46 of them participated. Agenda 21 called for a global conference on their special condition. The General Assembly agreed and convened the first global conference on the subject "at the highest level of representation," to take place in Bridgetown, Barbados, in 1994. 125 states and territories participated and adopted the Barbados Program of Action, a 14-point document that identified priority areas such as sea-level rise, coastal and marine resources, fresh water, biodiversity, administrative capacity, and human resource development. The UN Commission on Sustainable Development was given the responsibility to follow up on the implementation of these decisions and requested the convening of a Special Session of the General Assembly to undertake a comprehensive review and conduct an appraisal of the Barbados Program on its fifth anniversary. This took place in September 1999.[48] In addition, the special needs of developing island states were addressed by the 2000 UN Millennium Summit in New York. World leaders pledged to implement the Barbados Program of Action. Small island needs were included also in the Declaration issued at the 2002 Johannesburg World Summit on Sustainable Development. The Johannesburg World Summit devoted to them a chapter of its Plan of Implementation and called upon the General Assembly to convene an international meeting for a comprehensive review of the 1994 Barbados Program.

The UN General Assembly carried out the Johannesburg recommendation in December 2002 thereby calling a special diplomatic meeting in 2004, the

10th anniversary of the Barbados Program, to review its accomplishments and discuss further action by mobilizing resources and offering practical assistance. The Government of Mauritius offered to host the conference (in 2005). The General Assembly made plans for three preparatory meetings (August–October 2003) leading to the Mauritius Conference. These were to be regional: a meeting for the Pacific, another for the Atlantic, Indian Ocean, Mediterranean, and South China Sea, and the third for the Caribbean. The regional positions formulated in each meeting were to be discussed at an interregional gathering in Nassau, in January 2004. The Alliance of Small Island States[49] prepared a strategy paper of its own for the Nassau meeting. Adding to the preparatory work, four meetings of experts were convened (July–December 2003) to address technical issues, such as renewable energy needs. Expert reports were submitted to the Nassau gathering.

The General Assembly arranged for two days of informal diplomatic consultation, to take place just before the January 2005 Mauritius Conference. This was to facilitate assessment of the Barbados Program. Several rounds of informal conversations also took place among diplomats at the UN headquarters in New York. This extensive preparatory work is often part of conference diplomacy although it usually escapes public attention. The Mauritius Conference brought together 129 countries and territories and produced the Mauritius Strategy for the Further Implementation of the Program of Action for the Sustainable Development of Small Island Developing States.[50] The members of the Small Island States Network then planned a high-level five-year review of the Mauritius Strategy under the sponsorship of the UN. This took place during the 65th session of the UN General Assembly in September 2010. As was the case for the 10-year review of the Barbados Program, the meeting was preceded by extensive preparation at the regional and interregional levels. The UN General Assembly designated 2014 as the International Year of Small Island Developing States and held the Third International Conference on their well-being in September 2014, in Apia, Samoa. Thus, a great deal of work is now devoted to issues virtually ignored a few years ago. Interestingly, these review meetings bring together more than 100 diplomatic delegations indicating that small island problems are now well established on the global diplomatic agenda and are actively worked on.

3. Fish Stocks Conservation

The participants in the Rio Conference took another initiative, requesting the UN to find ways to conserve fish stocks on the high seas and prevent violence between fishing vessels. By the early 1990s, most stocks of commercially valued fish were running low and international incidents were occurring with increasing frequency. Britain and Norway, for example, sent naval units to protect their fishing fleets on the high seas. Many agreements have been negotiated, regulating fishing and specific fisheries. The monumental 1982 UN Convention on the Law of the Sea provided further regulation. But straddling and highly migratory fish stocks presented a special problem.[51] The UN therefore convened an International Conference on this special topic, which held its first full meeting in July 1993. Six negotiating sessions led to the signing of the Agreement on the Conservation and Management of Straddling and Highly Migratory Fish Stocks in December 1995.[52] More work has been done at the UN by the UN Division of Oceans Affairs and Law of the Sea,[53] and by the UNEP's Regional Seas Program.[54] Without continuing attention, economic pressure would lead to further depletion and more conflict.

4. Land-Based Sources of Marine Pollution

Finally, the governments assembled in Rio called on the United Nations to negotiate an agreement to reduce land-based sources of marine pollution. The UNEP Governing Council took up the issue in 1995 and an Intergovernmental Conference was convened in Washington, DC (October–November 1995). Diplomatic representatives of 108 states and the EU adopted a Global Program of Action for the Protection of the Marine Environment from Land-Based Activities in which states agreed to reduce marine pollution caused by sewage, heavy metals, oil, pesticides, nutrients, and litter, and to stop activities that physically alter and destroy marine habitats.[55] The UN General Assembly endorsed the Global Program of Action in December 1996 and made institutional arrangements for its implementation. The UNEP was mandated to provide Secretariat facilities for the Program of Action and to play a role in its implementation.

Review of Agenda 21 Implementation

As requested by the Earth Summit, the UN General Assembly held a Special Session (New York, June 2007 – Rio + 5) to maintain the momentum of global environmental work. It must be noted that the CSD and the GEF were instrumental in providing continuing assistance for the implementation of Rio projects. Additional momentum was soon forthcoming from another global campaign.

MORE SUMMITS

The arrival of the new millennium was the occasion for the UN to ponder its role in the world, and on December 17, 1998, the General Assembly decided to convene the Millennium Summit as an integral part of the Millennium Assembly at the UN headquarters in New York, from September 6–8, 2000, with the theme "The Role of the UN in the 21st Century." The Millennium Summit adopted eight Millennium Development Goals (MDGs), one of which was to "ensure environmental sustainability."[56] Interestingly, these goals were rooted in (or inspired by) Agenda 21 of the 1992 Earth Summit. To maintain the impetus of its environmental mission and generate additional support, the UN prepared another summit, Rio + 10 in Johannesburg, South Africa (2002). In preparation for this event, the CSD organized four meetings between April 2001 and June 2002. The UN secretary-general also convened a Panel of Eminent Persons to explore the challenges of sustainable development and formulate recommendations on how to meet them (to be negotiated at the Millennium Summit). Also convened in Johannesburg was a nongovernmental forum and numerous parallel events with representatives from local authorities, industry, academia, and the scientific community in an effort to involve a large variety of concerned people.[57] The United States refused to attend.

In September 2005, the UN held the Millennium + 5 Summit to evaluate progress toward the achievement of the MDGs. But it was a disappointment. Many governments had not acted on their original promises. Secretary-General Kofi Annan created the MDG Gap Task Force in May 2007 and diplomatic efforts continued. In September 2010, another UN summit at the headquarters in New York indicated better progress.[58] The 2010 Millennium Development Goals Report showed that much remained to be done on the four environmental targets constituting Goal 7, Environmental Sustainability.[59] But the UN campaign would continue and new goals would be selected for the period 2015–2030. In the meantime, Rio + 20 needed to be observed. The UN General Assembly decided upon another summit—back in Rio in June 2012. But the results were disappointing. The leaders of Germany, Britain, and the United States did not attend, although the French president did. The Conference recommended strengthening the UNEP and supported the development of a set of sustainable development goals to follow the MDGs after 2015. Rio + 20 also launched a high-level political forum to enable important environment stakeholders to dialogue and foster greater efforts in environment and development.[60] More summits are in the planning stage.

REGIONAL ACTIVITIES FOR
ENVIRONMENTAL PROTECTION

Beyond global efforts, many countries have worked to protect their own neighborhood, for example, their regional marine environment (see Textbox 9.1).

Doubtless, global endeavors have encouraged them to cooperate closer to home.

The EU was the most responsive. Starting in 1972, Europe produced a series of Environmental Action Plans and, step by step, created a remarkably extensive program.[61] 280 items of EU environmental legislation were enacted in the 1990s (applicable as law in EU member states).[62] EU environmental law now includes more than 500 legal instruments. Environmental impact assessments have been mandatory since 1985 for all public and private projects above a certain size.[63] The European Environment Agency was established in 1994 and its Environment Information and Observation Network involves approximately 900 experts and more than 300 national institutions.[64] European legislation is enforceable. In June 2010, the European Commission was in the process of taking four EU member states (Belgium, Luxembourg, Germany, and Greece) to the EU Court of Justice for failing to incorporate EU environmental legislation into their national laws.[65] Such remarkable developments are of course made possible by European integration and the supranational nature of many of its institutions.

The ASEAN, in a region of some 500 million people, has shown sustained interest in environmental protection. These countries are keenly aware of the increasing stress on their regional ecosystems due to growing population and increasing pollution resulting from accelerated industrialization and urbanization. In 1997, ASEAN launched a series of subregional environmental programs, followed by the Strategic Plan of Action on the Environment (1999–2004) and the Vientiane Action Program (2004–2010). ASEAN ministers responsible for environmental issues meet regularly. In 2002 they agreed on ten priority areas. In October 2011, they held their 13th informal meeting in Phnom Penh, Cambodia, in conjunction with the 7th meeting of the Conference of the Parties to the ASEAN Agreement on Transboundary Haze Pollution. They reviewed ongoing programs and discussed new activities to promote regional environmental cooperation.[66] ASEAN environment ministers also meet regularly with their counterparts from China and South Korea.[67] ASEAN leaders consider environmental protection to be essential to the long-term economic growth of the region and the ASEAN Secretariat plays an important role in integrating environmental factors into other ASEAN development activities.[68]

The other regional organizations have been less involved in environmental protection, but the AU, formerly OAU, is making progress. It contributed the African Convention on the Conservation of Nature and Natural Resources (1968, revised in 2003), and the 1991 Bamako Convention on the Ban on the Import into Africa and the Control of Transboundary Movement and Management of Hazardous Wastes within Africa.[69] The African Ministerial Conference on the Environment (AMCEN) was convened in 1985 to halt environmental degradation. The AMCEN has become institutionalized. It has a Bureau, a Trust Fund, a number of Regional Scientific and Technical Committees; the UNEP Regional Office for Africa serves as the AMCEN's Secretariat. AMCEN convenes every other year in regular meetings. Its fifteenth session was held in 2014 in Cairo;[70] it also meets in special sessions as needed. It is expected that the AMCEN will ultimately become a Specialized Technical Committee of the African Union Commission. The AMCEN's Secretariat has been working with the African Council on Water (established in 2002).[71] Some of the subregional African organizations have also taken steps to protect the environment. For example, the New Partnership for Africa's Development undertook to protect the marine and coastal environment of the Western Indian Ocean and negotiated, for that purpose, the Nairobi Convention in 1985, revised in 2010.

The OAS has created a Department of Sustainable Development to address the environmental issues of the region, particularly water resources, climate change, and biodiversity.[72] An interesting project for 2015–2016 is to get schools throughout Latin America and the Caribbean to lead their students to think of new ways of dealing with the environment. It is sponsored by UNESCO, the UN Office for Disaster Risk Reduction and the General Secretariat of the OAS.[73] The Summit of the Americas has encouraged the states of the region to participate in the global efforts to combat environmental degradation, and the Inter-American Development Bank helps member countries address environmental challenges by financing activities to improve the management of environmental projects—for instance, wind power in Peru.[74] The United States itself, by means of its Environmental Protection Agency, works with a number of Latin American and Caribbean countries to address their environmental problems. In 2013, it launched the South America Environmental Compliance and Enforcement Network, which holds annual meetings to help participating states improve the application of their environmental laws. Currently, six countries are involved.[75]

The Arab World has been slower in responding to the challenge but an Arab Water Council works for integrated water resource management in the region and a Council of Arab Ministers Responsible for the Environment meets annually. It must of course be noted that, aside from what regional organizations may do, states use their regular diplomatic process to address some regional environmental hazards as illustrated in Textbox 9.1.

Environmental degradation can be costly and hard to correct. The global population is growing, consumption is increasing, and the spread of industry is leaving its mark on nature. But the global society is better organized. Environmental diplomacy has escalated in the last twenty-five years. Many international institutions and conferences are addressing environmental

Textbox 9.1   Instruments for the Protection of the Regional Marine Environment

1. **Baltic**
   Convention for the Protection of the Marine Environment of the Baltic Sea Area, Helsinki, 1974, revised, 1992.

2. **North-East Atlantic**
   Convention for the Protection of the Marine Environment of the North-East Atlantic, Oslo and Paris, 1974, revised and combined, 1992.

3. **Wider Caribbean**
   Convention for the Protection and Development of the Marine Environment of the Wider Caribbean Region, Cartagena, 1983.

   Protocol Concerning Cooperation in Combating Oil Spills in the Wider Caribbean Region, 1983.

   Protocol Concerning Protected Areas and Wildlife, 1990.

   Protocol on the Prevention, Reduction and Control of Land-Based Sources and Activities, 1999.

4. **Middle Atlantic**
   Convention for Cooperation in the Protection and Development of the Marine and Coastal Environment of the West and Central African Region, Abidjan, 1981.

   Protocol Concerning Cooperation in Combating Pollution in Cases of Emergency, 1981.

5. **Mediterranean**
   Convention for the Protection of the Marine Environment and the Coastal Region of the Mediterranean, Barcelona, 1976, revised, 1995.

   Protocol for the Prevention and Elimination of Pollution of the Mediterranean Sea by Dumping from Ships and Aircraft, Barcelona, 1976, revised, 1995.

   Protocol Concerning Cooperation in Combating Pollution of the Mediterranean Sea by Oil and Other Harmful Substances in Cases of Emergency, Barcelona, 1976.

   Protocol for the Protection of the Mediterranean Sea against Pollution from Land-Based Sources, Athens, 1980, amended, 1996.

   Protocol Concerning Mediterranean Specially Protected Areas, Geneva, 1982, revised, 1995.

   Protocol for the Protection of the Mediterranean Sea against Pollution Resulting from Exploration and Exploitation of the Continental Shelf and the Seabed and Its Subsoil, Madrid, 1994.

   Protocol on the Prevention of Pollution of the Mediterranean Sea by Transboundary Movement of Hazardous Wastes and Their Disposal, Izmir, Turkey, 1996.

6. **Black Sea**
   Convention on the Protection of the Black Sea against Pollution, Bucharest, 1992.

Protocol on the Protection of the Black Sea Marine Environment against Pollution from Land-Based Sources, 1992.

Protocol on Cooperation in Combating Pollution of the Black Sea Marine Environment by Oil and Other Harmful Substances in Emergency Situations, 1992.

Protocol on the Protection of the Black Sea Marine Environment against Pollution by Dumping, 1992.

7. **Red Sea and Gulf of Aden**
Convention for the Conservation of the Red Sea and Gulf of Aden Environment, Jeddah, 1982.

Protocol Concerning Regional Cooperation in Combating Pollution by Oil and Other Harmful Substances in Cases of Emergency, 1982.

8. **Kuwait Region**
Kuwait Regional Convention for Cooperation on the Protection of the Marine Environment from Pollution, 1978.

9. **Eastern Africa (Indian Ocean)**
Convention for the Protection, Management and Development of the Marine and Coastal Environment of the Eastern African Region, Nairobi, 1985.

Protocol Concerning Protected Areas and Wild Fauna and Flora in the Eastern African Region, 1985.

Protocol Concerning Cooperation in Combating Marine Pollution in Cases of Emergency in the Eastern African Region, 1985.

10. **South Pacific**
Convention for the Protection of Natural Resources and Environment of the South Pacific Region. Noumea, 1986.

Protocol for the Prevention of Pollution of the South Pacific Region by Dumping, 1986.

Protocol Concerning Cooperation in Combating Pollution Emergencies in the South Pacific Region, 1986.

11. **South-East Pacific**
Convention for the Protection of the Marine Environment and Coastal Area of the South-East Pacific, Lima, 1981.

Agreement on Regional Cooperation in Combating Pollution of the South-East Pacific by Hydrocarbons or Other Harmful Substances in Cases of Emergency, 1981. Supplementary Protocol, 1983.

Protocol for the Protection of the South-East Pacific against Pollution from Land-Based Sources, 1983.

Protocol for the Conservation and Management of Protected Marine and Coastal Areas in the South-East Pacific, 1989.

Protocol for the Protection of the South-East Pacific Against Radioactive Contamination, 1989.

Protocol on the Program for the Regional Study on the El Niño Phenomenon in the South-East Pacific, 1992.

12. **North-East Pacific**
Convention for Cooperation in the Protection and Sustainable Development of the Marine and Coastal Environment of the North-East Pacific, 2002.

13. **Western and Central Pacific**
Convention on the Conservation and Management of the Highly Migratory Fish Stocks of the Western and Central Pacific, 2000.

14. **Antarctica**
Convention on the Conservation of Antarctic Marine Living Resources, 1980.

Source: www.unep.ch/regionalseas/main/hconlist (Accessed August 24, 2010).

issues and civil society is supporting international action. The environment is well established on the diplomatic agenda. Spectacular global conferences have grappled with the problem. Significantly, *development* is now part of the picture—*sustainable* development. The struggle for development now involves environmental protection. It is a central part of global governance. A surprising number of issues have been alleviated even when some, like global warming, remain intractable. In the final analysis, the "environment problem" cannot be "solved." It is a matter of working at it and learning how to do it better. It is going to take a good deal of diplomacy.

NOTES

1. For example, the Treaty to Regulate the Transportation of Toxic Substances on the Rhine River concluded among littoral states, 1900.

2. Lorraine Elliott, *The Global Politics of the Environment* (New York: New York University Press, 1998), pp. 8–10. See Gino J. Marco, Robert M. Hollingworth and William Durham, eds. *Silent Spring Revisited* (Washington, DC: American Chemical Society, 1987).

3. Paul R. Ehrlich, *The Population Bomb* (New York: Ballantine, 1968).

4. See Wolfgang Sachs, ed. *The Global Ecology: A New Arena of Political Conflict* (London: Zed Books, 1993), and in the same volume, "The Landscape of Diplomatic Conflicts," by Tariq Banuri.

5. The diplomatic work of Maurice Strong can be found in "Engaging the Developing Countries: The Fournex Initiative." www.mauricestrong.net/20100213146/fournex/fournex/fournex-environment-conference-1971/all-pages (Accessed July 17, 2010).

6. Elliott, p. 12. www.folkrorelser.nu/inenglish/stockholm-rio (Accessed July 24, 2010).

7. www.unep.org/documents.multilingual/default (Accessed July 26, 2010).

8. Ibid.

9. www.unep.org/roa (Accessed July 16, 2012).

10. http/web.mit.edu/urbanupgrading/upgrading/resources/organizations/UNCHS (Accessed January 1, 2013).

11. www.un.org/Conferences/habitat (Accessed February 3, 2011).

12. www.unhabitat.org/about/history (Accessed July 26, 2010).

13. Forum VII Medellin, Colombia, 2014 www.unhabitat.org/content (Accessed August 30, 2014).

14. www.unhabitat.org/7th-world-urban-forum-medellin (Accessed May 28, 2015).

15. Thomas Princen and Matthias Finger, eds. *Environmental NGOs in World Politics : Linking the Local and the Global* (London: Routledge, 1994).

16. www.aip.org/history/climate/internat (Accessed July 30, 2010).

17. http://nobelprize.org/nobel_prize/peace/laureates/2007 (Accessed February 8, 2011).

18. See text at: www.unep.org/ozone/pdf/montreal-protocol20 (Accessed February 17, 2011).

19. See Rio Summit in this chapter. See also Irving M. Mintzer and J. Amber Leonard, eds. *Negotiating Climate Change: The Inside Story of the Rio Convention* (New York: Cambridge University Press, 1994).

20. http://unfccc.int/kyoto_protocol/items (Accessed February 5, 2011).

21. See Daniel Bodansky, "The History of the Global Climate Change Regime," in *International Relations and Global Climate Change*, edited by Urs Luterbacker and Detlef F. Sprinz (Cambridge, MA: MIT Press, 2001).

22. http://unfccc.int/essential_background/items (Accessed February 2, 2011).

23. See Alan E. Boyle, "The Convention on Biological Diversity," in *the Environment After Rio: International Law and Economics,* edited by Luigi Campiglio and others (London: Graham and Trotman, 1994).

24. www.cbd.int/history (Accessed January 23, 2011).

25. www.cbd.int/abs/nagoya-protocol/signatories/default (Accessed July 17, 2015).

26. www.un-document.net/wced-oef (Accessed July 30, 2010).

27. www.un.org/documents/ga/res/44/ares44-228 (Accessed August 2, 2010).

28. www.thegef.org/gef/whatisgef (Accessed July 28, 2010).

29. See Mostafa K. Tolba, Osama A. El-Kholy and others, *The World Environment: 1972–1992. Two Decades of Challenge* (London: Chapman and Hall, 1992).

30. See Shanna Halpern, *The United Nations Conference on Environment and Development: Process and Documentation* (Providence, RI: Academic Council on the United Nations System, 1992).

31. http://info.bahai.org/print/article-1-8-1-20 (Accessed January 20, 2012).

32. www.un.org/geninfo/bp/enviro2 (Accessed August 3, 2010).

33. See Caroline Thomas, "The United Nations Conference on Environment and Development (UNCED) of 1992 in Context." *Environmental Politics* Vol. 1, No. 4 (Winter 1992), pp. 250–261.

34. Elliott, pp. 87–89.

35. www.un.org/esa/forests/about-history (Accessed August 20, 2010).

36. www.un-redd.org/AboutUNREDDProgramme (Accessed February 2, 2011).

37. Ibid.

38. www.un.org/esa/dsd/csd/csd_aboucsd (Accessed August 9, 2010).

39. sd.issd.org/events (Accessed January 5, 2015).

40. http://207.190.239.143/monitoringandevaluation/meabout/meabout (Accessed August 11, 2010).

41. Joyeeto Gupta, "The Global Environmental Facility in its North-South Context," *Environmental Politics* Vol. 4, No. 1 (Spring 1995), pp. 19–43.

42. *About the Global Environmental Facility* www.thegef.org/gef/sites.thegef-org/files/publication/GEF-Fact-Sheets-June09 (Accessed July 28, 2010).

43. P. Haas, Marc A. Levy, and Edward A. Parsons, "Appraising the Earth Summit: How Should We Judge UNCED Success?" *Environment* Vol. 34, No. 8 (1992), pp. 6–11, 26–33.

44. www.un.org/geninfo/bp/envirp3 (Accessed August 3, 2010).

45. www.unced.int/convention/menu (Accessed January 29, 2011).

46. www.unced.int/convention/menu (Accessed January 29, 2011).

47. See *Basic Facts on Desertification*, www.nyo.unep.org/action/15f (Accessed January 29, 2011).

48. 22nd Special Session of the UN General Assembly. www.iisd.ca/sids (Accessed August 5, 2010).

49 AOSIS' website lists 40 member states and 4 observers. http://aosis.info (Accessed January 2, 2013).

50. www.sidsnet.org/docshare/other/20050622163242_English (Accessed August 13, 2012).

51. See Evelyne Meltzer, Global Overview of Straddling and Highly Migratory Fish Stocks. www.dfo-mpo.gc.ca/fgc-cap/index.

52. www.un.org/ecosocdev/geninfo/sustdev/fishery (Accessed August 9, 2010).

53. www.un.org/Depts/los/reference_files/status2005 (Accessed February 15, 2011).

54. www.unep.org/regionalseas (Accessed February 15, 2011).

55. www.imo.org/dynamic/mainframe (Accessed August 12, 2010). See also David L. VanderZwaag and Ann Powers, "The Protection of the Marine Environment from Land-Based Pollution and Activities: Gauging the Tides of Global and Regional Governance," *Journal of Marine and Coastal Law* Vol. 23 (2008), pp. 423–452.

56. The eight Millennium Development Goals to be reached by 2015 were:

1. Eradicate extreme hunger and poverty.
2. Achieve universal primary education.
3. Promote gender equality and empower women.
4. Reduce child mortality.
5. Improve maternal health.
6. Combat HIV/AIDS, malaria, and other diseases.
7. Ensure environmental sustainability.
8. Develop a global partnership for development.

www.unmillenniumproject.org/goals/index (Accessed February 1, 2011).

57. www.johannesburgsummit.org/html/basic_info/basicinfo (Accessed July 23, 2015).

58. www.un.org/en/mdg/summit2010 (Accessed February 1, 2011).

59. www.un.org/millenniumgoals/environ (Accessed January 31, 2011).

60. https://sustainabledevelopment.un.org (Accessed July 24, 2015).

61. www.civitas.org.uk/eufacts/FSENV/ENV1 (Accessed August 30, 2010).

62. www.mta.ca/faculty/socsci/geograph/genv4111/International%20laws (Accessed July 15, 2010), p. 7.

63. Margaret P. Karns and Karen A. Mingst, *International Organizations: The Politics and Processes of Global Governance* (2nd ed. Boulder, CO: Lynne Rienner, 2010), p. 525.

64. http://eionet.europa.eu (Accessed August 30, 2010).

65. http://europa.eu/rapid/pressReleasesAction (Accessed August 30, 2010).

66. See projects at www.aseansec.org (Accessed July 18, 2012).

67. Their tenth meeting took place in October 2011. Ibid.

68. Ibid.

69. www.africa-union.org/official_documents/Treaties (Accessed August 30, 2010).

70. Amcen.eeaa.gov.eg/en-us/session2014 (Accessed January 11, 2015).

71. http://africasd.iisd.org/institutions/african-ministerial-conference-on-envirnment-amcen (Accessed July 18, 2012).

72. See www.oas.org/en/topics/environment; and www.oas.org/en/sedi/dsd (Accessed July 19, 2012).

73. www.oas.org/en/sedi/dsd/EN_Overview_Schools_with_a_Sustainable_Future (Accessed June 1, 2015).

74. www.iadb.org/en/topics/environment-in-latin-america-and-the-caribbean (Accessed June 1, 2015).

75. www2.epa.gov/international-cooperation/epa-efforts-latin-america-and-caribbean (Accessed June 1, 2015).

Chapter 10

The Future of Global Governance Diplomacy

Global society is likely to become more complex and is also likely to face a multiplicity of challenges requiring collective attention—such as environmental degradation. The need for global governance will thus increase and with it, the use of diplomacy. The diplomatic agenda will expand. More aspects of life in society that used to be strictly domestic will have international dimensions. The world is becoming more interdependent and more issues will need to be addressed internationally—such as disease control. The distinction between what is domestic and what is international will become more blurred. Diplomats will be negotiating a wider variety of issues and the mix of international actors is bound to become more elaborate.

States will remain most important as they wield power, even when underdeveloped. Their conflicts can destabilize entire regions—take, for example, the current situation in the Middle East. They strive for freedom of action, often seen as a sovereign right, which complicates the need for international cooperation. Some are woefully governed and afflicted by corruption. Even the better-run states have different notions of the common good and different views of their self-interest. Getting them to work together may remain problematic and may require a great deal of diplomacy. Ideology and technology have given some groups, such as the al-Qaeda or the Islamic State of Iraq and Syria (ISIS), the capacity to spread chaos, challenging former concepts of governance. Global governance is not going to be any easier.

International organizations will continue playing a highly significant role. In fact, they are likely to become more significant. They are not a panacea, but they render services beyond the capacity of nation states. They will remain very diverse. They will retain their dual function—first, as forums where member states dialogue, debate issues, and make joint decisions, and second, as international actors, taking initiatives of their own, participating in

239

international affairs and causing their role to escalate, for example, by engaging in peacekeeping and peace building. This international actor function will remain of capital importance. Many of the problems facing international society cannot be solved once and for all. They need continuing attention and many international organizations are well suited to doing that—"managing" international situations as they evolve, and by using their own diplomatic means. Thus international organizations can be expected to be important *instruments* of global governance. Some international organizations will add to their effectiveness by working together, forming partnerships. Regional or limited membership organizations can also be helpful for the future of global governance. They enable states with common interests and affinities to achieve greater cooperation and greater problem-solving capacity leading to some experimentation, for example, the creation of international banking systems—thereby making use of so many tools of global governance once thought utopian. As global society organizes it seems more willing to try new mechanisms.

Old-fashioned tools, however, remain promising. The international conference is a prime example. It is flexible and versatile. The participants can be chosen to suit the purpose at hand. Conferences can be convened by states, by international organizations, or even by civil society institutions and NGOs. New forms have been devised and, as international society evolves, new practices will emerge. The Cold War led to small summit meetings and this form of dialogue proved constructive. Some of it, such as the G7, was institutionalized. The problem is that new powers have emerged, particularly among the rapidly developing states, but there is a limit to the number of participants one can add to these summits while still retaining their effectiveness. A new variety of small meetings has been added: specialized ministerial meetings. Many summits have preconference meetings of officials to prepare for the main event and there are postsummit proceedings to make better use of what was done at the summit. The UN has called meetings "at the highest level." A new variety of conference that seems to have a future is built into some important treaties, such as "Conferences of the Parties (COPs)," in which representatives of the parties to a given treaty are mandated to meet periodically, not only to assess implementation but also to negotiate revisions. This does not work for all agreements. Some are intended to remain as initially agreed upon. However, it does show how established diplomatic tools can be modified. More innovations will take place in the future as with informal forums, open to states and other actors and civil society representatives. Informal forums are now convened on the occasion of large diplomatic conferences to enable those who are not participating in the proceedings to be heard and perhaps present a collective statement to the diplomatic conference. These forums are likely to remain popular. They widen international dialogue and permit the exploration of new ideas. Regional forums are helpful in preparation for global conferences.

Increasing interdependence and the communication revolution are leading the private sector and its NGOs to seek greater involvement in global governance. This will escalate. The UN has greatly contributed to this development. Kofi Annan, former secretary-general, was fond of the idea of partnership with the private sector. A number of UN bodies are more open to NGO contribution. The private sector fosters openness in international affairs and gives a new dimension to some international dialogues. Informal forums will permit even broader participation. But it may not be appropriate to speak of the democratization of global governance. Private-sector institutions may be quite open to grassroots input but they are not representative. They are very diverse. What they can contribute varies widely. Some are poorly informed; others are ideological. But they are likely to become more prominent on the international scene.

A different way of expanding the international dialogue is likely to grow in the form of interparliamentary bodies (attached to regional organizations), composed of members of national parliaments, often representing the political diversity found there. These delegations do not speak for national governments. They do not have to abide by national policy and do not take orders from their national leadership. Their functions depend upon the regional organizations creating them, but they are seldom part of the organizations' decision-making process. They are mostly deliberative and advisory. They are nevertheless another channel of public expression on international issues, likely to expand in the future.

The experience of global society since the Second World War indicates a trend toward extensive collective activity in dealing with international phenomena. As new challenges emerge, new tools will be devised. Will it give the world more peace and security? Confrontations with the Soviet Union could have led to war. Diplomacy contributed to the maintenance of peace, along with a good deal of inventiveness including the UN's Uniting for Peace Resolution and the "Hot Line." But the world remains conflict-oriented. Peacekeeping was a remarkable achievement and it will continue to be used in many parts of the world. This form of international response is receiving unusual support. The quality of the units deployed needs to be strengthened. Peacekeeping is not suited for large conflicts such as the civil war in Syria. Peace observation, supervision, or monitoring will remain most useful in many situations. Peacebuilding is an enormous step in the right direction, but hard to do and without standard methodology. It has to be attempted one step at a time. International organizations can make a serious contribution in this area.

And there is the issue of terrorism, a special challenge, fostered by revolution, ideology, and religious fanaticism. Modern weapons make it more dangerous. Diplomacy is critical to mobilize international support in combating it. A major problem is that each terrorist movement has different origins, political objectives, and even international allies. Creating coalitions to fight terrorists will often have to vary with the movements concerned and perhaps also the region affected. The UN will remain extremely helpful in addressing the problem, getting more states involved in the struggle, cooperating in intelligence gathering, and stopping money laundering. Some regional organizations may also provide assistance in doing that. In the end, terrorism is easy to carry out and tempting to resort to. International society will remain challenged by some forms of it.

International peace has another dimension that can be served by the old-fashioned method of peaceful settlement, that is, accommodation, keeping conflict under control, or finding alternatives for what states are fighting over. This will remain an attractive method. In fact, the world is better equipped to make it work in the future because of the expanding role of international organizations. Now there is nothing automatic in conflict management and the best efforts may always fail. But there are more international actors prepared to help, including NGOs. Mediation will remain an important procedure. As in the past, the critical element is diplomacy. But more actors are prepared to intervene and serve as intermediaries even when the contenders refuse to negotiate. Peace observation or some forms of peacekeeping may now be available to let diplomacy try to produce results. International organizations bring states together where sources of conflict can be discussed and future problems explored. In some cases, international courts can effectively settle disputes and states are less reluctant to use them. International society has created an unprecedented number of them, particularly at the regional level.

Can arms control make peace more secure in the future? It helped during the Cold War. Effectively supervised arms agreements contribute to international confidence building. Preventing arms races creates a better international climate. Keeping weapons of mass destruction from falling into the hands of terrorists is indispensable for international security and it will require continuing diplomatic efforts. An agreement has even been reached to control trade in conventional arms, an important step given the activities of radical groups destabilizing entire regions. The problem remains one of enforcement. The arms trade is very lucrative. And international society is still faced with a number of governments providing arms to revolutionary groups they are determined to support.

Some states are likely to remain ambitious and may, in the future, use military power to acquire a more dominant role, at least regionally. North Korea is still bellicose and militaristic. Russia proved expansionist in Ukraine, and the self-proclaimed ISIS embarked upon outright military conquest. Military preparedness for self-defense and collective security remains a necessity for the foreseeable future. The UN has done better than the League of Nations in fostering security. But peacekeeping is ineffective in large-scale conflict and aggression by powerful states. Much more work is needed in the future to lead states to carry out what the UN Charter wanted to do with the Security Council. True collective security remains a necessity. Even NATO is an imperfect alternative.

Interestingly, over the years, security has grown to encompass a larger meaning: *human security.* This is not intended to replace protection from aggression, but it includes an economic and social dimension that is already found in the UN Charter, especially with the ECOSOC and the creation of the Specialized Agencies. Economic and social matters are now an integral part of global governance efforts and are certain to expand in the future. Much greater economic cooperation and coordination are needed. The ICAO, now a UN Specialized Agency, was given unusual legislative powers to create new rules of the air to permit the expansion of international civil aviation after the Second World War, and revise them as aviation technology evolved. The ICAO was also given enforcement authority. Such unusual powers in a world of sovereign states reflect the vital need for regulation for safe air travel.

In the realm of global finance, the IMF and the World Bank have led the way, trying to foster financial stability and reduce economic inequality. But they still have much to learn and many states are far from acting responsibly. These banking institutions have contributed to the financing of development and humanitarian projects and this kind of work will expand in the future. Regional international banks have been created showing that international society is adjusting to this kind of international function. The EU, with its more integrated system, is also trying to learn how to generate financial stability. In the meantime, global banking is contributing to economic and social development. The promotion of global trade has also been a major pursuit of the international system. But many states are still clinging to various forms of protectionism. Freer trade will probably require years of difficult negotiations. But the creation of the WTO should be viewed as an achievement with its system of compulsory settlement of trade disputes. Regional organizations will continue to promote special trade relationships in their parts of the world.

The reduction of poverty and the achievement of sustainable development are now major goals for global governance—a monumental task. The UN's MDGs were perhaps too ambitious for the target date of 2015. However, the remarkable campaign continued over the years by the world organization generated such unusual global support and success in reaching some of the goals that the Millennium Project will be continued beyond 2015 with reformulated objectives. The reduction of inequality and attendant battle against poverty are now a well-established part of the global agenda—a notable development. The task remains monumental. But as more international actors participate in the common effort, international society is likely to derive substantial benefits. The results already achieved show that this project is more than pie in the sky.

The UN and its Specialized Agencies have shown the way in a large variety of activities that belong to the broad social category—many of them contributing to the attainment of the MDGs and their future iteration. The future of global governance includes a well-established social agenda likely to grow. Global health care is an important endeavor in an interdependent world. Disease does not respect boundaries. And then, there is the challenge of making modern medicine available to the millions who do not even have clean drinking water in their remote villages. The WHO has done pioneering work in the field. A number of UN bodies have health concerns in their own specialized missions. They enjoy a natural partnership with the WHO. The challenge is to channel enough resources through these organizations to get the job done—and the World Bank is here to help. It is always frustrating to realize that so many important tasks exceed the means available. However, we must appreciate that there is in place a network of organizations already contributing something to a more distant "solution"—although the word "solution" is probably inappropriate. Many of these problems have no final solution. It is more a matter of working at them and keeping them under control as they evolve. And we are better equipped today to do that. Much has been done to educate international society about the population explosion, and progress has been made despite cultural and religious barriers. However, much more remains to be done, particularly in destitute nations. There is now greater understanding that the issue is tied to the emancipation of women and the protection of their human rights. The rapid expansion of the role of civil society in the international dialogue will make a difference. Poverty and hunger remain dominant in many parts of the world, but many organizations are working on sustainable development.

A different area of the social order is the abuse of the labor force, for too long viewed as just a consequence of the industrial revolution rather than exploitation. Labor unrest, the communist movement, and revolution jolted parts of international society before there was much thinking about the international protection of human rights and before steps were taken to address the situation. The ILO, now a UN Specialized Agency, created the International Labor Code with the unusual participation of independent labor representatives—showing how some organizations can innovate. These labor representatives challenge member states during the annual Labor Conference on the manner in which they enforce labor standards, thus applying public international pressure for decent labor treatment. This must be acknowledged as a noteworthy contribution to the improvement of working conditions. In another sector of the social order, the UN has created highly successful programs to protect children (with UNICEF), particularly in poor countries. It has also taken the initiative to lead global society to be more diligent with regard to the well-being of young and the aged, two groups that many countries have neglected. The UN is creating greater awareness of unmet needs that domestic societies are invited to address. Continued international dialogue with regard to these neglected groups will foster needed concern.

The UN is also generating global dialogue in education, science, and culture. UNESCO, the UN Specialized Agency, is fostering international cooperation in these areas, although such efforts are not without controversy, which illustrates the importance of having an organization engaged in such pursuits. Many states are not very proficient doing it on their own. Education is receiving increasing attention. It is of course a critical element in the pursuit of economic and social development. UNESCO's "Education for All" campaign in cooperation with several international organizations will generate new programs at all educational levels and generate additional funding. It is likely to be a long-term endeavor despite efforts in the Millennium Project to hasten the process. The UNU, an earlier venture, provides higher education tailored to the needs of developing societies.

The mass movement of people to escape violence, oppression, or poverty is occurring on an unprecedented scale and creating a humanitarian crisis. The states in which they are seeking refuge also need help. The UNHCR is making a remarkable contribution. But the continuing migration of people trying to escape destitution is causing social destabilization in many countries in which they seek resettlement. They are a different kind of refugees, and international society is still looking for ways to address this growing problem as well as the related issue of organized human trafficking. In another humanitarian issue, the UN has tried to help with disaster relief by providing assistance to the victims without delay and coordinating the help offered. It is an attempt to be ready whenever and wherever disaster strikes. The availability of experienced personnel is particularly important. The UN has also attempted the more problematic task of disaster reduction. Disasters may be hard to predict but some regions are disaster prone and steps are worth taking to reduce the potential impact on the most vulnerable. Global society is trying to be better prepared.

Still in the category of social endeavors, how to respond to the problem of drugs and crime will remain a major challenge. Global society took a long time to address drugs. But, even now, a great deal of money can still be made in the trade. There is plenty of corruption around to prevent effective control, and there will probably always be addicts. More comprehensive efforts against money laundering will help. The fact that such efforts are also needed to fight terrorism is useful. International society has been concerned about the growth and diversification of transnational organized crime, and the

UN increased its efforts to fight it with the negotiation of new international conventions, one of them on the problem of corruption. The UNODC keeps the issue of law enforcement on the global agenda and provides assistance for more effective crime fighting. But the issue will remain an international challenge.

More encouraging is the protection of human rights, although abuses are still a widespread reality around the world. But there is a solid foundation for future international efforts. The UN made human rights an important matter of global concern and defined them in the Universal Declaration even including economic, social, and cultural rights—a significant contribution. It is true that the ILO created the International Labor Code following the First World War, but the world was not ready to view international labor protection as a matter of human rights, which shows how much remained to be done. The international protection of human rights is now well established in the global diplomatic agenda. Some regional organizations have created means of enforcement, which serve as models for other organizations.

Violating human rights is becoming a political liability. The UN and its global conferences provide forums in which abuses and the need for reforms will be brought up and discussed inviting new initiatives, for example, launching the MDGs and the impressive global campaign to achieve them. Reform in the field of human rights is no longer primarily focused on legal protection and the negotiation of new conventions. A global trend offering promise for the future includes the creation of conditions in which more people can enjoy their fundamental rights such as freedom from hunger and destitution, access to health care and education, and women's rights. This should not be exclusively focused on the developing world. Dismal conditions exist in "rich" countries, as can be witnessed in their urban slums. Civil society and the expanding role of its NGOs will be an increasingly important factor in the protection of human rights, particularly their use of global "forums" widely open to stakeholders of all kinds in addition to official representatives. International organizations are also likely to increase the role of civil society in their decision making. Protecting human rights will remain monumental. But the world is better equipped to carry it out.

Environmental protection is another global challenge. Some of it will remain intractable. It took diplomacy to catch the attention of governments. The UN was ahead of its time when it convened the Stockholm Conference, and it succeeded in placing the environment on the global diplomatic agenda. Civil society found in environmental protection a new cause. Many countries, however, believe that they have more urgent problems to address and this is likely to be the case in the future. Nevertheless, international dialogue and diplomatic efforts generated many initiatives. The UNEP's Urban Environment Program and companion UN-Habitat are frameworks for future work in the field as the problem evolves. This will remain the advantage of creating agencies specialized in specific issues. They foster continuing efforts in their respective programs.

The UN's 1992 Rio Summit was spectacular, generating more diplomatic work, linking environment and development, and helping new nations see the relevance of environmental protection to their own condition. Their future progress toward development requires environmental sustainability. Moreover, as is often the case, global conferences, with all their elaborate preparatory work, are media events. The Rio Conference energized civil society and its NGOs. Efforts were made by the UN to involve NGOs in the global dialogue. Some 17,000 attended the civil society Parallel Forum. Thirteen NGOs were invited to address the Conference plenary meeting. Concern for the environment was seen as gaining momentum. This will have a positive effect on future efforts. The Rio Conference generated such global interest in environmental protection that the UN's Millennium Summit included environmental sustainability among its celebrated MDGs. The massive global effort to reach these goals created remarkable popular enthusiasm for the project and, in the process, gave environmental protection additional support. Regional initiatives added to these global environmental endeavors. None of this existed fifty years ago. Environmental diplomacy is now well established and more projects will be launched.

In the end, is the future more promising? The world is better organized for joint efforts. More international actors are taking part in this diplomacy. Useful tools of international governance have been created and a number of problems have been successfully addressed. Inevitably, there will be more crises in the future, some probably worse. Given the evolution of technology and growing interdependence, more people will be affected by such developments. However, it must be acknowledged that the global system has changed Nations interact on a grand scale. The amount of diplomatic work is beyond quantification. Of course there is disagreement. But the opportunity for negotiations is unprecedented—in international organizations, in a growing number of conferences and consultations, and in response to NGOs more anxious than ever to play a role. The multiplication of international actors means that a greater diversity of initiatives is available to address international problems. This may complicate governance, but offers more alternatives. Success is never guaranteed but we can learn from all this experience.

Appendix

ARMS CONTROL AGREEMENTS AND
RELATED ARRANGEMENTS SINCE 1945

M = Multilateral; B = Bilateral (US-USSR/Russia); * = with UN involvement

1959   Antarctic Treaty (M). Demilitarizes the Antarctic continent.
1957   International Atomic Energy Agency (IAEA), Vienna (M*). Verifies the peaceful use of nuclear power and safe storage of nuclear material.
1963   Partial Test-Ban Treaty (M*).
1967   Outer Space Treaty (M*). Demilitarizes outer space.
1967   Latin America Nuclear-Free Zone Treaty. Tlatelolco Treaty (M).
1968   Nuclear Non-Proliferation Treaty (M*).
1969   Strategic Arms Limitation Talks. SALT I (B).
1971   Zangger Committee established to implement the Nuclear Non-Proliferation Treaty (M).
1971   Seabed Treaty (M*). Prohibits emplacing weapons of mass destruction (WMDs) on the seabed.
1972   Biological Weapons Convention (M*).
1972   Anti-Ballistic Missile Treaty (B). Limits strategic missile defenses.
1972   Interim Agreement. Capped intercontinental ballistic missile (ICBM) and submarine-launched ballistic missile (SLBM) forces (B).
1974   Threshold Test-Ban Treaty (B). Limits underground nuclear weapon tests.
1975   Conference for Security and Cooperation in Europe (CSCE) (M). Fosters East-West dialogue on military activities and disarmament.
1975   Nuclear Suppliers Group agreed to coordinate nuclear export controls (M).

1976   Peaceful Nuclear Explosion Treaty (B). Prohibits peaceful underground nuclear tests having a yield exceeding 150 kilotons.
1977   Environmental Modifications Convention (M*).
1977   U.S.-IAEA Safeguards Agreement (B*).
1979   Strategic Nuclear Arms Limitation Talks (SALT II) (B).
1979   Moon and other Celestial Bodies treaty (M*). Ensures their demilitarization.
1980   Protection of Nuclear Material Convention (M*).
1981   Inhumane Weapons Convention (CCW Convention) (M*).
        CCW Protocol I. Prohibits weapons with fragments not detectable in the human body by X-rays.
        CCW Protocol II. Restricts the use of mines, booby-traps and other devices.
        CCW Protocol III. Restricts the use of incendiary weapons.
        CCW Protocol IV. Prohibits laser weapons to cause permanent blindness.
        CCW Protocol V. To minimize the effects of explosive remnants of war.
1984   Australia Group. 30-state informal group to impede chemical weapon proliferation (M).
1985   South Pacific Nuclear Weapon Free Zone. Rarotonga Treaty (M).
1986   Stockholm Agreement (CSCE) (M). Confidence- and Security-Building Measures and Disarmament in Europe.
1987   Intermediate-Range Nuclear Forces Treaty (INF) (B). To destroy ground-launched missiles of a specified range. 2,692 missiles were eliminated by May 1991.
1989   Bilateral Verification Experiment and Data Exchange Agreement (B). Pertains to chemical weapons.
1990   Bilateral Destruction Agreement (B). Pertains to chemical weapons.
1990   Conventional Forces in Europe (CFE Treaty) (M). Sets ceilings on equipment.
1991   Presidential Nuclear Initiatives.
1991   Strategic Arms Reduction Treaty (START I) (B).
1991   UN Register of Conventional Arms (M*).
1992   Agreement on Personnel Strength of Conventional Armed Forces in Europe (CFE-1A Agreement) (M).
1992   CSCE Forum for Security Cooperation (M). Pertains to military matters.
1992   Open Skies Treaty (NATO-Warsaw Pact). Permits surveillance aircraft overflights.
1993   Strategic Arms Reduction Treaty (START II) (B). Eliminates some strategic missiles and reduces number of nuclear warheads.

1993 Chemical Weapons Convention (CWC) (M*).

1993 Fissile Material Disposition Treaty (B).

1994 CSCE Agreement on Confidence and Security-Building in Europe (M). Pertains to the exchange of military information.

1994 Agreement transforming the Conference for Security and Cooperation in Europe (CSCE) into the Organization for Security and Cooperation in Europe (OSCE) (M). Expands cooperation for arms control.

1994 OSCE Code of Conduct on political-military aspects of security (M).

1995 Wassenaar Export Control Treaty (M). Pertains to conventional weapons.

1995 Southeast Asia Nuclear Weapon-Free Zone Treaty. Bangkok Treaty (M).

1996 African Nuclear-Weapon-Free Zone Treaty. Pelindaba Treaty (M).

1996 Florence Agreement (M) (per 1995 Dayton Accord). Sets arms ceilings on the parties to the war in Bosnia.

1996 Comprehensive Nuclear Test-Ban Treaty (CTBT) (M*). A global moratorium on nuclear tests is effectively in place since 1998.

1996 Comprehensive Nuclear-Test Ban Treaty Organization (CTBTO) (M*). Will monitor implementation of the comprehensive nuclear-test ban.

1996 Mutual Reduction of Military Forces in the Border Areas (Russia, China, Kazakhstan, Kyrgyzstan, and Tajikistan) (M).

1996 US-Russia-IAEA Agreement (M*).Verifies weapon-origin nuclear materials.

1997 Preparatory Commission for the CTBTO and Provisional Technical Secretariat (M*). Provisionally operates the international monitoring system (321 monitoring stations) until the CTBT Organization is operational.

1997 Strategic Arms Reduction Treaty Framework (START III) (B).

1997 Inter-American Convention against Illicit Manufacturing of and Trafficking in Firearms, Ammunition, Explosives, and Related Materials (M).

1997 Anti-personnel Landmine Treaty (M*).

1997 Organization for the Prohibition of Chemical Weapons (OPCW) (M).

1997 Small arms moratorium in Africa (part of the Program for Coordination and Assistance for Security and Development in Africa (PCASED)) (M).

1998 International Convention for the Suppression of Terrorist Bombings (M*).

1998 Informal Global Moratorium on Nuclear-Weapons Testing (M).

1999 Inter-American Convention on Transparency in Conventional Weapons Acquisitions (M) for the purpose of confidence building.

1999 Vienna Agreement (OSCE) on Confidence- and Security-Building Measures (M).
2000 OSCE Agreement on small arms (M).
2001 Protocol Against the Illicit Manufacturing of, and Trafficking in, Firearms, Their Parts and Components and Ammunition (M*).
2002 US-Russia Strategic Offensive Reductions Treaty (SORT) (B).
2002 International Code of Conduct against Ballistic Missile Proliferation (M).
(The Hague Code of Conduct). Supplements the Missile Technology Control Regime of 1987.
2003 Proliferation Security Initiative. An association of more than 80 countries to restrict nuclear shipments (M).
2003 OSCE Document on Stockpiles of Conventional Ammunition (M).
2005 Nuclear Terrorism Convention (M*).
2006 Economic Community of West African States (ECOWAS) Convention on Small Arms (M).
2006 Central Asia Nuclear-Weapon-Free Zone Treaty. Semipalatinsk Treaty (M).
2008 Convention on Cluster Munitions (M*).
2008 European Union Common Rules to Control Exports of Military Technology and Equipment (M).
2010 Measures for the Further Reduction and Limitation of Strategic Offensive Arms (New START) (B).
2013 Arms Trade Treaty (M*) Regulates international trade in conventional arms.

BILATERAL RISK REDUCTION AGREEMENTS

1963 US-Soviet Hot Line Agreement.
1971 US-Soviet Accidents Measures Agreement to reduce the risks of nuclear war.
1972 US-Soviet Incidents at Sea Agreement.
1987 US-Soviet Nuclear Risk Reduction Centers Agreement. Does not replace previously established hot line.
1988 US-Soviet Ballistic Missile Launch Notification Agreement.
1991–2004 Cooperative Threat Reduction: 9 agreements to dismantle nuclear, chemical, and biological weapons between the United States and Russia, Ukraine, Belarus, Kazakhstan, and, subsequently, Moldova, Georgia, Uzbekistan, Azerbaijan, and Albania (2004).
1994 US-Russia Mutual Detargeting of ballistic missiles.

2000   US-Russia Joint Data Exchange Center (JDEC) for the exchange of missile data.

2008   US-China Military Hotline Agreement.

2008   China-Russia Military Hot Line Agreement.

2008   China-South Korea Hot Line Agreement linking their air forces and navies to prevent military incidents and promote cooperation in emergency situations.

Note: A number of these agreements were subsequently revised; some have provisions for periodic review conferences.

Source: Stockholm International Peace Research Institute (SIPRI) Yearbook, 2008. Annex A. Arms Control and Disarmament, pp. 517–542. Also, Federation of American Scientists, *Arms Control Agreements*. www.fas.org/nuke/control/index (Accessed July 14, 2009).

Bibliography

Acharya, Amitan. "The Emerging Regional Architecture of World Politics," *World Politics*, LIX (July, 2007), 629–52.

———, and Johnston, Alastair Ian, eds. *Crafting Cooperation: Regional International Institutions in Comparative Perspective*. New York: Cambridge University Press, 2007.

Ahmad, Ayaz, ed. *Disaster Management: Through the New Millennium*. New Delhi: Anmol Publications, 2003.

Alger, Chadwick. "The Emerging Roles of NGOs in the UN System: From Article 71 to a People's Millennium Assembly," *Global Governance*, VIII (January–March, 2002), 93–117.

Alvarez, José E. *International Organizations as Law-Makers*. New York: Oxford University Press, 2005.

Avant, Deborah D., Finnemore, Martha, and Sell, Susan K., eds. *Who Governs the Globe?* New York: Cambridge University Press, 2010.

Ba, Alice D., and Hoffmann, Matthew. *Contending Perspectives on Global Governance: Coherence, Contestation, and World Order*. New York: Routledge, 2005.

Bache, Ian, and Flinders, Matthew. *Multi-Level Governance*. New York: Oxford University Press, 2004.

Barabasi, Albert-Lazslo. *Linked: The New Science of Networks*. New York: Basic Books, 2002.

Barnett, Michael, and Duvall, Raymond, eds. *Power in Global Governance*. New York: Cambridge University Press, 2005.

Barnett, Scott. *Why Cooperate? The Incentive to Supply Global Public Goods*. New York: Oxford University Press, 2007.

Basher, Reid. *Global Early Warning Systems for Natural Hazards: Systematic and People-Centered*. London: Philosophical Transactions of the Royal Society, 2006.

Bass, Stephen, and Dalal-Clayton, Barry. *Small Island States and Sustainable Development: Strategic Issues and Experience*. London: International Institute for Environment and Development, 1995.

Baylis, John, and Smith, Steve, eds. *The Globalization of World Politics.* 2nd ed. New York: Oxford University Press, 2001.

Bayne, Nicholas, and Woolcock, Stephen, eds. *The New Economic Diplomacy: Decision-Making and Negotiations in International Economic Relations.* 3rd ed. Burlington, VT: Ashgate, 2011.

Bercovitch, Jacob. *Theory and Practice of International Mediation.* New York: Routledge, 2011.

Berridge, G. R. *Diplomacy: Theory and Practice.* 3rd ed. London: Palgrave, 2005.

Bilal, Sanoussi, de Lombaerde, Philippe, and Tussie, Diana, eds. *Asymmetric Trade Negotiations.* Burlington, VT: Ashgate, 2011.

Bindi, Federiga, ed. *The Foreign Policy of the European Union: Assessing Europe's Role in the World.* Washington, DC: Brookings Institution, 2009.

Bjola, Cornelu, and Kornprobst, Markus. *Understanding International Diplomacy: Theory, Practice, and Ethics.* New York: Routledge, 2013.

Bjorgo, Einar. *Space Aid: Current and Potential Uses of Satellite Imagery in Humanitarian Organizations.* Washington, DC: US Institute of Peace, 2002.

Boyd-Judson, Lyn. *Strategic Moral Diplomacy: Understanding the Enemy's Moral Universe.* Sterling, VA: Kumarian Press, 2011.

Broadhead, Lee-Ann. *International Environmental Politics: The Limits of Green Diplomacy.* Boulder, CO: Lynne Rienner, 2002.

Brown-Shafi, Susan. *Promoting Good Governance, Development and Accountability: Implementation and the WTO.* New York: Palgrave Macmillan, 2011.

Buergenthal, Thomas, Shelton, Dinah, and Stewart, David P. *International Human Rights in a Nutshell.* St. Paul, MN: West Publishing, 2009.

Burt, Richard, and Fulton, Barry. *Reinventing Diplomacy in the Information Age.* Washington, DC: Center for Strategic and International Studies, 1998.

Cahill, Kevin M. *Preventive Diplomacy: Stopping Wars Before They Start.* New York: Basic Books, 1996.

Caldwell, Dan, and Williams, Robert E., Jr. *Seeking Security in an Insecure World.* 2nd ed. New York: Rowman and Littlefield, 2011.

Cameron, Maxwell A., Lawson, Robert J., and Tomlin, Brian W., eds. *To Walk Without Fear: The Global Movement to Ban Landmines.* New York: Oxford University Press, 1998.

Center on International Cooperation, New York University. *Annual Review of Global Peace Operations.* Boulder, CO: Lynne Rienner Publishers, 2014.

Chasek, Pamela S., Downie, David L., and Brown, Janet Welsh. *Global Environmental Politics.* 6th ed. Boulder, CO: Westview Press, 2013.

Chayes, Abram, and Chayes, Antonia Handler, eds. *Preventing Conflict in the Post-Communist World: Mobilizing International and Regional Organizations.* Washington, DC: Brookings, 1996.

Chesterman, Simon. *Secretary or General? The UN Secretary-General in World Politics.* New York: Cambridge University Press, 2007.

Christoff, Peter, and Eckersley, Robyn. *Globalization and the Environment.* New York: Rowman and Littlefield, 2013.

Clapp, Jennifer. *Hunger in the Balance: The New Politics of International Food Aid.* Ithaca, NY: Cornell University Press, 2012.

Cohen, Raymond. *Negotiating Across Cultures: International Communication in an Interdependent World.* Washington, DC: US Institute of Peace, 1997.

Collier, Paul, ed. *Globalization and Poverty.* 3 vols. Northampton, MA: Elgar Publishing, 2008.

Coomer, Erin Leslie. *Women's Rights as Human Rights: The Role of NGOs in Integrating Women's Rights into Human Rights Theory and Advocacy.* London: Greenwood, 2000.

Cooper, Andrew F., English, John, and Thakur, Ramesh, eds. *Enhancing Global Governance: Toward a New Diplomacy?* Tokyo: UN University Press, 2002.

Coppola, Damon P. *Introduction to International Disaster Management.* Burlington MA: Elsevier, 2007.

Corbin, Jane. *Gaza First: The Secret Norway Channel to Peace Between Israel and the PLO.* London: Bloomsbury, 1994.

Cortright, David, and Lopez, George A., eds. *Uniting Against Terror: Cooperative Nonmilitary Responses to the Global Terrorist Threat.* Cambridge, MA: MIT Press, 2007.

Crocker, Chester A., Hampson, Fen Osler, and Aall, Pamela, eds. *Herding Cats: Multiparty Mediation in a Complex World.* Washington, DC: US Institute of Peace, 1999.

———. *Managing Global Chaos: Sources of and Responses to International Conflict.* Washington, DC: US Institute of Peace, 1996.

Cronin, Bruce, and Hurd, Ian, eds. *The UN Security Council and the Politics of International Authority.* New York: Routledge, 2008.

Dannreuther, Roland. *International Security: The Contemporary Agenda.* 2nd ed. Indianapolis: Polity Books, 2013.

De Sombre, Elizabeth R. *The Global Environment and World Politics: International Relations in the 21st Century.* 2nd ed. Continuum Publishing Group, 2007.

Dicken, Peter. *Global Shift: Mapping the Changing Contours of the World Economy.* New York: Guilford Publications, 2010.

Dizard, Wilson, Jr. *Digital Diplomacy: US Foreign Policy in the Information Age.* Westport, CT: Praeger, 2001.

Donais, Timothy. *Peacebuilding and Local Ownership: Post-Conflict Consensus Building.* New York: Routledge, 2012.

Dunn, David H. ed. *Diplomacy at the Highest Level: The Evolution of International Summitry.* New York: St. Martin, 1996.

Edwards, Michael, and Gaventa, John, eds. *Global Citizen Action.* Boulder, CO: Lynne Rienner, 2001.

Elliott, Emory, Payne, Jasmine, and Ploesch, Patricia. *Global Migration, Social Change, and Cultural Transformation.* New York: Palgrave Macmillan, 2007.

Finger, Seymour Maxwell. *American Ambassador at the UN: People, Politics and Bureaucracy in Making Foreign Policy.* 2nd ed. New York: Holmes and Meier, 1988.

Florini, Ann M., ed. *The Third Force: The Rise of Transnational Civil Society.* Washington, DC: Carnegie Endowment for International Peace, 2000.

Franda, Marcus. *The United Nations in the Twenty-First Century: Management and Reform Processes in a Troubled Organization.* New York: Rowman and Littlefield, 2006.

Freytag, Andreas, Kirton, John J., Sally, Razeen, and Savona, Paolo, eds. *Securing the Global Economy: G-8 Global Governance for a Post-Crisis World.* Burlington, VT: Ashgate, 2011.

Fulton, Barry, ed. *Net Diplomacy: Beyond Foreign Ministries.* Washington, DC: US Institute of Peace, 2001.

————. *Net Diplomacy III: 2015 and Beyond.* Washington, DC: US Institute of Peace, 2005.

Galbreath, David J. *The Organization for Security and Co-operation in Europe.* New York: Routledge, 2007.

Gilmore, William C. *Dirty Money: The Evolution of International Measures to Counter Money Laundering and the Financing of Terrorism.* Strasbourg: Council of Europe Publications, 2004.

Ginsberg, Roy H. *Demystifying the European Union: The Enduring Logic of Regional Intergration.* 2nd ed. New York: Rowman and Littlefield, 2011.

Glendon, Mary Ann. *A World Made New: Eleanor Roosevelt and the Universal Declaration of Human Rights.* New York: Random House, 2001.

Glynn, Ian, and Glynn, Jenifer. *The Life and Death of Small Pox.* New York: Cambridge University Press, 2004.

Green, Michael, and Gill, Bates, eds. *Asia's New Multilateralism: Cooperation, Competition, and the Search for Community.* New York: Columbia University Press, 2009.

Hajnal, Peter I. *The G-8 System and the G-20: Evolution, Role, and Documentation.* Burlington, VT: Ashgate, 2007.

Hamilton, Keith, and Langhorne, Richard. *The Practice of Diplomacy: Its Evolution, Theory, and Administration.* New York: Routledge, 1995.

Harper, S. *Ageing Societies: Myths, Challenges, and Opportunities.* London: Hadder Arnold, 2006.

Hatton, Timothy J., and Williamson, Jeffrey A. *Global Migration and the World Economy: The Centuries of Policy and Performance.* Cambridge, MA: MIT Press, 2006.

Held, David, and McGrew, Anthony, eds. *The Global Transformations Reader: An Introduction to the Globalization Debate.* Madden, MA: Blackwell, 2000.

————. *Governing Globalization: Power, Authority, and Global Governance.* Madden, MA: Blackwell, 2002.

————. Goldblatt, David, and Perraton, Jonathan. *Global Transformation: Politics, Economics and Culture.* Cambridge, UK: Polity Press, 1999.

Henderson, D. A., and Preston, Richard. *Smallpox, the Death of a Disease: The Inside Story of Eradicating a Worldwide Killer.* Amherst, NY: Prometheus Books, 2009.

Henkin, Louis, Neuman, Gerald L., Orentlicher, Diane F., and Leebron, David W. *Human Rights.* New York: Foundation Press, 1999.

Hewitt de Alcántura, Cynthia. "Uses and Abuses of the Concept of Governance," *International Social Science Journal,* L (1998), 105–13.

Hewson, Martin, and Sinclair, Timothy, eds. *Approaches to Global Governance Theory.* Albany, NY: SUNY, 1999.

Hocking, Brian, Melissen, Jan, Riordan, Shaun, and Sharp, Paul. *Futures for Diplomacy: Integrative Diplomacy for the 21ˢᵗ Century.* The Hague: Netherlands Institute of International Relations, "Clingendael," 2012.

International Instruments Related to the Prevention and Suppression of International Terrorism. New York: UN Publications, 2008.

Ivanov, Ivan Dinev. *Transforming NATO: New Allies, Missions, and Capabilities.* Lanham, MD: Lexington Books, 2011.

Jolly, Richard, Emmerij, Louis, and Weiss, Thomas G. *The United Nations: A History of Ideas and their Future.* Bloomington, IN: Indiana University Press, 2009.

Jönsson, Christer, and Langhorne, eds. *Diplomacy.* 3 vols. London: Sage, 2004.

Karns, Margaret P., and Mingst, Karen A. *International Organizations: The Politics and Processes of Global Governance.* 2nd ed. Bouolder, CO: Lynne Rienner, 2010.

Kay, Sean. *Global Security in the Twenty-First Century: The Quest for Power and the Search for Peace.* New York: Rowman and Littlefield, 2011.

Kegley, Charles W., Jr., and Blanton, Shannon L. *World Politics: Trends and Transformation.* 14th ed. Belmont, CA: Wadsworth, 2013.

Kennan, George F. "Diplomacy without Diplomats?" *Foreign Affairs,* LXXVI (September-October, 1997), 198–212.

Keohane, Robert O., and Nye, Joseph S. *Power and Interdependence.* 2nd ed. Glenview, IL: Scott, Foresman, 1989.

Kerr, Pauline, and Wiseman, Geoffrey, eds. *Diplomacy in a Globalizing World, Theories and Practices.* New York: Oxford University Press, 2012.

Koplow, David A. *Smallpox: The Fight to Eradicate a Global Scourge.* Berkeley, CA: University of California Press, 2003.

Krau, Edgar. *Toward Globalization with a Human Face.* Lanham, MD: University Press of America, 2009.

Langholtz, Harvey J., and Stout, Chris E. *The Psychology of Diplomacy.* Westport, CT: Greenwood Publishing, 2004.

Lauren, Paul Gordon, Craig, Gordon A., and George, Alexander L. *Force and Statcraft: Diplomatic Challenges of our Time.* 5th ed. New York: Oxford University Press, 2013.

Leguey-Feilleux, Jean-Robert. *Dynamics of Diplomacy.* Boulder, CO: Lynne Rienner, 2009.

Levi, Michael A., and O'Hanlon, Michael E. *The Future of Arms Control.* Washington, DC: Brookings, 2005.

Lomperis, Timothy J. "Flawed Realism: Hans Morgenthau and Kenneth Waltz on Vietnam. The Case for a Regional Level of Analysis," Unpublished. St. Louis: St. Louis University, Political Science Department, 2005.

Lynch, David A. *Trade and Globalization: An Introduction to Regional Trade Agreements.* New York: Rowman and Littlefield, 2011.

MacKenzie, Heather, ed. *Democratizing Global Governance: Ten Years of Case Studies and Reflections by Civil Society Activists.* New Delhi: Mosaic Books, 2009.

Mathiason, John. *Invisible Governance: International Secretariats in Global Politics.* Bloomfield, CT: Kumanian, 2007.

Mautner-Markhof, Frances, ed. *Processes of International Negotiations.* Boulder, CO: Westview, 1989.

McAllister, William B. *Drug Diplomacy in the Twentieth Century.* New York: Routledge, 2000.

Melissen, Jan, ed. *Innovation in Diplomatic Practice.* New York: St. Martin's, 1999.

Minear, Larry, and Smith, Hazel, eds. *Humanitarian Diplomacy: Practitioners and their Craft.* Tokyo: UN University Press, 2007.

Mingst, Karen A., and Karns, Margaret P. *The United Nations in the 21ˢᵗ Century.* 4th ed. Boulder, CO: Westview, 2011.

Mittelman, James H. *The Globalization Syndrome: Transformation and Resistance.* Princeton, NJ: Princeton University Press, 2000.

Morin, Ann Miller. *Her Excellency: An Oral History of American Women Ambassadors.* New York: Twayne, 1995.

Muldoon, James P., Jr., Aviel, Jo Ann Fagot, Reitano, Richard, and Sullivan, Earl, eds. *Multilateral Diplomacy and the United Nations Today.* Boulder, CO: Westview, 1999.

———. *The New Dynamics of Multilateralism: Diplomacy, International Organization and Global Governance.* Boulder, CO: Westview, 2010.

Nassar, Jamal R. *Globalization and Terrorism: The Migration of Dreams and Nightmares.* 2nd ed. New York: Rowman and Littlefield, 2010.

Pécoud, Antoine, and de Guchteneire, eds. *Migration without Borders: Essays on the Free Movement of People.* Paris: UNESCO Publishing, 2007.

Pigman, Geoffrey Allen. *Contemporary Diplomacy.* Cambridge, UK: Polity, 2010.

Princen, Thomas, and Finger, Matthew, eds. *Environmental NGOs in World Politics: Linking the Local and the Global.* New York: Routledge, 1994.

Ripinsky, Sergey, and Bossche, Peter van den. *NGO Involvement in International Organizations: A Legal Analysis.* London: British Institute of International and Comparative Law, 2007.

Rosenau, James N. *Distant Proximities: Dynamics Beyond Globalization.* Princeton, NJ: Princeton University Press, 2003

———, and Singh, J. P., eds. *Information Technologies and Global Politics: The Changing Scope of Power and Governance.* Albany, NY: State University of New York Press, 2002.

Ross, Dennis. *The Missing Peace: The Inside Story of the Fight for Middle Eas Peace.* New York: Farrar, Straus, and Giroux, 2004.

Ross, Sandy. *The World Food Programme and Global Politics.* Boulder, CO: First Forum Press, 2011.

Rupert, Mark. *Ideologies of Globalization: Contending Visions of a New World Order.* New York: Routledge, 2000.

Russett, Bruce, Starr, Harvey, and Kinsella, David. *World Politics: The Menu for Choice.* 9th ed. Belmont, CA: Thomson Wadsworth, 2010.

Sachs, Wolfgang, ed. *Global Ecology: A New Arena of Political Conflict.* London: Zed Books, 1993.

Sagafi-Nejad, Tagi, with Dunning, John. *The UN and Transnational Corporations: From Code of Conduct to Global Compact.* Bloomington, IN: Indiana University Press, 2008.

Sandre, Andreas. *Digital Diplomacy: Conversations on Innovation in Foreign Policy.* New York: Rowman and Littlefield, 2015.

Schechter, Michael G., ed. *United Nations-Sponsored World Conferences: Focus on Impact and Follow-up.* Tokyo: UN University Press, 2001.

Sethi, S. Prakash. *Multinational Corporations and the Impact of Public Advocacy on Corporate Strategy: Nestlé and the Infant Formula Controversy.* The Netherlands: Kluwer Academic Publishers Group, 1994.

Severino, Rodolfo C. *The ASEAN Regional Forum.* Singapore: Institute for Southeast Asian Studies, 2009.

———. *Southeast Asia in Search of an ASEAN Community.* Singapore: ISEAS Publishing, 2006.

Shaw, Timothy M. *Commonwealth Inter- and Non-state Contributions to Global Governance.* New York: Routledge, 2008.

Shelton, Dinah, ed. *Commitment and Compliance.* New York: Oxford University Press, 2000.

Simmons, P. J., and de Jonge Oudraat, eds. *Managing Global Issues: Lessons Learned.* Washington, DC: Carnegie Endowment for International Peace, 2001.

Sinclair, Timothy. *Global Governance.* Indianapolis, IN: Polity Books, 2012.

Slaughter, Anne Marie. *A New World Order.* Princeton, NJ: Princeton University Press, 2004.

Smith, Gordon S. *Reinventing Diplomacy: A Virtual Necessity.* Washington, DC: US Institute of Peace, 1999.

Smith, Jackie, Chatfield, Charles, and Pagnucco, eds. *Transnational Social Movements and Global Politics: Solidarity beyond the State.* Syracuse, NY: Syracuse University Press, 1997.

Smock, David, ed. *Private Peacemaking: USIP-Assisted Peacemaking Projects of Nonprofit Organizations.* Washington, DC: US Institute of Peace, 1998.

Solomon, Richard, and Brown, Sheryl J. *Creating a Common Communication Culture: Interoperability in Crisis Management.* Washington, DC: US Institute of Peace, 2005.

Spector, Bertram I., Sjöstedt, Gunnar, and Zartman, I William, eds. *Negotiating International Regimes: Lessons Learned from the United Nations Conference on Environment and Development.* London: Graham and Trotman, 1994.

Staab, Andreas. *The European Union Explained: Institutions, Actors, Global Impact.* Bloomington, IN: Indiana University Press, 2008.

Starkey, Brigid, Boyer, Mark A., and Wilkenfeld, Jonathan. *International Negotiation in a Complex World.* 4th ed. New York: Rowman and Littlefield, 2015.

Starr, Harvey. *Anarchy, Order, and Integration: How to Manage Interdependence.* Ann Arbor, MI: University of Michigan Press, 1997.

Stiglitz, Joseph E. *Globalization and Its Discontents.* New York: Norton, 2002.

Talberg, Jonas, Sommerer, Thomas, Squatrito, Theresa, and Jönsson, Christer. *The Opening Up of International Organizations: Transnational Access in Global Governance.* New York: Cambridge University Press, 2013.

Tamas, Kristof, and Palme, Joakim. *Globalizing Migration Regimes: New Challenges to Transnational Cooperation.* Burlington, VT: Ashgate Publishing, 2006.

Thompson, Leigh. *The Mind and Heat of the Negotiator.* 2nd ed. Upper Saddle River, NJ: Prentice-Hall, 2001.

United Nations Institute for Disarmament Research. *The Value of Diversity in Multilateral Disarmament Work.* New York: UN Publications, 2009.

United Nations Office on Drugs and Crime. *A Century of International Drug Control.* New York: UN Publications, 2008.

———. *United Nations Congresses on Crime Prevention and Criminal Justice, 1955–2010: 55 Years of Achievement.* Vienna: UN Information Service, 2010.

US Institute of Peace. *The Challenge of Virtual Diplomacy.* Washington, DC: US Institute of Peace,,2012.

Van Naerssen, Ton, Spaan, Ernst, and Zoomers, Annelies, eds. *Global Migration and Development.* New York: Routledge, 2008.

Verdirame, Guglielmo. *The UN and Human Rights: Who Guards the Guardians?* New York: Cambridge University Press, 2011.

Vogl, Frank. *Waging War on Corruption: Inside the Global Movement Fighting the Abuse of Power.* New York: Rowman and Littlefield, 2012.

Weiss, Thomas G. *Governing the World? Addressing "Problems without Passports."* Boulder, CO: Paradigm Publishers, 2014.

———, ed. *Thinking About Global Governance: Why People and Ideas Matter?* New York: Routledge, 2011.

———, Forsythe, David P., and Coate, Roger A. *The United Nations and Changing World Politics.* 6th ed. Boulder, CO: Westview, 2009.

———, and Wilkenson, Rorden, eds. *International Organization and Global Governance.* New York: Routledge, 2014.

Whalan, Jeni. *How Peace Operations Work: Power, Legitimacy, and Effectiveness.* New York: Oxford University Press, 2014.

Willetts, Peter. *Non-Governmental Organizations in World Politics: The Construction of Global Governance.* New York: Routledge, 2011.

Zanotti, Laura. *Governing Disorder: UN Peace Operations, International Security, and Democratization in the Post-Cold War Era.* University Park, PA: Penn State University Press, 2011.

Ziring, Lawrence, Riggs, Robert E., and Plano, Jack C. *The United Nations: International Organization and World Politics.* 4th ed. Belmont, CA: Thomson, Wadsworth, 2005.

Index

About the Author

Jean-Robert Leguey-Feilleux received his MBA from the École Supérieure de Commerce de Marseille, France, following which, he received a U.S. Fulbright Grant to study at the University of Florida, where he received an MA in political science. After receiving a fellowship from Georgetown University, he obtained his Ph.D. in political science. He became director of research at the Institute of World Polity, Georgetown University, then joined the political science department, at St. Louis University where he taught international affairs; became department chair for thirteen years and directed the foreign service certificate. On a St. Louis University sabbatical, became visiting researcher at Harvard University. During another sabbatical, attended an entire session of the UN General Assembly in New York. He is the author of articles in international studies, and the author of *The Dynamics of Diplomacy* (2009), 401 pages, which was selected as "2009 *Choice* Outstanding Academic Title."